CICERO

ON STOIC GOOD AND EVIL

De Finibus Bonorum et Malorum Liber III
and
Paradoxa Stoicorum

Edited with Introduction, Translation & Commentary by

M.R. Wright

ARIS & PHILLIPS Ltd

© 1991.

British Library Cataloguing in Publication Data
Cicero, Marcus Tullius *106 B.C. - 43 B.C.*
    On Stoic Good and Evil. - (Classical Texts 0953-7961)
    1. Roman Republic philosophy. Stoicism
    I. Title II. Wright M.R. III Series
188

ISBN *0 85668 467 8* (cloth)
      0 85668 468 6 (limp)

Published and printed by Aris & Phillips Ltd, Teddington House, Warminster, Wiltshire, BA12 8PQ, England

CONTENTS

filiis filiabusque carissimis

Tom, Cathy, Edward, Helen

INTRODUCTION

I BACKGROUND

After the defeat of the Pompeians at Pharsalus and Munda there was no satisfactory public role for Cicero at Rome, and his consequent despondency was compounded by events in his private life. In 46 b.c. he divorced his first wife Terentia after thirty years together; the following year his daughter Tullia died, and a second marriage finished almost immediately. Grieving and disheartened (as we learn from his letters at the time) Cicero left Rome for his country villa at Tusculum where he devoted all his energies to writing. He returned to the capital eighteen months later, after the death of Caesar, and there made his last stand for the Republic. Because of his speeches against Mark Antony, and in particular the publication of the brilliant and virulent second *Philippic*, he was proscribed by the second triumvirate and eventually brutally murdered on Antony's orders in 43 b.c.[1]

Cicero had been interested in philosophy throughout his life. In his youth he had been instructed by the blind Stoic Diodotus at his father's house,[2] and was taken by Atticus to attend the Roman lectures of the Epicurean Phaedrus and of Philo of Larissa, the leading figure of the Academics (as Plato's later successors in the Academy were called). During a subsequent visit to Greece and Asia Minor he toured the main schools on their home ground, and was particularly impressed by Antiochus in Athens and Posidonius in Rhodes. Above all Cicero was influenced by the writings of Plato. He translated the *Protagoras* and *Timaeus* into Latin, and, in his *De Republica* and *De Legibus*, he adapted to a Roman context Plato's philosophic interests in government, law and the workings of justice. The study of rhetoric, which the sophists had initiated in the fifth century, was another subject of Platonic analysis and development. This had been further advanced by Isocrates, Aristotle and the Peripatetic tradition, and reached its peak in the combination of Greek theory with native Roman skills delineated in Cicero's *De Oratore*, *Brutus* and *Orator*. In particular Cicero found a new relevance and role for the Platonic philosopher-king: the ideal guide and guardian of the body politic (*reipublicae rector*) might well be realised in the wise and persuasive Roman statesman.

The main body of Cicero's philosophical works was produced in his short retirement from the political scene, from February 45 to September 44 b.c., and we have his own explanation for his reasons for starting on them: 'I began to interest myself anew in the study of philosophy, so that my mind might thereby be lightened of the burden of its cares and I might serve my fellow citizens in the most effective way'.[3] Accordingly, he proceeded to cover a wide range of philosophical problems methodically, energetically, and in detail. As well as the five books of *De Finibus* on ethical theory, his output included three books on the nature of the gods (*De Natura Deorum*), a further five on suffering, death and immortality (*Disputationes Tusculunae*, known generally as the *Tusculans*), essays on fate and free will (*De Fato* and *De Divinatione*) and on friendship and old age (*De Amicitia* and *De Senectute*); there were also two versions of a technical work on scepticism and probability (*Academica*), and an adaptation of Aristotle's *Topica*. The series finished with the three books on practical duties (*De Officiis*), written as Cicero was returning to the political scene. If the crisis of Caesar's assassination had not intervened, Cicero claimed that there would no longer be any philosophical topic that he had not opened to treatment in Latin.[4]

Cicero's general approach in these works was to present the theories of the great Hellenistic schools – Epicurean, Stoic and Sceptic – in speeches and dialogues set earlier in the century, and with parts taken by distinguished and cultured Romans, many of whom were his personal friends.[5] The case of the *De Finibus* is particularly poignant in that the Epicurean speakers in the first two books were Pompeians who had died fighting for the Republic at Pharsalus and in Africa, and Cato, the Stoic exponent in the third book, had recently committed suicide at Utica rather than submit to Caesar. The whole work, like the *Tusculans* and the later *De Officiis*, was dedicated to Marcus Brutus, and would have reached him as he was pondering the conflicting loyalties to friendship, family and state in his decision to join the anti-Caesarian conspiracy.

II GOODNESS, KNOWLEDGE AND HAPPINESS

De Finibus Bonorum et Malorum is an account of different theories of the greatest good and the worst evil in life. *Finis* translates the Greek *telos*, the end or purpose of the structure, function and activity of living organisms, and *finis bonorum*, like *summum bonum*, is the goal of *human* endeavour. The five books are an analysis and assessment of different ways in which a man can achieve a successful, complete and happy life, and the extent to which such a life can be independent of external circumstance. The theories discussed derive directly from the Hellenistic philosophies of the late fourth and early third centuries b.c., but these in turn were rooted in the work of previous thinkers.

Socrates

In the early dialogues of Plato, Socrates had been shown exploring ways in which knowledge relates necessarily to the happy life, both with regard to goodness – *aretē* – as a whole (especially in the *Protagoras* and *Meno*) and in discussions of particular virtues (as of courage in the *Laches* and *sōphrosunē* in the *Charmides*). Despite the negative conclusions reached, the recognition of some essential connection is acknowledged, and the kind of knowledge involved is shown to link with one's specific humanity. Only through knowledge of oneself, of the characteristic functioning of a man individually and in relation to gods and other men, can the fulfilled and therefore happy life be achieved. The complementary consequence was that a failure in goodness was due not to intentional delinquency but to a basic ignorance, and the redress therefore was not through punishment but by means of an enlightened education based on dialectic persuasion.

Plato

Plato expanded and then partially rejected a theory that the best type of individual and political life was one guided according to an infallible knowledge of eternal and unchanging moral forms. In the *Republic* these forms had been shown to depend ultimately on the form of the good, but it was Plato's later reflections in the *Philebus* that are most relevant to the fundamental assumption of a connection between goodness and knowledge for human happiness. In his mature contribution to the debate, Plato, through Socrates as his spokesman, rejected a straight antithesis of intelligence versus pleasure in the totality of the good life. Intellectual activity *tout court* belongs to the divine, whereas the non-intellectual enjoyment of pleasures could characterise only the simplest forms of animal species. The satisfactory and commendable life for man requires both ingredients in an approved combination. Reason is aligned with order, truth and what is appropriate (*to kalon*) in the pattern of right living, involving not only theorising and dialectic but the application of knowledge in sciences and crafts. Pleasures 'true and pure' come with these activities and are constituents of the best type of life 'along with pleasures that go with health and self-control (*to sōphronein*), and in general with those that, like attendants on a goddess, always accompany virtue'.[6]

Aristotle

Aristotle notoriously attacked the Platonic form of the good, in particular for its failure to take account of the various uses of the word 'good' (*agathos*). His own analysis of the different applications of the adjective and the relationship between them resulted in the recognition of a primary meaning around which other senses cluster.[7] Further clarification distinguished what is good as means from what is good as an end or aim; and this end or aim was found to admit of a hierarchy of distinctions culminating in an ultimate good for which no further explanation could be given. At this level all is done for the sake of happiness (*eudaimonia*), and it is pointless to ask then why a man wishes to be happy. The happy man has fulfilled his desires and achieved his end, but the *content* of his happiness is open to question and indeed dispute. Aristotle gives his own conclusion in the first book of the *Nicomachean Ethics*: 'The happy man is one who is able to realise perfect virtue in action, and who is adequately provided with external goods, not just for a time but throughout his life; and we should perhaps add that his death will be in accord with the pattern of his life.'[8]

Aristotle also incorporated contemplation as the ingredient contributed by reason in the functioning of what is both specifically human and shared with the divine. The result reflects the tripartite division of the *psychē* that had been developed in Plato's *Republic*: the successful and happy life satisfies the whole man in its combination of reasoned contemplation, considered action and the enjoyment of external goods. The most important component for happiness, Aristotle argues, is virtue, and, in the Socratic and Platonic tradition of the essential involvement of the intellect in ethics, reason both ensures the realisation of virtue in particular choices of modes of conduct and finds a happiness of its own in *theōria*. Reason however can only flourish in conditions of leisure and moderate comfort.

Cyrenaics and Cynics

Since Socrates himself wrote nothing, the method and content of his philosophising were open to different interpretations, and were responsible for developments in directions other than those taken by Plato and Aristotle. With Aristippus and his followers the Cyrenaics (so named after Aristippus' home town of Cyrene), the search for happiness and the best life became the search for the life of greatest pleasure. The sources are unsatisfactory, but it seems that Aristippus started from the Socratic principle of the importance of self-knowledge and the limitations of human wisdom. If the past is no longer real and the future is uncertain, then human good has to be in the present. The only available knowledge rests then in immediate consciousness of the self, and, through sense experience, of its relation to what is external to it. The function of reason therefore is to control sense experience and harmonise its effects in the continual best adaptation of the self to continually changing circumstances. In practice this would be achieved by maximising pleasure and minimising pain, aiming at 'smoothness' in the physical constitution and avoiding 'roughness'. The resulting life was seen as one of 'sybaritic hedonism' based on natural desire, where one was best engaged in securing feelings of intense enjoyment at every consecutive moment. And yet there was still the attempt to combine this hedonism in some way with the Socratic inheritance of moral independence, self-mastery and calm optimism.[9]

The early Cynics, like the Cyrenaics, saw themselves as followers of Socrates, but they were more interested in the Socratic linking of knowledge with virtue, and proceeded to strengthen this link in the idealisation of the 'wise man' and his ascetic way of life. Pleasure was despised: 'it is better to be mad than pleased' was one of the many deliberately provocative remarks attributed to their founder Antisthenes.[10] For them the goal of the only truly human life was virtue, and this brought its own reward. The Cynics regarded material goods as irrelevant and worthless, and they were ready to demonstrate their independence of them in an ostentatiously simple and open street life. They deliberately courted hardship on the grounds that it provided an opportunity to assert their individual self-sufficiency and moral superiority, and, with a missionary zeal which was often taken to extremes, they attempted to impose their views on others by aggressive confrontation, preaching and shaming example.[11]

III EPICURUS

Epicurus was most sympathetic to the Cyrenaics among the philosophic successors of Socrates, but the sophisticated hedonism which he developed in the late fourth and early third centuries b.c. was firmly based on the physics of an atomic theory derived from Democritus and supported with a *Canōn* or 'criterion of truth'. Since his physical theory demonstrated that there was no divine government of the cosmos, or any survival of the soul after death, he concluded that happiness had to be found solely by human endeavour and within the limits of human potential.

Epicurean ethics started from the fundamental Aristotelian assumption that living things tend towards, or seek to obtain, the good appropriate to their own kind. Looking therefore at human nature Epicurus found that the basic instinct is to approach what is pleasant and avoid what is painful. This instinct, since it *is* grounded in human nature, must be for what is of benefit to man, and so he established his first principle, that pleasure is good and pain evil. This principle does not have to be proved, but it is an immediate subjective experience, a direct perception that is not liable to error. Epicurus was not concerned with obligation, with what 'ought' to be done, but claimed instead to give a factual description: it is the case that in a natural condition, or 'in a free hour, when our power of choice is untrammelled, and nothing prevents us acting on our choice' we do act for pleasure. A practical mode of life could then be drawn up, based on the universal experience of pleasure being of our nature (*oikeia*) and good, and pain alien (*allotrios*) and bad.[12]

Epicurus defined pleasure broadly as the fulfilment of desire, but then classified desires into two types, those that are natural and those that are 'vain'. The natural were then sub-divided into the necessary and unnecessary, with a further division of the necessary into the physical that are concerned with life itself (as for food and drink) and with the minimum comfort of the body (as for warmth, clothing and shelter), and those that bring confidence and freedom from fear for the repose of the mind. When the means of satisfying the necessary bodily desires are available and adopted, pleasure is the actual process of achieving satisfaction, a 'smooth and gentle motion in the flesh', known technically as 'kinetic'. It is followed by 'static' pleasure, the feeling of general well-being consequent on the removal of pain.

For natural but unnecessary desires, where there is no actual deficiency and therefore no pain, Epicurus says 'it is not difficult either to obtain their satisfaction or to forego them'. He is thinking in terms of small luxuries which 'are easily set aside whenever their satisfaction appears difficult or likely to cause injury'. Our attitude will be to make a moderate use of them, guided by *phronēsis* – 'practical wisdom'. The 'vain' desires however, which are unnatural and unnecessary, and include those for great wealth or power, deliberately upset the body's equilibrium. They are wholly kinetic, and, instead of resulting in a feeling of euphoria on their attainment, cause further disturbance by inviting an onrush of further vain desires.[13]

Excess of any kind is liable to interrupt and endanger the

body's state of well-being. 'Not continual drinking and dancing and enjoying sex with boys and women and eating fish and the other delights of a luxurious table bring about the pleasant life; rather it is produced by sober reasoning, which examines the motive for every choice and rejection, and which drives away all those opinions which throw the soul into the greatest confusion.'[14] The restriction of unnecessary pleasures by practical wisdom prevents any attempt to exceed the limit of moderation and to introduce gratuitous disturbance. A life of bodily repose results in a pleasant life within the reach of all.

All pleasures may be good, but not all are to be chosen. On occasion pain can be viewed as good if it will result in an increase of pleasure, and pleasure evil if the consequence is greater pain. Often though it is the case that one seizes on an immediate pleasure and is caught by it 'as by a bait', without looking ahead. Epicurus follows Socrates in assuming that no one does or suffers evil willingly, but can be misled by specious appearance. So practical wisdom, as well as guiding us in the moderate use of luxuries and restricting unnecessary pleasures, has a third function, that of hedonistic calculation. To this end it discriminates between pleasures and pains, evaluates and balances them, and then makes the decisions which will lead to the attainment of long-term happiness.

It will however be found that in the end the instructions from *phronēsis* recommend the practice of the traditional virtues, for it will show that the life in which they are practised is in fact the most pleasant, and also that 'immediate delight' may eventually accompany them. Virtue as a whole cannot exist apart from activity, and on its own it is 'an empty name'.[15] But when the two combine, then virtuous action becomes a means to the end or goal of happiness, and the most useful means on the broad view, despite the appearance of being laborious and painful. Epicurus however went further, and regarded virtuous activity not only as one of several means, but as *the* necessary and overriding way to the pleasant life, and inseparable from it. 'It is not possible' he said 'to live pleasantly without living prudently, honourably and justly, nor to live prudently, honourably and justly without living pleasantly ... the virtues have grown up in close union with the pleasant life, and the pleasant life cannot be separated from them.'[16] Epicureanism started as a theory of hedonism based on the most fundamental of human instincts and desires, and resulted in practice in the recommendation of a restrained and virtuous life that was proof against the vagaries of fortune.

IV THE STOICS

The Stoics, like the Epicureans, saw themselves in direct descent from Socrates, whom they were inclined to canonise as one of the very few to achieve the status of 'Wise Man'. They approved his ascetic way of life, and continued his interest in the rigorous analysis of ethical terms. But their logic was able to profit from the later developments made by the Megarians and by Aristotle, and to advance on them, while they based their physics on the divine fire that the Presocratic Heraclitus had propounded. Their overriding interest however, and the fruit of the garden of their philosophy, was ethics, based on the twin Socratic foundations of care for the soul and alliance of virtue with knowledge. The Stoic aim was a virtuous way of life guided by reason, self-sufficient and independent of the vagaries of fortune, that would fulfil human nature and bring happiness with it.

Whereas the Epicureans claimed that the primary natural instinct was to approach what is pleasant and eschew the painful, the Stoics countered with an instinct for self-preservation, which impels the animal and young child towards what is life-giving and away from what would cause or contribute to its destruction.[17] Since nature had brought the living creature into being and 'endeared it to itself', it was to be expected that she would ensure its survival by providing both the necessary means and the impulse to adopt those means and avoid their opposite. It is instinctive and appropriate behaviour for children and animals alike to make for what will foster, protect and nourish them and to turn from all that might endanger their well-being, as they struggle to gain a foothold in life and overcome their initial weakness.

As the child grows, however, while still retaining this natural and appropriate behaviour which he shares with the animal world, he begins to show himself specifically human in his awareness of and attachment to rational processes. He starts to think about his behaviour, on its own and in relation to the outside world, and then the workings of nature and his own particular place in a wider scheme become clearer. He acts now from choice rather than instinct, and his maturing reason should then encourage him to choose consistently what is appropriate and in accord with nature as a whole. When such a pattern of behaviour has been established then finally the true good comes to be present in him and to be understood. This is none other than virtue (*aretē*), which alone has intrinsic merit and is to be desired for its own sake. The adult now understands that virtue is the one good and its opposite, vice, the one evil, and that only in practising virtue under the guidance of reason will he realise his humanity to the full and so be truly happy.

Those who reach the highest good are few, and in the daily life of most men moral issues are not always pressing or dominant; advice is needed on how to make decisions on a non-moral level. Provided it is always recognised that there is no good but virtue and no evil but vice, the Stoics were ready to divide the rest into what is to be preferred, what rejected, and what is of no consequence at all. What is preferable accords with nature and so most obviously includes life itself as well as health and physical well-being, and these are to be chosen if there is no conflict with morality and the dictates of reason. It is also according to nature, though less immediately so, to have a moderate amount of wealth for one's comfort, and also to enjoy the respect of others. In addition property, position and power give scope for particular aspects of virtue such as justice and generosity, whereas the poor and lowly, even if they should possess the one good, would have limited means for its display and practice. The continual selection by reason of what is to be preferred and the rejection of the opposite according to the criterion of conformity with nature make up the sum of 'appropriate actions' that are open to all. But only when they are performed by the truly wise man, who has attained virtue and comprehensive knowledge with it, do they become definitively right.

The intellectualising of virtue – the recognition of a fundamental connection between knowing right and doing right – was, as we have seen, a distinctive feature of Greek ethics, from its tentative beginnings in Socratic dialectic through its developments in the Socratic schools and in Plato and Aristotle down to the Hellenistic era. The Stoics adopted it whole-heartedly, made it the pivot of morality and did not shrink from a ruthless deduction of the consequences entailed. The related suggestion that the particular standard virtues of wisdom, courage, moderation and justice were essentially related had been raised by Socrates in Plato's *Protagoras* and continually interested his successors. The Stoics again took up the extreme position that the virtues were all basically one, being particular applications in particular areas of the theory of conduct (or 'art of living') known by reason, and each ultimately requiring the others. The inevitable conclusion was that a man was either completely virtuous, knowing the principles of right action in every situation, or, being ignorant, was not merely foolish but also vicious in every respect.

There is no denying that the Stoic system of ethics was uncompromising, and it was generally mocked as paradoxical and out of touch with reality. But there are four implications which redeem its harshness and show that its idealism was not hopeless. The first is that man is fundamentally good. It is in accord with human nature that reason develops from sound foundations, and the life of virtue to which it will lead us is consistently in harmony with our nature and indispensable to happiness. If we do not reach the goal the fault is likely to lie with ill-health, unsympathetic environment, bad company and in particular misguided education, all of which compound our own error. Secondly the merit of an action can only be truly judged by the 'state of soul' of the agent, and inner motive is more important than the outward result. When that which sustains and guides a man is concordant with itself (which in a physical sense means that the warm breath or *pneuma* of which the soul consists is in the correct 'tension') then the actions performed will always be rational and right, but, where there is discord within, vicious actions follow. There is no point therefore in meting out punishment for treason, murder and the like, but attention should be given to the individual's psychological state and the underlying *pathos* – the sickness or disorder that caused the eruption into violence. Thirdly more emphasis came to be placed on progress towards the goal than on the unlikelihood of reaching it, so that education and exhortation had a role in the continual and consistent choice of appropriate actions in accordance with nature. And finally, in the exposition of the practical duties that resulted from the ethical theory, in particular in the exhortation to a life of service to one's country and then to the whole human race that made up the *cosmopolis*, the Stoics had a vision that went far beyond the sheltered garden of the Epicureans.

V PHILOSOPHY AT ROME

The accompanying diagram shows in a simplified way the descent of the Greek schools of philosophy from Socrates, their various developments, and the transition to the Roman world.

The Aristotelian or Peripatetic school lost its distinction soon after Aristotle's immediate successors in the Lyceum. Little is known of its work in the following years until there was a revival in the first century b.c. under the leadership of Andronicus of Rhodes, who repossessed Aristotle's treatises by a circular route involving their transfer to Rome by Sulla and their subsequent return to Athens by one of Cicero's friends. Andronicus then initiated a series of commentaries on the works which were to

The Later Development of the Greek Schools of Philosophy

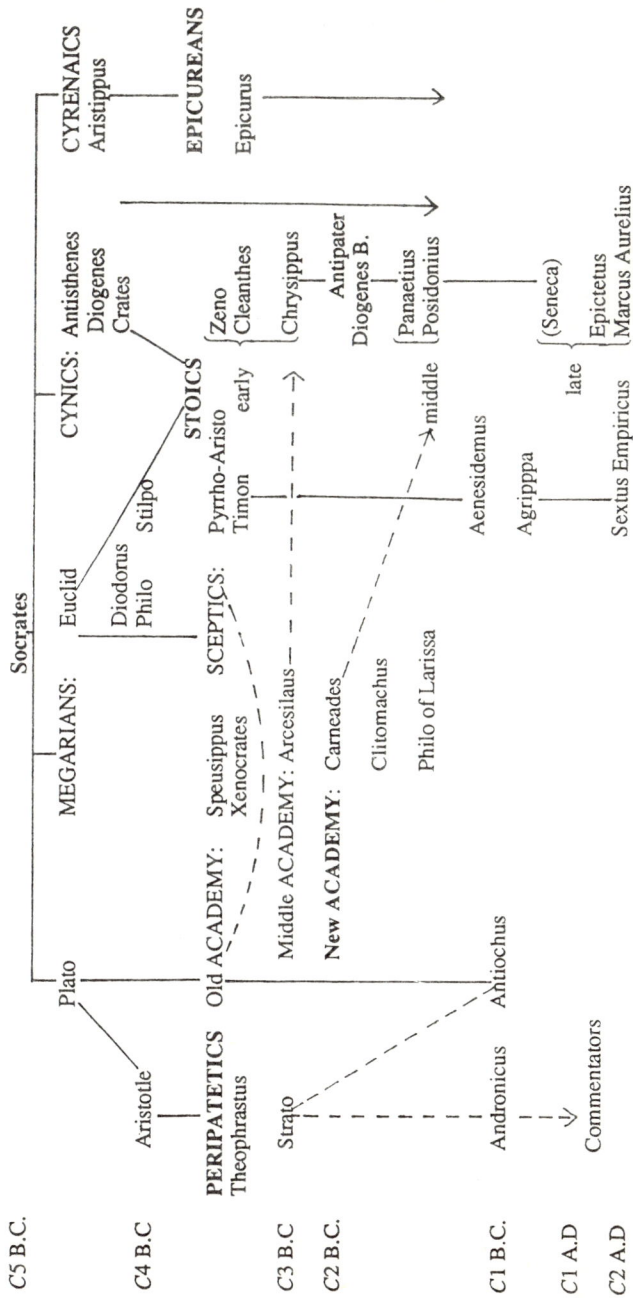

Socrates

CYRENAICS
Aristippus

EPICUREANS
Epicurus

CYNICS: Antisthenes
Diogenes
Crates

STOICS
{ Zeno
Cleanthes
{ Chrysippus
Antipater
Diogenes B.
{ Panaetius
Posidonius

(Seneca)
Epictetus
Marcus Aurelius

MEGARIANS: Euclid
Diodorus
Philo Stilpo

SCEPTICS: Pyrrho-Aristo early
Timon →

→ middle

Aenesidemus
Agripppa

late

Sextus Empiricus

Plato

PERIPATETICS
Theophrastus

Old ACADEMY: Speusippus
Xenocrates

Middle ACADEMY: Arcesilaus

New ACADEMY: Carneades
Clitomachus
Philo of Larissa

Aristotle

Strato

Antiochus

Andronicus

Commentators

C5 B.C.

C4 B.C

C3 B.C

C2 B.C.

C1 B.C.

C1 A.D

C2 A.D

occupy the Peripatetics over the following centuries and become their most important legacy. But generally, by Cicero's time, the Peripatetics were no longer philosophically original, and their views were not distinguished sharply from those of the Academics. Eventually the two schools were to converge when the mammoth task of writing commentaries on Aristotle was taken over by the Neoplatonists.

The Academy itself had a divided history after Speusippus and Xenocrates, Plato's successors in the Academy. The most important work was done by what was in effect a breakaway movement (known eventually as the 'New' Academy) headed by Arcesilaus and Carneades and heavily influenced by the original Sceptics. Philo of Larissa succeeded these, but the last head of the Academy, Antiochus, abandoned the sceptical slant, and reverted to the teaching of the 'Old' Academy. Cicero attended lectures by both Philo and Antiochus.

The Megarians, who hardly rank as a 'school', were a group loosely centred round Euclid of Megara, not the famous mathematician, but a follower of Socrates and slightly older than Plato. They seem to have been particularly interested in critical argument of varying degrees of seriousness, including both eristic attacks on opponents' conclusions and the generation of puzzles and paradoxes. The great philosophers of scepticism, starting with Pyrrho and continuing down to Sextus Empiricus, are likely to have owed their original impetus to them, and they were linked to the Stoics through the logician Stilpo, who taught Zeno of Citium dialectic.

This Zeno was the founder of the Stoic school, and the author of its fundamental doctrines. He was however, as we have seen, partially indebted to the Cynics for his moral outlook, to the Presocratic Heraclitus for the inspiration for his physics, and to earlier logicians for his skills in presentation. One of his students Aristo of Chios concentrated his interests solely on ethics, and allowed no rank or value at all to the non-virtuous; another was Cleanthes, who breathed life and feeling into Zeno's austere dogma, especially in his presentation of Stoic theology in his famous 'Hymn to Zeus'. Cleanthes was succeeded by Chrysippus, one of the most prolific and influential of all ancient philosophers. In over three hundred works (of which only a few lines survive) he elaborated, emended and clarified the whole of Stoic philosophy, sharpened its logical tools and defended its orthodoxy against repeated onslaughts from the sceptical Academy under Arcesilaus and from the Epicureans. On all aspects of Stoic teaching his word was the final authority. He was succeeded by Antipater and

Diogenes of Babylon, and then Stoicism moved into its important 'middle' stage, during which it was brought to Rome.

Epicureanism was a complete and practically unalterable philosophy, passed on as a comprehensive system from Epicurus to his companions and followers, and it stayed intact over the following centuries. Lucretius, its great Roman advocate, made no fundamental innovations, but used his poetic gifts to explain the principles of atomic physics, cosmology and psychology in the avowed Epicurean aim of alleviating universal fears of divine interference during life and of horrors after death. The Roman influence of Lucretius was not so much on philosophy as in his use of the satiric tradition to turn the sharp weaponry of invective and ridicule against the ambition, corruption, superstition and avarice that so dominated the last decades of the Republic. The 'middle' Stoics on the other hand considerably modified early Stoic dogmatism, and Panaetius in particular, who introduced the philosophy to the Scipionic circle on his arrival at Rome in 144 b.c., shifted the main emphasis to the more practical aspects, and those features of duty, service and endurance which appealed directly to the Roman statesman and soldier. Posidonius, a student of Panaetius, only came to Rome once, to plead the cause of Rhodes before Marius (to whom he took an instant dislike), but his school in Rhodes was on the itinerary of every educated Roman, and he had, through his writings and teachings, the greatest influence of all on Roman thought.[18]

From the third century b.c., when Rome became aware of the Greek world through the initial contacts with the Greek colonies of south Italy and Sicily, and the widening spheres of trade and conquest (which sent back to the capital an influx of Greek slaves), the first reactions were ambiguous. Distinguished Romans began to introduce Greek slaves into their households as private tutors to supplement the traditional Roman education of their children with the study of grammar, rhetoric, physical training and the arts. Moral dangers however were seen here, and especially in the open practice of Greek philosophy, and preventive measures were attempted. Two Epicureans were expelled in 173 b.c., and a general decree against philosophers was passed in 161, but the tide could not be stemmed. The climax was the embassy of the three philosophers in 155 b.c., when Carneades, the star of the New Academy, along with the Stoic Diogenes and the Peripatetic Critolaus, came as ambassador for Athens before the Roman senate, and gave public lectures while the petition was being considered. The success of these lectures ensured the future of philosophy at Rome, but a problem immediately arose – what language was to be its medium?

In the first century b.c. those working in philosophy would, as philhellenes, expect to discourse and write in Greek. Varro's *dictum* is typical: 'One who knows Greek prefers to read philosophy in Greek, and one who does not know Greek cannot do philosophy in any language'.[19] Despite the incredible difficulties of putting Greek technical terms into Latin, and especially into Latin hexameters, Lucretius, as philosopher and poet, chose to write in his own language mainly because he wanted to take philosophy from the upper classes and give it popular appeal, so that the message of Epicurus would be available to all. But speaking and writing in Latin was also a question of national pride. At the very beginning of the *De Finibus* Cicero defended his choice of language against those who maintained that Greek philosophy should only be studied in Greek. In other genres Latin writers were beginning to match their Greek predecessors, and he too would write in a spirit of friendly rivalry with the older language, extending the range of Latin, and proving it as capable as Greek of expressing complex ideas and subtle argument; Cicero taught philosophy to speak Latin, and, as it were, 'gave her Roman citizenship'.[20] This success in establishing Latin as a philosophical language was so complete that it continued as the accepted medium for seventeen centuries, with Erasmus, Bacon and Descartes, for example, still writing in Latin, and using the philosophical vocabulary and syntax forged by Cicero.

VI *DE FINIBUS BONORUM ET MALORUM*

On Supreme Good and Evil is the most philosophically interesting of Cicero's works. It takes us to the heart of the Hellenistic debates about the good life, set in the context of the last years of the Roman Republic. Cicero claimed no originality for himself, and it is true that large stretches of the argument have been taken over from primary and secondary Greek sources. The Stoic exposition in book 3, for example, is probably based on summaries by Diogenes of Babylon, whereas its refutation in book 4 is generally agreed to be derived from Antiochus. But rather than worry futilely about the non-extant sources, it is preferable to accept the whole for itself, as an exposition of a civilised debate between recognisable points of view on the ultimate values of life, given relevance and urgency by the unmentioned but crucial political background.

In the prologue, Cicero defends the practice of philosophy

against those who see it as an unworthy and unsuitable occupation for statesmen. Surely, he claims, a study of good and evil, of the principles of human behaviour and the criteria for the management of life, is more important for those who are to govern a state than expertise in the niceties of law and other such practical matters. Although Cicero's detractors suspected a whiff of sour grapes in such claims for philosophy over politics, it was the case that Brutus went on to join the tyrannicides and lead the last major defence of the Republic after receiving the book, and Cicero did not later flinch from what he saw as right action in opposing Antony, whatever the consequences for himself.

Lucretius chose the epic hexameter as the medium most suited to the presentation of his philosophy, following in the tradition of the Presocratics Parmenides and Empedocles. Cicero set out his debates in the form of prose dialogues, not in the cut and thrust of Platonic dialectic, when philosophy was in the making, but in the more sedate extended explanation and refutation of known philosophical systems. *On Supreme Good and Evil* presents the ethical views of all the main schools[21] in the form of three dialogues, in which the presentations are given by Cicero's friends and the refutations by himself; there are no final verdicts.

Books 1 and 2 form the first dialogue, set in 50 b.c. at Cicero's villa north of Naples. The Pompeian L. Manlius Torquatus undertakes to speak for Epicurus against the deliberately provocative charges of error, incompetence and lack of originality. The defence covers the range of Epicurean ethics, starting from pleasure as the supreme good and criterion of conduct, and the move towards it as the primary natural instinct. Virtue is not desirable for itself but as the best means to the pleasant life, and, in the practice of individual virtues, especially in the cultivation of wisdom and the control of emotion, independence of fortune and a tranquil life are achieved; the enjoyment of such a life is enhanced by the company of friends. Cicero counters this position with criticisms drawn mainly from the Stoics: self-interest is not an adequate motive either for virtue in general or for individual acts of justice, prudence and courage – in fact the Epicureans are interested in the appearance and not the reality of virtue. Pleasure is not grounded in rational human nature and so cannot relate to the original instinct or to the final end of human life; absence of pain is unattainable and utilitarian friendship short-lived.

Books 3 and 4 make up the second dialogue, set a year or two earlier and held between Marcus Cato and Cicero in Lucullus' villa, which Cicero visits from his Tusculan home. After some preliminaries, book 3 settles down to the most important and extended presentation of Stoic ethics that has survived. Cato takes the reader through 'the whole system of Zeno and the Stoics'.[22] He emphasises in particular the instinct for self-preservation, the emergence of reason and the processes of thought, the predominance of virtue and the character and duties of the wise man. But he also enlarges on the idea of progress, the place for wealth and reputation, the 'art of living', self-sufficiency, world citizenship and the brotherhood of man. These, and many other issues that are barely touched on in passing, transcend the narrowness of the quarrels between the schools, and their interest is enhanced with a wealth of similes and analogies. Then the fourth book deliberately undermines the effect of the whole with a series of criticisms of Stoic theory and practice put forward by Cicero in his own character.

The third dialogue, which occupies the last book, is set much earlier, in 79 b.c., and outside of Italy in Athens. There is a sense of excitement as Cicero presents his younger self, with his brother and friends, in a more innocent age, eagerly absorbing all the philosophy they can in the heady atmosphere of the Greek cultural capital. Marcus Piso is persuaded to take the stage and give a lecture on the combined ethical position of the old Academy and the Peripatetics which he had just heard himself from Antiochus, and this again is criticised by Cicero, now acting the part of the Stoic. The whole ends with a compliment on the skill with which the Greek ideas have been discussed in Latin.

VII *PARADOXA STOICORUM*

Paradoxes of the Stoics consists of short essays (preceded by a preface) on six famous Stoic pronouncements. They are not paradoxes in the strictly logical sense in which apparently sound argument leads to an outright contradiction. The most perplexing of this type had been put forward by the Presocratic Zeno of Elea (concluding for example that 'the flying arrow is at rest' and 'the faster runner cannot overtake the slower') and by the Megarian Eubulides in the fourth century with the 'Liar' (i.e. 'if a liar says that he is lying he both lies and tells the truth'). The general method of bringing a respondent to contradictory conclusions by seemingly innocuous moves had also been a characteristic of Socrates' *elenchus*. In the third century b.c. paradoxography was the name given to the literary genre of graphic accounts of 'unbelievable' natural wonders; it appears to have begun with Callimachus, and continued through Roman times to a work on the

Seven Wonders of the World by Philo of Byzantium. The Stoics also knew about the so-called paradoxes of material implication, and used them extensively in their propositional logic, but Cicero's essays are in the original sense of paradox – that which runs counter to generally accepted opinion (*doxa*). The apparent surprise in statements like 'the wise man is rich if poor' or 'only the wise man is free' is easily resolved by filling in the implied limitations: the wise man is rich (spiritually) if poor (materially), or he is (really) free even if in (apparent) slavery. The initial shock is produced by the 'pithy' and arresting style of the propositions, typical of the provocative rhetoric of both Cynics and Stoics, but having its origins in the enigmas of Heraclitus.

The *Preface* engagingly discounts any grandiose claims for the *Paradoxes* – they are certainly not to be compared with Pheidias' statue of Athena, but are at least from the same workshop! Written in 46 b.c., probably between *Brutus* and *Orator*, they are essays in popularising some of the most extreme tenets of Stoicism in the conviction that the art of persuasion, discussed in the longer accompanying treatises, can make even the most uncompromising material acceptable.

The rival claims to virtue for the title of 'good' are countered in the first Paradox ('Only what is right is good') with *exempla* from Roman history and legends of great men motivated in their great deeds not by pleasure, which reduces our human status, nor by riches but by the desire to excel. Conversely, according to the second Paradox, threats of death, exile and the like do not trouble the heroic nature or affect its self-sufficiency and happiness. The third essay is a commendable and convincing attempt to open up the arguments on which the difficult proposition 'All sins are equal' is based. The fifth ('Only the wise man is free') is a lively and witty attack on contemporary forms of genuine slavery – to women, to works of art, to wealth, to political and military ambition, and to fear. The remaining two are elaborated in a personal and vituperative manner, more in the tradition of Roman satire than Hellenistic philosophy. The fourth Paradox ('Every fool is mad') is used to justify Cicero's own position vis-à-vis Clodius in the political events of 58 b.c. which resulted in Cicero's temporary exile; seven years after his adversary's death the events of that year still rankle. The last Paradox ('Only the wise man is rich') may have been directed particularly at Crassus, another adversary who died in the same year as Clodius, as well as at Roman corruption in general; Cicero's own thrift is contrasted with others' extravagance, and past virtue with present decadence. As a whole the *Paradoxes* find a new context and justification for Stoic ethics in the social, political and economic life of the late Republic.

A section from Cicero's speech *In defence of Murena* has been added in the Appendix, because in it Cicero satirises some of the Stoic precepts that he later defended in the *Paradoxes*. The speech was delivered in 63 b.c. in the last month of Cicero's consulship, and later revised for publication. Cato was prosecuting Murena for malpractice (bribery in particular) at the consular elections for the following year. In the section of the defence usually given to a rebuttal of the prosecution's charges, Cicero side-stepped the main issue (a sign that the defendant was probably guilty), and concentrated instead on satirising the prosecution and emphasising the political advantage the Catilinarians would gain if Murena was condemned. Cicero's basic kindliness towards the young Cato is shown in the bantering tone with which he treats the consequences of Stoic extremism, and the implied compliment in the reference to Cato's natural courtesy which will in time temper the austerity he has just adopted from the Stoics. Cato took the banter in good part, and the growing friendship between the two was not affected. Plutarch reports that Cato's reaction to this onslaught was to smile and say 'what a witty consul we have' (*Cato* 21).

VIII THE TEXT

The Latin of *De Finibus* III given here derives from that of Madvig's edition, but with considerable alteration, so that there is virtually a new text. I have not hesitated to change presentation, punctuation and paragraphing in the interests of clarity, and there has been a thorough revision of orthography. Any significant variant readings, deletions, additions and conjectures, as well as two major transpositions, are noted and explained in the commentary; this seemed preferable to giving an orthodox, but in this case generally unhelpful, critical apparatus. The space saved has been used to insert headings to guide the reader through the work. The aim has been to unfold in the most direct way, for Latinists and philosophers alike, the concentration and richness of thought in what may otherwise appear as daunting stretches of text, and thereby to increase interest both in the ideas and in the medium in which they are presented. The text of the *Paradoxes* is based on the Leipsig edition of the complete *opera* by Nobbe, which took account of earlier collations and editions. Punctuation, paragraphing and general presentation have here too been drastically changed in the interests of clarity and consistency. The latest editions of both works are those for the Budé series, *De Finibus* by Jules Martha and *Paradoxa* by Jean Molager (Paris 1961 and 1971), but there are very few new readings which require significant alterations to the older texts; where the meaning may be affected due acknowledgments have been made in the discussions in the commentary.

On orthography in the texts generally, I have removed the anachronistic distinction between 'u' and 'v', reduced the use of capital letters and dealt with the notorious fluidity of consonantal forms by preferring consistent intelligibility to fidelity to manuscript erraticisms. So the appropriate assimilations of prepositional prefixes are accepted throughout, in particular aff- (adf-), ass- (ads-), att- (adt-), coll- (conl-), comp- (conp-), corr- (conr-), eff- (ecf-), ill- (inl-), imm- (inm-), off- (obf-), opt- (obt-) and supp- (subp-). The aspirate is retained, double 'p' and 't' are preferred (as in 'opportunitas' and 'litterae'), and the Greek *phi* is transliterated by 'ph', not 'f'. In accordance with majority usage there is 'quicquam' but 'quidquid', 'm' rather than 'n' in 'numquam' and 'tamquam', and 'cum' and 'uult' rather than 'quom' or 'volt'. Second declension genitive singulars are with a single 'i', third declension accusative plurals are in '-es', and superlative endings in '-imus'. Two works which offer some guidelines on this topic are: P. Schwenke, 'Apparatus criticus ad Ciceronis libros *De Natura Deorum*', *CR* 4 (1890), 347–55, and Louis Havet, *Règles pour éditions critiques*, Paris: Budé, 1920.

Greek words, usually technical terms, given in Greek letters in the Latin manuscripts, have been transliterated. The translation leaves the same transliteration when Cicero himself explains the term, otherwise an appropriate English word is given in quotation marks, and there is a note in the relevant commentary. The Glossary lists Stoic technical terms that are used in the texts – in Greek, transliteration, Latin and English forms. The translation aims throughout to be consistent with the glossary in the use of these terms, and any difficulties are also noted in the commentary.

The manuscripts

The manuscripts derive from a single, lost archetype. The oldest and best of those extant is A (Palatinus 1, 11th c., which also contains the *Academica*), but it finishes at the seventh chapter of book 4. Two others, from the same copy, but descended from the archetype independently of A, are B (Palatinus II) and E (Erlangensis), both from the 15th c. They are generally inferior, with standard faults of omission, repetition and transposition, but are valuable in that the copy from which they both derive was written by a scribe with more accuracy than understanding. Two others from the 12th c. are P (Paris) and R (Rotterdam), from a second but less trustworthy stemma from the archetype. Another group with a common source further back on this stemma also needs to be taken into account. (I am grateful to Leighton Reynolds for drawing my attention to this group. They will be fully explained in his forthcoming Oxford Classical Text of *De Finibus*; for a transitional account, cf. Jules Martha's introduction to the Budé edition, xxv-xxxi.) The first printed edition of the work, by Cratander (Basle, 1528), was taken from the B tradition, but with marginalia from A.

The main editions are:

of *De Finibus Bonorum et Malorum:*

Thomas Bentley (Cambridge 1738), J. Davison (Cambridge 1741), R.G. Rath (Halis Saxon 1804), I.A. Goerenz (Leipsig 1813), J.N. Madvig (Hauniae 1876), C.F. Müller (Leipsig 1878: Teubner), W.M. Hutchinson (London 1909), Th. Schiche (Leipsig 1915: Teubner), Jules Martha (Paris 1928: Budé, Latin-French), Alexander Kabza (Munich 1960, Latin-German), H. Rackham (Harvard 1961: Loeb, Latin-English), Karl Atzent (Stuttgart 1964: Latin-German)

and of *Paradoxa Stoicorum:*

A.G. Gernhard (Leipsig 1819), M.N. Bouillet (Paris 1828), J.C. Orelli (Zurich 1831), C.F. Müller (Leipsig 1879: Teubner), O. Plasberg (Leipsig 1908: Teubner), H. Rackham (London 1942: Loeb), A.G. Lee (London 1953), Jean Molager (Paris 1971: Budé).

NOTES TO THE INTRODUCTION

1. For a general survey of Cicero's life and writings, and of his place in the history of philosophy, cf. the introduction to the first volume of this series by A.E. Douglas: Cicero *Tusculan Disputations* 1, Warminster 1985, 4-15.

2. Cicero's respect for Diodotus continued into later life, and he transferred him to his own house on his father's death, cf. *Brutus* 309, *Att* 2.20.6, *Tusc* 5.113; for his regard for Plato cf. *Leg* 1.15, and for other teachers *ND* 1.6; Cicero's personal preference, reinforced by his legal experience, was to remain eclectic, cf. *Tusc* 4.7.

3. Cicero *Div* 2.7, and cf. *Ac* 1.11, *Off* 2.2-5.

4. *Div* 2.6, and the whole preface in *Fin* 3, chs. 1-2; also *ND* 1.7.

5. The main exceptions are the *Tusculans*, where the speakers are marked in the MSS as M and A (possibly for Magister and Adulescens), and *De Officiis*, which is in the form of a letter of exhortation to Cicero's son Marcus.

6. Plato *Philebus* 63e.

7. For the classic demonstration of Aristotle's use of 'focal meaning' with reference to 'good' cf. G.E.L. Owen: 'Logic and Metaphysics in early Aristotle' in *Logic, Science and Dialectic* London 1986, ch.10.

8. Aristotle *EN* 1101a14-20; 'to realise perfect virtue in action' means something like 'to perform excellently what one is best capable of'.

9. Cf. in particular E. Mannebach *Aristippi et Cyrenaicorum Fragmenta*, Leiden 1961.

10. Antisthenes fr. 108a-f (F.D. Caizzi *Antisthenis Fragmenta*, Milan 1966).

11. cf. Xenophon *Symp* 4.39, Antisthenes frs. 22, 69-71; there was not a Cynic 'school' in any official sense, but the life-style of Diogenes of Sinope (and the more sympathetic Crates of Thebes) immediately attracted imitators. They were called Cynic or 'dog' philosophers because of their open street life and the ferocity of their diatribe or 'bark'.

12. DL 10.34, and cf. 10.129; the argument that the natural condition provides the impulse towards pleasure and avoidance of pain goes back to Eudoxus, cf. Aristotle *EN* 1172b9-23, and commentary, notes 1 and 57.

13. DL 10. 127-31, *KD* 26, 30, *SV* 25, 51, 59, frs. 29, 39, 68 (Bailey), and cf. note 16.

14. DL 10. 131-32.

15. frs. 12 and 23, DL 10.138.

16. *KD* 5, DL *loc. cit.* The 'Letter to Menoeceus' (DL 10. 122-35) is an epitome of Epicurean ethics, and with two other letters, the epigrammatic *Kyriai Doxai* ('Key Doctrines', also in Diogenes) and *Sententiae Vaticanae* (fragments from a Vatican manuscript referred to as *SV*) as well as a few other fragments are all that survive from Epicurus' extensive writings.

17. Cf. commentary, notes 53 and 54, and the discussion of *oikeiōsis*.

18. The importance of Posidonius and the extent of his influence is in dispute, cf. in particular L. Edelstein 'The philosophical system of Posidonius' *AJP* 57 (1936), 286-325, A.D. Nock 'Posidonius' *JRS* 49 (1959), 1-16 and A. Dihle 'Posidonius' system of moral philosophy' *JHS* 93 (1973) 50-57; I.G. Kidd's revised text of the fragments and two volumes of commentary have now appeared (Cambridge 1989).

19. Varro in Cicero *Ac* 1.4; on the topic generally cf. J. Kaimio *The Romans and the Greek Language*, Helsinki 1979, esp. ch. 52 on 'Roman authors and Greek writing'.

20. *Fin* 3.40.

21. Cf. *Fin* 1.12: 'In this work I think I have given a practically exhaustive account of views on supreme good and evil; I set out to include, as far as I could, not only those of which I approve, but the teaching of all the different schools of philosophy.'

22. *Fin* 3.15.

DE FINIBUS BONORUM ET MALORUM III

M. TULLI CICERONIS

De finibus bonorum et malorum

LIBER TERTIUS

Pleasure has been eliminated as a good

[I] 1. Voluptatem quidem, Brute, si ipsa pro se loquatur nec tam pertinaces habeat patronos, concessuram arbitror conuictam superiore libro dignitati. etenim sit impudens, si uirtuti diutius repugnet, aut si honestis iucunda anteponat aut pluris esse contendat dulcedinem corporis ex eaue natam laetitiam quam grauitatem animi atque constantiam. quare illam quidem dimittamus et suis se finibus tenere iubeamus, ne blanditiis eius illecebrisque impediatur disputandi seueritas. 2. quaerendum est enim, ubi sit illud summum bonum, quod reperire uolumus, quoniam et uoluptas ab eo remota est, et eadem fere contra eos dici possunt, qui uacuitatem doloris finem bonorum esse uoluerunt, nec uero ullum probetur summum bonum, quod uirtute careat, qua nihil potest esse praestantius.

No subtle argument was needed

Itaque quamquam in eo sermone, qui cum Torquato est habitus, non remissi fuimus, tamen haec acrior est cum Stoicis parata contentio. quae enim de uoluptate dicuntur, ea nec acutissime nec abscondite disseruntur; neque enim qui defendunt eam uersuti in disserendo sunt nec qui contra dicunt causam difficilem repellunt. 3. ipse etiam dicit Epicurus ne argumentandum quidem esse de uoluptate, quod sit positum iudicium eius in sensibus, ut commoneri nos satis sit, nihil attineat doceri. quare illa nobis simplex fuit in utramque partem disputatio. nec enim in Torquati sermone quicquam implicatum aut tortuosum fuit, nostraque, ut mihi uidetur, dilucida oratio.

The Stoics' discourse uses a sophisticated terminology

Stoicorum autem non ignoras quam sit subtile uel spinosum potius disserendi genus, idque cum Graecis tum magis nobis, quibus etiam uerba parienda sunt imponendaque noua rebus nouis nomina. quod quidem nemo mediocriter doctus mirabitur cogitans in omni arte, cuius usus uulgaris communisque non sit, multam nouitatem nominum esse, cum constituantur earum rerum uocabula, quae in

M. TULLIUS CICERO

On supreme good and evil

BOOK THREE

[I] 1. If pleasure[1] of course were to speak for herself, Brutus, and did not have such determined defenders,[2] she would I think admit that she had been beaten by the previous book and had lost the contest to merit. She would be quite shameless if she struggled any longer with virtue,[3] continuing to prefer what is agreeable to what is right,[4] or claiming that physical gratification or its consequent feeling of delight[5] is of greater value than a sense of responsibility and tenacity of purpose.[6] Let us then say good-bye to her, and tell her to keep to her own quarters so that our serious debate is not diverted by her attractions and charms. 2. We have to find out where that supreme good[7] is which is the subject of our investigation, now that pleasure has been eliminated from it, and objections on more or less the same lines can be made against those who have assumed that absence of pain[8] is the greatest of goods; in fact no supreme good is acceptable that does not include virtue, which nothing can excel.

So, although we did not slacken in the discussion which we had with Torquatus,[9] the contest now awaiting us with the Stoics is even more formidable. For what is said on the subject of pleasure is not material for a very subtle or profound discourse; those who defend her are not skilled in debate[10] nor are those who oppose her refuting a difficult motion. 3. Epicurus himself actually says that no proof at all is required in the case of pleasure, because the verdict there depends on the senses,[11] so that it is enough for us to be made aware - exposition is unnecessary. That is why our earlier debate was a direct account of the two positions. There was nothing perplexing or involved in Torquatus' speech, and my delivery was, I think, straightforward.[12]

With the Stoics on the other hand you know quite well how sophisticated or 'spiky'[13] their style of discourse is, even more so for us than the Greeks, since we also have to coin words and match new terms to new discoveries.[14] Anyone with a smattering of culture will find this unremarkable, when he considers that in every branch of learning which does not have a common or everyday

quaque arte uersentur. **4.** itaque et dialectici et physici uerbis utuntur iis, quae ipsi Graeciae nota non sint. geometrae uero et musici, grammatici etiam more quodam loquuntur suo. ipsae rhetorum artes, quae sunt totae forenses atque populares, uerbis tamen in docendo quasi priuatis utuntur ac suis.

Problems in Latinising Greek philosophy

[II] Atque ut omittam has artes elegantes et ingenuas, ne opifices quidem tueri sua artificia possent, nisi uocabulis uterentur nobis incognitis, usitatis sibi. quin etiam agri cultura, quae abhorret ab omni politiore elegantia, tamen eas res, in quibus uersatur, nominibus notauit nouis. quo magis hoc philosopho faciendum est. ars est enim philosophia uitae, de qua disserens arripere uerba de foro non potest. **5.** quamquam ex omnibus philosophis Stoici plurima nouauerunt, Zenoque, eorum princeps, non tam rerum inuentor fuit quam uerborum nouorum. quodsi in ea lingua, quam plerique uberiorem putant, concessum est ut doctissimi homines de rebus non peruagatis inusitatis uerbis uterentur, quanto id nobis magis est concedendum, qui ea nunc primum audemus attingere?

Et quoniam saepe diximus (et quidem cum aliqua querela non Graecorum modo, sed eorum etiam, qui se Graecos magis quam nostros haberi uolunt) nos non modo non uinci a Graecis uerborum copia, sed esse in ea etiam superiores, elaborandum est ut hoc non in nostris solum artibus, sed etiam in illorum ipsorum assequamur. quamquam ea uerba, quibus instituto ueterum utimur pro Latinis, ut ipsa philosophia, ut rhetorica, dialectica, grammatica, geometrica, musica, quamquam Latine ea dici poterant, tamen, quoniam usu percepta sunt, nostra ducamus. atque haec quidem de rerum nominibus.

The dedication to Brutus

6. De ipsis rebus autem saepenumero, Brute, uereor ne reprehendar, cum haec ad te scribam, qui cum in philosophia tum in optimo genere philosophiae tantum processeris. quod si facerem quasi te erudiens, iure reprehenderer. sed ab eo plurimum absum, neque ut ea cognoscas quae tibi notissima sunt ad te mitto, sed quia facillime in nomine tuo acquiesco et quia te habeo aequissimum eorum studiorum, quae mihi communia tecum sunt, existimatorem et iudicem. attendes igitur, ut soles, diligenter,

application there are a number of strange terms, since a vocabulary has to be constructed for the concepts which relate to each branch of learning. 4. That is why scholars of logic or natural science use words which are not well known even in Greece. Geometricians too and musicians as well as grammarians all speak in their own idiom. Even those skilled in public speaking, which is totally public and practical, still use their own esoteric jargon[15] in teaching.

[II] Not to mention the cultured and liberal arts, even common craftsmen would not be able to preserve their traditional occupations if they did not use a vocabulary that was strange to us but familiar to them. You see that agriculture,[16] which is remote from any cultural refinement, still coins terms for the subjects with which it deals. All the more so must the philosopher do this. For philosophy is the art of life,[17] and the words for discussing it cannot be picked up from the market-place. 5. And of all philosophers, the Stoics have been the greatest innovators. Zeno, their founder, was not so much the inventor of new ideas as of new words.[18] So if in that language which many think the richer an allowance has been made for learned men to use uncommon words for uncommon subjects, how much more allowance must be made for us who are now venturing to tackle the discipline for the first time?[19]

Since we have often claimed (with some protest it is true not only from the Greeks but also from those who would rather be considered Greek than of our country) that we are not only not inferior to the Greeks in wealth of language but even surpass them[20] in this, we must make the effort to overtake them in their accomplishments as well as our own. Although all their words which we traditionally treat as Latin,[21] for example 'philosophy' itself, 'rhetoric', 'dialectic', 'grammar', 'geometry' and 'music', could all be given a Latin translation, we may adopt them as our own because of their long familiarity. That is enough on terminology.

6. On the discipline itself, Brutus, I often feel nervous of being criticised for writing this for you, since you have become so proficient not only in philosophy but in its most important field. If I were to behave as if I were teaching you, I would be justly criticised. But I am far from that, and I am not dedicating my work to you for you to learn what you already well know, but because it is a great comfort for me to use your name, and I find you a most fair commentator and reviewer in those subjects in which we both have a keen interest. So please give me as always

eamque controuersiam diiudicabis, quae mihi fuit cum auunculo tuo, diuino ac singulari uiro.

The meeting with Marcus Cato

7. Nam in Tusculano cum essem uellemque e bibliotheca pueri Luculli quibusdam libris uti, ueni in eius uillam, ut eos ipse ut solebam depromerem. quo cum uenissem, M. Catonem, quem ibi esse nescieram, uidi in bibliotheca sedentem, multis circumfusis Stoicorum libris. erat enim, ut scis, in eo auiditas legendi nec satiari poterat – quippe qui ne reprehensionem quidem uulgi inanem reformidans in ipsa curia soleret legere saepe, dum senatus cogeretur, nihil operae rei publicae detrahens. quo magis tum in summo otio maximaque copia quasi helluari libris (si hoc uerbo in tam clara re utendum est) uidebatur.

8. Quod cum accidisset ut alter alterum necopinato uideremus, surrexit statim. deinde prima illla, quae in congressu solemus: 'Quid tu' inquit 'huc? a uilla enim credo', et: 'Si ibi te esse scissem, ad te ipse uenissem'. 'Heri,' inquam, 'lusis commissis ex urbe profectus ueni ad uesperum. causa autem fuit huc ueniendi ut quosdam hinc libros promerem. et quidem, Cato, hanc totam copiam iam Lucullo nostro notam esse oportebit; nam his libris eum malo quam reliquo ornatu uillae delectari. est enim mihi magnae curae (quamquam hoc quidem proprium tuum munus est) ut ita erudiatur, ut et patri et Caepioni nostro et tibi tam propinquo respondeat. laboro autem non sine causa; nam et aui eius memoria moueor (nec enim ignoras quanti fecerim Caepionem, qui – ut opinio mea fert – in principibus iam esset, si uiueret) et Lucullus mihi uersatur ante oculos, uir cum uirtutibus omnibus excellens tum mecum et amicitia et omni uoluntate sententiaque coniunctus.'

9. 'Praeclare' inquit' facis cum et eorum memoriam tenes, quorum uterque tibi testamento liberos suos commendauit, et puerum diligis. quod autem meum munus dicis non equidem recuso, sed te adiungo socium. addo etiam illud, multa iam mihi dare signa puerum et pudoris et ingenii, sed aetatem uides.' 'Video equidem,' inquam, 'sed tamen iam infici debet iis artibus quas si, dum est tener, combiberit, ad maiora ueniet paratior.' 'Sic, et quidem diligentius saepiusque ista loquemur inter nos agemusque

your careful attention, and chair the debate which I had with that remarkably gifted man, your uncle.

7. When I was staying at Tusculum[22] and wanted to consult some books from the library of the young Lucullus,[23] I went to his house to borrow them as usual. When I arrived I saw Marcus Cato[24] – I had not known he was there – sitting in the library surrounded by piles of books on Stoicism. He had, as you know, a great appetite for reading, and could never have enough of it – he did not care what silly things people said against him but would often read right in the senate-house while the senators were assembling, but not during government business. All the more so then, when he was on holiday and in a well-stocked library, he looked as if he was having a rare old time[25] (if this expression can be used in such an intellectual context).

8. On each of us being surprised to see the other he stood up at once. Then we exchanged the usual remarks on meeting. 'What brings you here?' he said. 'I suppose you have come from your country house', and 'If I had known you were there I would have come to you.' 'I left the city yesterday,' I replied, 'once the games had started, and arrived early in the evening. I came here to borrow some books from the library. Our Lucullus, Cato, should soon be getting to know this great collection, and I hope he will enjoy these books more than any of the other adornments to the house. For I am very concerned (although the responsibility is really yours) that he should be brought up to be a credit to his father,[26] to our friend Caepio,[27] and to yourself, his close relation. There is good reason for my concern, for I respect his grandfather's memory (for you know my high opinion of Caepio, who I think would be one of our leaders if he were still alive), and Lucullus is always before me, a gentlemen of outstanding merit, close to me in friendship and sharing my every preference and opinion.'

9. 'You do well' he said 'to cherish the memory of the two men who bequeathed to you the trust of their children,[28] and you have an affection for the boy. I do not disown my responsibility as you call it, but I am inviting you to share it. I notice too that the boy is already showing signs of propriety and talent. But you see how young he is.' 'I do indeed,' I said, 'but still, while he is young, he should be given a taste of those subjects which will make him better equipped for greater things in the future.' 'Yes,' he said, 'and of course we shall discuss the matter further, and in more

communiter. sed residamus,' inquit, 'si placet.' Itaque fecimus.

Is Stoicism original only in terminology?

[III] 10. Tum ille: 'Tu autem cum ipse tantum librorum habeas, quos hic tandem requiris?' 'Commentarios quosdam' inquam 'Aristotelios, quos hic sciebam esse, ueni ut auferrem, quos legerem dum essem otiosus – quod quidem nobis non saepe contingit.' 'Quam uellem' inquit 'te ad Stoicos inclinauisses! erat enim, si cuiusquam, certe tuum nihil praeter uirtutem in bonis ducere.' 'Vide ne magis' inquam 'tuum fuerit, cum re idem tibi quod mihi uideretur, non nova te rebus nomina imponere. ratio enim nostra consentit, pugnat oratio.' 'Minime uero' inquit ille 'consentit. quicquid enim praeter id quod honestum sit expetendum esse dixeris in bonisque numeraueris, et honestum ipsum quasi uirtutis lumen exstinxeris et uirtutem penitus euerteris.' 11. 'Dicuntur ista, Cato, magnifice,' inquam, 'sed uidesne uerborum gloriam tibi cum Pyrrhone et cum Aristone, qui omnia exaequunt, esse communem? de quibus cupio scire quid sentias.'

The only good life is the life of virtue

'Egone quaeris' inquit 'quid sentiam? quos bonos uiros, fortes, iustos, moderatos aut audiuimus in re publica fuisse aut ipsi uidimus, qui sine ulla doctrina naturam ipsam secuti multa laudabilia fecerunt – eos melius a natura institutos fuisse quam institui potuissent a philosophia, si ullam aliam probauissent praeter eam quae nihil aliud in bonis haberet nisi honestum, nihil nisi turpe in malis. ceterae philosophorum disclipinae – omnino alia magis alia sed tamen omnes – quae rem ullam uirtutis expertem aut in bonis aut in malis numerent, eas non modo nihil adiuuare arbitror neque firmare quo meliores simus, sed ipsam deprauare naturam. nam nisi hoc obtineatur, id solum bonum esse quod honestum sit, nullo modo probari possit beatam uitam uirtute effici. quod si ita sit, cur opera philosophiae sit danda nescio. si enim sapiens aliquis miser esse possit, ne ego istam gloriosam memorabilemque uirtutem non magno aestimandam putem.'

Pyrrho and Aristo allow no exercise of choice

[IV] 12. 'Quae adhuc, Cato, a te dicta sunt, eadem' inquam 'dicere possis si sequerere Pyrrhonem aut Aristonem. nec enim ignoras his istud honestum non summum modo sed etiam – ut tu uis – solum bonum uideri. quod si ita est, sequitur id ipsum quod te

detail, and work together on it. But let's sit down, if you like.' And we did so.

[III] 10. Then he continued: 'But what books do you need from here, when you have such a large library of your own?' 'I came to fetch some treatises of Aristotle,' [29] I answered,'which I knew were here, to read while I had some time to myself[30] – a rare event for me.' 'How I wish' he said 'that you had been converted to the Stoics! for surely you, if anyone, would consider nothing but virtue as a good.'[31] 'Shouldn't you rather' I said 'have avoided introducing new terms[32] for the subject, when in substance you think as I do? Our logic agrees, our expressions are at variance.' 'There is no agreement at all,' he said. 'For should you say that anything is to be our goal or count as a good apart from what is right, you extinguish, in what is right, that which illuminates virtue, and in fact you demolish virtue.[33]' 11. 'Wonderfully put, Cato,' I said, 'but do you realise that the value you attach to terminology is shared with Pyrrho and Aristo,[34] who put everything on the same level? I would like to know what you think about this.'

'You want to know what I think?' he repeated. 'It is that those men in public life,[35] good and courageous, just and self-restrained, whom we have either heard of in our state's history or seen for ourselves, who without any formal training followed nature herself[36] and carried out many noteworthy achievements – such men have been better educated by nature than they could have been by philosophy, if, that is, they had been satisfied with any other philosophy than the one which holds nothing to be good except what is right, nothing bad except what is wrong. The other schools of philosophy[37] – some more so than others, but still without exception – which count anything that is not related to virtue as either good or evil[38] I think do not only not give us aid or support in self-improvement, but actually corrupt our human nature. For unless the principle that only what is right is good prevails, it is impossible to demonstrate that the happy life is achieved through virtue. And if this is the case I see no reason for any attention being given to philosophy. For if a wise man can be unhappy[39] I would not think[40] that your honoured and famous virtue was worth much.'

[IV] 12. 'What you have said so far, Cato,' I replied 'you could still say just as effectively if you were a disciple of Pyrrho or Aristo. For you know quite well that they see what is right not only as the greatest but – as you would – the only good.[41] And if this is

uelle uideo, omnes semper beatos esse sapientes. hosne igitur laudas et hanc eorum' inquam 'sententiam sequi nos censes oportere?' 'Minime uero istorum quidem,' inquit. 'cum enim uirtutis hoc proprium sit, earum rerum quae secundum naturam sint habere delectum, qui omnia sic exaequauerunt, ut in utramque partem ita paria redderent, uti nulla selectione uterentur, hi uirtutem ipsam sustulerunt.'

13. 'Istud quidem' inquam 'optime dicis, sed quaero nonne tibi faciendum idem sit nihil dicenti bonum, quod non rectum honestumque sit, reliquiarum rerum discrimen omne tollenti.' 'Si quidem' inquit 'tollerem, sed relinquo.' 14. 'Quonam modo?' inquam. 'si una uirtus, unum istud quod honestum appellas, rectum, laudabile, decorum – erit enim notius quale sit pluribus notatum uocabulis idem declarantibus – id ergo, inquam, si solum est bonum, quid habebis praeterea quod sequare? aut, si nihil malum nisi quod turpe, inhonestum, indecorum, prauum, flagitiosum, foedum – ut hoc quoque pluribus nominibus insigne faciamus – quid praeterea dices esse fugiendum?' 'Non ignoranti tibi' inquit 'quid sim dicturus, sed aliquid, ut ego suspicor, ex mea breui responsione arripere cupienti non respondebo ad singula; explicabo potius, quoniam otiosi sumus, nisi alienum putas, totam Zenonis Stoicorumque sententiam.' 'Minime id quidem' inquam 'alienum, multumque ad ea quae quaerimus explicatio tua ista profecerit.'

An exposition of Stoic ethics in Latin is required

15. 'Experiamur igitur,' inquit 'etsi habet haec Stoicorum ratio difficilius quiddam et obscurius. nam cum in Graeco sermone haec ipsa quondam rerum nomina nouarum noua uidebantur, quae nunc consuetudo diuturna triuit, quid censes in Latino fore?' 'Facillimum id quidem est,' inquam. 'si enim Zenoni licuit, cum rem aliquam inuenisset inusitatem, inauditum quoque ei rei nomen imponere, cur non liceat Catoni? nec tamen exprimi uerbum e uerbo necesse erit – ut interpretes indiserti solent – cum sit uerbum quod idem declaret magis usitatum. equidem soleo etiam quod uno Graeci, si aliter non possum, idem pluribus uerbis exponere. et tamen puto concedi nobis oportere ut Graeco uerbo utamur, si quando minus occurret Latinum, ne hoc *ephippiis* et *acratophoris* potius quam *proēgmenis* et *apoproēgmenis* concedatur; quamquam haec quidem "praeposita" recte et "reiecta" dicere licebit.' 16. 'bene facis' inquit 'quod me adiuuas, et istis quidem, quae modo dixisti, utar potius Latinis, in ceteris subuenies, si me haerentem uidebis.' 'Sedulo'

so, that proposition follows which I see you want, namely that all
wise men are always happy.[42] So do you approve of them and do
you think that we should follow their way of thinking?' 'Certainly
not their way,' he answered. 'For since it is an essential property of
virtue[43] to exercise choice among the things that are according to
nature, those who put all on a level, so as to make everything the
same one way or another with no exercise of choice,[44] actually
abolish virtue.'

13. 'Very well put,' I said. 'But my question is: aren't you taking
up a similar position when you say that nothing is good which is
not moral and right, and remove all other distinctions?' 'Yes,' he
said, 'if I were removing them, but I leave them.'[45] 14. 'How is
that?' I asked.[46] 'If virtue alone, that alone which you call right,
moral, praiseworthy, fine[47] – for the character is better understood
if it is denoted by a number of synonyms – if, I ask, that alone is
good, what else will you have to aim at? or again, if nothing is evil
except what is shameful, wrong, disgraceful, immoral, criminal and
foul – to make this, too, explicit by using a number of terms –
what else will you say should be avoided?' 'You know quite well'[48]
he said 'what my reply will be. But since, as I suspect, you want to
catch me out in a short answer, I shall not deal with particular
points. Instead, since we have plenty of time, and if you have no
objection, I shall expound the whole system of Zeno and the
Stoics.' 'I certainly do not have any objection,' I replied, 'and your
exposition will be of great help in our present investigation.'

15. 'Well, let's try,' he said, 'although this system of the Stoics is
not very easy or clear. For when in Greek these terms for what
were once strange ideas seemed strange,[49] but now constant use has
made them routine, what do you think will happen in Latin?[50]' 'No
trouble at all,' I answered. 'for if Zeno was allowed to give some
outlandish name[51] to his uncommon discoveries, why can't Cato?
But still a word for word correspondence – which inexpert
translators adopt – isn't necessary when there is a familiar term
which can mean the same. I often use several expressions for one
Greek one, if I can't convey the meaning otherwise. But also I
think that we can be allowed to use the Greek word if a suitable
Latin one is not available. We have *ep῾npia* ("saddles") and
acratophoria ("jars for undiluted wine"), so why not *proēgmena*
and *apoproēgmena*, even though it would be acceptable to call
these *praeposita* and *reiecta*?' 16. 'Thank you for your help,' he
said. 'In those cases I shall certainly prefer to use the Latin
equivalents you have just given; for the rest, you must help me if

inquam 'faciam. sed "fortuna fortis". quare conare, quaeso. quid enim possumus hoc agere diuinius?'

The primary instinct is for self-preservation

[V] 'Placet his', inquit, 'quorum ratio mihi probatur, simulatque natum sit animal – hinc enim est ordiendum – ipsum sibi conciliari et commendari ad se conservandum et ad suum statum eaque, quae conseruantia sint eius status, diligenda, alienari autem ab interitu iisque rebus quae interitum uideantur afferre. id ita esse sic probant: quod ante quam uoluptas aut dolor attigerit, salutaria appetant parui aspernenturque contraria – quod non fieret, nisi statum suum diligerent, interitum timerent. fieri autem non posset ut appeterent aliquid nisi sensum haberent sui eoque se diligerent. ex quo intellegi debet principium ductum esse a se diligendo.

The primary instinct is not for pleasure

17. In principiis autem naturalibus plerique Stoici non putant uoluptatem esse ponendam. quibus ego uehementer assentior, ne, si uoluptatem natura posuisse in iis rebus uideatur quae primae appetuntur, multa turpia sequantur. satis esse autem argumenti uidetur quam ob rem illa quae prima sunt ascita natura diligamus, quod est nemo quin, cum utrumuis liceat, aptas malit et integras omnes partes corporis quam, eodem usu, imminutas aut detortas habere.

There is intrinsic merit in rational activity

Rerum autem cognitiones (quas uel comprehensiones uel perceptiones uel, si haec uerba aut minus placent aut minus intelleguntur, katalēpseis appellemus licet) eas igitur propter se asciscendas arbitramur, quod habeant quiddam in se quasi complexum et continens ueritatem. id autem in paruis intellegi potest, quos delectari uideamus, etiamsi eorum nihil intersit, si quid ratione per se ipsi inuenerint. 18. artes etiam ipsas propter se assumendas putamus, cum quia sit in iis aliquid dignum assumptione, tum quod constent ex cognitionibus et contineant quiddam in se ratione constitutum et uia. a falsa autem assensione magis nos alienatos esse quam a ceteris rebus, quae sint contra naturam, arbitrantur.

you see me stuck.' 'I shall do my best,' I said. 'But "fortune favours the brave",[52] so please make the attempt, for what more god-like than this could we do?'

[V] 'It is', Cato began, 'the theory of those whose philosophy I accept, that as soon as a living creature is born[53] – for this should be our starting point – it feels an attachment for itself;[54] it has an instinct for self-preservation and concern about its own condition and what keeps that condition stable, but sets itself against death and what obviously contributes to death. The Stoics demonstrate this[55] in the following way: before pleasure or pain affects them, infants make for what is health-giving and reject the opposite – and this would not be the case unless they felt an affection for their own condition and feared its destruction.[56] But it would be impossible for them to have any desires unless they were conscious of themselves, and so had self-love. Consequently the primary instinct should be recognised as based on self-love.

17. Many Stoics maintain that pleasure should not even be included[57] in what is naturally primary. I am in earnest agreement with them, from fear of the numerous immoral consequences[58] of the assumption that nature has included pleasure among the objects of instinctive desires. There is however obviously sufficient evidence of our feeling of affection for what is first gained at nature's prompting[59] in the fact that there is no one who, given the choice either way, would not prefer[60] to have all the parts of his body well-formed and sound, rather than enfeebled and maimed, although equally serviceable.

Furthermore, cognitions[61] (which we may call comprehensions or perceptions or, if these terms are unpleasing or unintelligible, *katalēpseis*) can therefore, we think, be taken up for their own sake,[62] because they contain something in themselves which, as it were, embraces truth and holds it fast. This can be observed in children[63] who we see are delighted at making a discovery for themselves by the use of reason, even if they gain nothing by it. **18.** We think too that the arts should be adopted[64] on their own account, because they have that in them which is worth the adoption, and because they are built up from cognitions, and are themselves a product of logical method. The Stoics claim that we are more repelled by an assent to what is false[65] than by anything else contrary to nature.

The style must suit the subject matter

19. Haec dicuntur fortasse ieiunius; sunt enim quasi prima elementa naturae, quibus ubertas orationis adhiberi uix potest, nec equidem eam cogito consectari. uerum tamen, cum de rebus grandioribus dicas, ipsae res uerba rapiunt; ita fit cum grauior, tum etiam splendidior oratio.' 'Est ut dicis,' inquam, 'sed tamen omne quod de re bona dilucide dicitur, mihi praeclare dici uidetur. istius modi autem res dicere ornate uelle puerile est, plane autem et perspicue expedire posse docti et intellegentis uiri.'

The classification 'value-plus' and 'value-minus'

[VI] 20. 'Progrediamur igitur, quoniam' inquit, 'ab his principiis naturae discessimus, quibus congruere debent quae sequuntur. sequitur autem haec prima diuisio: "aestimabile" esse dicunt (sic enim, ut opinor, appellemus) id, quod aut ipsum secundum naturam sit aut tale quid efficiat, ut selectione dignum propterea sit, quod aliquod pondus habeat dignum aestimatione (quam illi *axian* uocant), contraque "inaestimabile", quod sit superiori contrarium. initiis igitur ita constitutis, ut ea, quae secundum naturam sunt, ipsa propter se sumenda sint contrariaque item reicienda, primum est "officium" (id enim appello *kathēkon*) ut se conseruet in naturae statu, deinceps ut ea teneat, quae secundum naturam sint, pellatque contraria. qua inuenta selectione et item reiectione sequitur deinceps cum officio selectio, deinde ea perpetua, tum ad extremum constans consentaneaque naturae, in qua primum inesse incipit et intellegi quid sit, quod uere bonum possit dici.

Reason and conformity

21. Prima est enim conciliatio hominis ad ea, quae sunt secundum naturam. simul autem cepit intellegentiam uel notionem potius (quam appellant *ennoian* illi) uiditque rerum agendarum ordinem et, ut ita dicam, concordiam, multo eam pluris aestimauit quam omnia illa quae prima dilexerat, atque ita cognitione et ratione collegit, ut statueret in eo collocatum summum illud hominis per se laudandum et expetendum bonum. quod cum positum sit in eo quod *homologian* Stoici (nos appellemus "conuenientiam" si placet), cum igitur in eo sit id bonum quo omnia referenda sint, honeste facta ipsumque honestum – quod solum in bonis ducitur, quamquam post oritur – tamen id solum ui sua et dignitate expetendum est; eorum autem, quae sunt prima naturae, propter se nihil est expetendum.

19. Perhaps all this is put rather baldly; but it is like the ABC of nature.[66] Richness of style is scarcely applicable here, and I do not intend to attempt it. However, when the subject-matter is more elevated the words keep pace, and the brilliance of the style then matches the increased dignity of the theme.' 'That is so,' I said, 'but still I think that anything said clearly on a serious topic is well said. It would be childish to expect a high style in a theme of that kind, but an educated and intelligent man will be able to express himself plainly and clearly.'[67]

[VI] **20.** 'Let us continue then' he said, 'after our digression from the subject of primary natural instincts, for the next stage must be consistent with the first. There comes now the following fundamental classification:[68] the Stoics call "of plus value"[69] (that, I think, is a permissible translation) whatever is either inherently according to nature, or productive of what is according to nature, so that it is worth choosing because it has a certain amount of positive value (which they term *axia*); its opposite they call "of minus value".[70] Once the foundation is thus established, namely that what is according to nature is to be taken up for its own sake and its opposite similarly rejected, the first "appropriate action"[71] (for so I translate *kathēkon*) is to keep in one's natural condition, the second is to hold fast to what is according to nature, and to drive off its opposite. When such a method of choice and rejection has been discovered, there follows choice conditioned by appropriate action;[72] this then becomes habitual, and finally unwavering and in harmony with nature. Then, for the first time, what can truly be called good begins to be apparent,[73] and its character to be understood.

21. Man's first attraction[74] is towards what is according to nature. Then, as soon as he is capable of reasoning, or rather of conceptual understanding[75] (which the Stoics call *ennoia*), and recognises order and, I might almost say, harmony in action, he regards that far above all that he had liked at first;[76] so, by the acquisition of knowledge and by reasoning, he reaches the decision that man's chief good,[77] praiseworthy and desirable for its own sake, rests here. Since it does reside in what the Stoics term *homologia*[78] (which, if you like, we shall call "conformity"), and in this then there is that good which is the standard of reference for everything else, the combination of right acts and right itself[79] – which alone is counted as a good, although arising later – is yet the only thing to be desired for its intrinsic power and merit; none of the primary natural objects is desirable for its own sake.[80]

Moral action is according to nature

22. Cum uero illa, quae officia esse dixi, proficiscantur ab initiis naturae, necesse est ea ad haec referri, ut recte dici possit omnia officia eo referri, ut adipiscamur principia naturae – nec tamen ut hoc sit bonorum ultimum, propterea quod non inest in primis naturae conciliationibus honesta actio; consequens enim est et post oritur, ut dixi. est tamen ea secundum naturam multoque nos ad se expetendum magis hortatur quam superiora omnia.

There is only one supreme good

Sed ex hoc primum error tollendus est, ne quis sequi existimet, ut *duo* sint ultima bonorum. etenim, si cui propositum sit colliniare hastam aliquo aut sagittam, sicut nos ultimum in bonis dicimus: huic in eius modi similitudine omnia sint facienda, ut colliniet, et tamen, ut omnia faciat, quo propositum assequatur, sit hoc quasi ultimum (quale nos summum in uita bonum dicimus) illud autem, ut feriat, quasi "seligendum", non "expetendum".

Wisdom begins from primary natural instincts

[VII] **23.** Cum autem omnia officia a principiis naturae proficiscantur, ab iisdem necesse est proficisci ipsam sapientiam. sed quem ad modum saepe fit ut is, qui commendatus sit alicui, pluris eum faciat, cui commendatus sit, quam illum a quo, sic minime mirum est primo nos sapientiae commendari ab initiis naturae, post autem ipsam sapientiam nobis cariorem fieri, quam illa sint, a quibus ad hanc uenerimus. atque ut membra nobis ita data sunt, ut ad quandam rationem uiuendi data esse appareant, sic appetitio animi (quae *hormē* Graece uocatur) non ad quoduis genus uitae, sed ad quandam formam uiuendi uidetur data, itemque et ratio et perfecta ratio.

The 'art' of living

24. Vt enim histrioni actio, saltatori motus non quiuis, sed certus quidam est datus, sic uita agenda est certo genere quodam, non quolibet; quod genus conueniens consentaneumque dicimus. nec enim gubernationi aut medicinae similem sapientiam esse arbitramur, sed actioni illi potius, quam modo dixi, et saltationi, ut in ipsa insit, non foris petatur extremum, id est artis effectio. et tamen est etiam aliqua cum his ipsis artibus sapientiae dissimilitudo, propterea quod in illis quae recte facta sunt non continent tamen omnes partes, e quibus constant. quae autem nos aut "recta" aut "recte facta" dicamus, si placet (illi autem appellant *katorthōmata*) omnes numeros uirtutis continent. sola enim

22. But since what I have called appropriate actions arise from natural first impulses,[81] they must be referred to these same impulses, so that one would be correct in saying that all appropriate actions are means to obtaining primary natural objects – not however that this is the ultimate good, for right action is not included[82] among the primary natural inclinations; it is, as I said, a consequence coming to light later. Nonetheless right action is according to nature, and stimulates our desire for itself[83] much more forcibly than all that came before.

A possible source of error must be removed here: could it not be assumed that it follows that there are *two* supreme goods?[84] Not at all,[85] if we compare the supreme good to the case of a man who has set himself to aim at some mark with a spear or arrow:[86] in such an illustration the man has to do everything possible to shoot straight, nevertheless the actual doing of all he can to accomplish his purpose is in this instance *his* supreme good[87] (comparable to what we call the chief good in life), whereas his hitting of the target is "to be chosen", and not "to be desired".[88]

[VII]   23. Now since all appropriate actions start from primary natural instincts,[89] wisdom too must have the same beginnings. But just as it is often the case that a man who is introduced to another[90] esteems him more highly than the one who made the introduction, so it is not surprising that once we have been introduced to wisdom on the first occasion by natural instincts, later that wisdom becomes dearer to us[91] than the instincts by means of which we came to know her. Moreover, as the parts of our body are clearly given to us with a view to a particular way of life, so the mind's instinctive desire[92] (which the Greeks term *hormē*) is obviously given not for any kind of life, but for life with a particular design,[93] as also are reason and perfected reason.

24. As the actor is assigned gestures[94] and the dancer movements not at random but with a fixed pattern, so life must be lived according to a definite plan, and not in any way you like; such a life we call harmonious and consistent.[95] Further, we do not consider that wisdom resembles navigation or medicine, but it is more like the gestures just mentioned, and like dancing, in that the actual exercise of the skill is in itself,[96] and does not aim at an external object. But the practice of wisdom is not quite like these skills, in particular because correctly performed gestures or steps do not involve all that make up these arts, but acts which we may call, if you like, "right" or "rightly done"[97] (*katorthōmata* in Stoic terminology) involve every category of virtue.[98] Wisdom alone is

sapientia in se tota conuersa est, quod idem in ceteris artibus non fit. 25. inscite autem medicinae et gubernationis ultimum cum ultimo sapientiae comparatur. sapientia enim et animi magnitudinem complectitur et iustitiam, et ut omnia, quae homini accidant, infra se esse iudicet, quod idem ceteris artibus non contingit.

32. Sed in ceteris artibus cum dicitur "artificiose", posterum quodam modo et consequens putandum est (quod illi *epigennēmatikon* appellant); cum autem in quo "sapienter" dicimus, id a primo rectissime dicitur. quicquid enim a sapientia proficiscitur, id continuo debet expletum esse omnibus suis partibus; in eo enim positum est id, quod dicimus expetendum. nam ut peccatum est patriam prodere, parentes uiolare, fana depeculari, quae sint in effectu, sic timere, sic maerere, sic in libidine esse peccatum est etiam sine effectu. uerum ut haec non in posteris et in consequentibus, sed in primis continuo peccata sunt, sic ea, quae proficiscuntur a uirtute, susceptione prima non perfectione recta sunt iudicanda.

Conclusion to V – VII

Tenere autem uirtutes eas ipsas, quarum modo feci mentionem, nemo poterit, nisi statuerit nihil esse, quod intersit aut differat aliud ab alio, praeter honesta et turpia. 26. uideamus nunc, quam sint praeclare illa his, quae iam posui, consequentia. cum enim hoc sit extremum (sentis enim, credo, me iam diu, quod *telos* Graeci dicant, id dicere tum extremum, tum ultimum, tum summum, licebit etiam "finem" pro extremo aut ultimo dicere) – cum igitur hoc sit extremum, congruenter naturae conuenienterque uiuere, necessario sequitur omnes sapientes semper feliciter, absolute, fortunate uiuere, nulla re impediri, nulla prohiberi, nihil egere. quod autem continet non magis eam disclipinam, de qua loquor, quam uitam fortunasque nostras, id est ut, quod honestum sit, id solum bonum iudicemus, potest id quidem fuse et copiose et omnibus electissimis uerbis grauissimisque sententiis rhetorice et augeri et ornari, sed consectaria me Stoicorum breuia et acuta delectant.

The syllogism for 'what is good is right'

[VIII] 27. Concluduntur igitur eorum argumenta sic: Quod est bonum, omne laudabile est; quod autem laudabile est omne est honestum; bonum igitur quod est, honestum est. satisne hoc conclusum uidetur? certe; quod enim efficiebatur ex iis duobus,

wholly directed towards itself, which is not the case with the other arts. **25.** A comparison of the aim of medicine or navigation with that of wisdom only shows ignorance, for wisdom includes high-mindedness, justice and that quality which deems the accidents to men's estate beneath contempt;[99] this sort of inclusion is not true of other skills.

32. In other skills, when we use the adverb "skilfully" we have to think of this as referring in some way to a chronological and logical result[100] (which the Stoics term *epigennēmatikon*); but when we use the adverb "wisely" this is correctly applied from the start. All that proceeds from wisdom must be complete in every respect throughout, for this is the condition of saying of anything that it is to be desired. Treason, violence to parents and sacrilege[101] are crimes on account of their external consequences, fear, grief and lust[102] are failings, even when there is no outward effect. Such passions are failings, not in their later results but right from the start, and similarly what proceeds from virtue is to be judged moral not in its completion but at its very adoption.[103]

No one will be able to maintain a hold on those virtues which I have just mentioned, unless he has made up his mind that the only difference and distinction which exists is that between right and wrong.[104] **26.** Let us look now at the striking results of the arguments which I have put forward. Since this is the ultimate aim (you realise I think that for some time now I have been translating the Greek word *telos* by aim, goal and highest point, and we can also say "end" for aim or goal) since then this is the ultimate aim, namely to live in conformity and harmony with nature,[105] it necessarily follows that all wise men are all their lives in a state of happiness, perfection and good fortune, without any restriction,[106] hindrance or need. The principle that we should consider only what is right as good, which is the foundation of our lives and fortunes as well as of the philosophy under discussion, could of course be enlarged on and decorated elaborately and extensively in a rhetorical manner[107] with all the choicest phrases and most imposing maxims, but I prefer the short and pointed proofs of the Stoics.

[VIII] 27. Their arguments are set out[108] in the following form: all that is good deserves praise, all that deserves praise is right, therefore what is good is right. Do you think that the conclusion is valid?[109] of course, for you can see that the conclusion follows from the two premises. However, against the first of the two premises from which the conclusion was drawn it is usually maintained that

quae erant sumpta, in eo uides conclusum. duorum autem e quibus effecta conclusio est contra superius dici solet non omne bonum est laudabile, nam quod laudabile sit honestum esse conceditur. illud autem perabsurdum bonum esse aliquid quod non expetendum sit, aut expetendum, quod non placens, aut, si id, non etiam diligendum, ergo ut probandum, ita etiam laudabile; id autem honestum. ita fit ut quod bonum sit id etiam honestum sit.

The happy life is the good life

28. Deinde quaero: quis aut de misera uita possit gloriari aut de non beata. de sola igitur beata. ex quo efficitur gloriatione, ut ita dicam, dignam esse beatam uitam, quod non possit nisi honestae uitae iure contingere; ita fit ut honesta uita beata uita sit. et quoniam is, cui contingit ut iure laudetur, habet insigne quiddam ad decus et ad gloriam, ut ob ea quae tanta sint beatus dici iure possit, idem de uita talis uiri rectissime dicetur. ita si beata uita honestate cernitur, quod honestum est id bonum solum habendum est.

The only evil is vice

29. Quid uero? negarine ullo modo possit <numquam> quemquam stabili et firmo et magno animo, quem fortem uirum dicimus, effici posse, nisi constitutum sit non esse malum dolorem? ut enim qui mortem in malis ponit non potest eam non timere, sic nemo ulla in re potest id quod malum esse decreuerit non curare idque contemnere. quo posito et omnium assensu approbato illud assumitur: eum, qui magno sit animo atque forti, omnia, quae cadere in hominem possint, despicere ac pro nihilo putare. quae cum ita sint, effectum est nihil esse malum, quod turpe non sit.

No evil can befall the good man

Atque iste uir – altus et excellens, magno animo, uere fortis, infra se omnia humana ducens – is, inquam, quem efficere uolumus, quem quaerimus, certe et confidere sibi debet ac suae uitae et actae et consequenti, et bene de sese iudicare statuens nihil posse mali incidere sapienti. ex quo intellegitur idem illud solum bonum esse quod honestum sit, idque esse beate uiuere, honeste – id est cum uirtute – uiuere.

Other theories

[IX] 30. Nec uero ignoro uarias philosophorum fuisse sententias, eorum dico, qui summum bonum, quod ultimum appello, in animo

it is not the case[110] that all that is good deserves praise, whereas it is admitted that what deserves praise is right. Yet it is silly to say that there is something which is good which is not to be desired, or which is to be desired but is not agreeable, or if agreeable not to be chosen, and therefore approved, and so deserving praise; but what deserves praise is right. So it follows[111] that what is good is indeed right.

28. I put this question next: who can be proud of a wretched or unhappy life?[112] It is only of a happy one. So it follows, if I may put it so, that the happy life is one to be proud of, and this can only be true of the righteous life; therefore the happy life is the righteous life.[113] And since the man who deservedly wins our approval has a certain characteristic which marks him out for distinction and renown, with the result that because of these great qualities he can truly be called happy, the same can quite correctly be said of the life of such a man. And so if happiness in life depends on what is right, what is right is to be considered the only good.

29. Well then, would it be at all possible to deny that there never could be anyone high-minded, steadfast and unwavering, a man of courage as we say, if it were not established that pain is not an evil?[114] For as it is impossible for anyone who considers death an evil not to be afraid of it, it is likewise impossible in any circumstances for a man to disregard and despise what he has decided is evil.[115] Once all this has been set out and universally approved a further assumption is made: the high-minded and courageous man[116] scorns and thinks of no account all that befalls the human race. This gives the conclusion that nothing is evil except vice.[117]

This man moreover – great and distinguished, high-minded and truly courageous, who thinks all human fortune beneath him – the man I say whom we want to bring to light, the object of our search,[118] must surely have confidence in himself and in his own life past and to come, and assess himself optimistically, being convinced that no evil can befall the wise man.[119] From this again we realise that only what is right is good, and that the righteous life – the one lived virtuously[120] – is the happy life.

[IX] 30. Now I know quite well that there is a difference of opinion[121] among those philosophers who maintain that the supreme good, which I call the final aim, depends on the mind. Although

ponerent. quae quamquam uitiose quidam secuti sunt, tamen non modo iis tribus, qui uirtutem a summo bono segregauerunt, cum aut (i) uoluptatem aut (ii) uacuitatem doloris aut (iii) prima naturae in summis bonis ponerent, sed etiam alteris tribus, qui mancam fore putauerunt sine aliqua accessione uirtutem ob eamque rem trium earum rerum, quas supra dixi, singuli singulas addiderunt, – his tamen omnibus eos antepono, cuicuimodi sunt, qui summum bonum in animo atque in uirtute posuerunt.

Difficulties even with the preferable alternatives

31. Sed sunt tamen perabsurdi et ii, (i) qui cum scientia uiuere ultimum bonorum, et (ii) qui nullam rerum differentiam esse dixerunt, atque ita sapientem beatum fore, nihil aliud alii momento ullo anteponentem, et (iii) qui – ut quidam Academici constituisse dicuntur – extremum bonorum et summum munus esse sapientis obsistere uisis assensusque suos firme sustinere. his singulis copiose responderi solet, sed quae perspicua sunt longa esse non debent. quid autem apertius quam, si selectio nulla sit ab iis rebus, quae contra naturam sint, earum rerum, quae sint secundum naturam, fore ut tollatur omnis ea, quae quaeratur laudeturque, prudentia?

Circumscriptis igitur iis sententiis, quas posui, et iis si quae similes earum sunt, relinquitur ut summum bonum sit uiuere scientiam adhibentem earum rerum, quae natura eueniant, seligentem quae secundum naturam et quae contra naturam sint reicientem – id est conuenienter congruenterque naturae uiuere.

The definition of 'good'

[X] 33. "Bonum" autem, quod in hoc sermone totiens usurpatum est, id etiam definitione explicatur; sed eorum definitiones paulum oppido inter se differunt et tamen eodem spectant. ego assentior Diogeni, qui bonum definierit id quod esset natura absolutum; id autem sequens illud etiam, quod prodesset (*ōphelēma* enim sic appellemus) motum aut statum esse dixit e natura absoluto. cumque rerum notiones in animis fiant, si aut (i) usu aliquid cognitum sit aut (ii) coniunctione aut (iii) similitudine aut (iv) collatione rationis; hoc quarto, quod extremum posui, boni notitia facta est. cum enim ab iis rebus quae sunt secundum naturam ascendit animus collatione rationis, tum ad notionem boni peruenit.

some of these have come to wrong conclusions, in placing the supreme good in virtue and the mind they are one and all preferable[122] to those three groups who have divorced virtue from the supreme good, identifying the chief good with (i) pleasure,[123] (ii) freedom from pain[124] or (iii) the primary natural state,[125] and also to a second set of three groups[126] who have supposed that virtue is defective without any accompaniments, and for that reason have added to it in each case one of the three conditions just mentioned.

31. But even those philosophers are rather ridiculous who claim (i) that a life of learning[127] is the supreme good, or (ii) that there are no distinctions to be made[128] in the world and that the wise man will be happy because he does not have a preference[129] for any one thing rather than another, or (iii) – as some Academics are said to have maintained – that the ultimate good and chief duty of the wise man is to resist, and steadfastly to withold his assent from appearances.[130] It is customary to give a lengthy refutation of each of these three points of view, but what is evident need not be dwelt upon. What could be plainer than the fact that, if there is no exercise of choice between what is contrary to nature and what is according to nature, all of that highly praised practical wisdom which is our aim will be useless?[131]

And so, if we eliminate[132] the theories I have described, and those like them, we are left with the conclusion that the supreme good consists in applying to the conduct of life a knowledge of the way nature operates, choosing what is according to nature and rejecting what is contrary – in sum in living in harmony and conformity with nature.[133]

[X]   **33.** The term "good", which has often been used in this discourse, is capable of definition;[134] certainly the definitions given by the Stoics differ a little in precise detail but they have the same general meaning. I agree with Diogenes who has defined "good" as what is naturally perfect;[135] following on this he called that which is beneficial[136] (as we may translate ōphelēma) a process or condition arising from what is naturally perfect. Concepts about the world arise in our minds when something has come to be known from (i) experience, (ii) combination, (iii) resemblance[137] or (iv) logical inference;[138] understanding of the good is reached by the fourth and last method. When the mind by means of logical inference passes beyond what is according to nature, it then reaches to an understanding of the good.

34. Hoc autem ipsum bonum non accessione neque crescendo aut cum ceteris comparando, sed propria ui sua et sentimus et appellamus bonum. ut enim mel, etsi dulcissimum est, suo tamen proprio genere saporis, non comparatione cum aliis dulce esse sentitur, sic bonum hoc de quo agimus, est illud quidem plurimi aestimandum, sed ea aestimatio genere ualet, non magnitudine. nam cum aestimatio (quae *axia* dicitur) neque in bonis numerata sit nec rursus in malis, quantumcumque eo addideris, in suo genere manebit. alia est igitur propria aestimatio uirtutis, quae genere, non crescendo ualet.

The emotions as mental disturbances

35. Nec uero perturbationes animorum, quae uitam insipientium miseram acerbamque reddunt (quas Graeci *pathē* appellant; poteram ego uerbum ipsum interpretans morbos appellare, sed non conueniret ad omnia; quis enim misericordiam aut ipsam iracundiam morbum solet dicere? at illi dicunt *pathos*; sit igitur "perturbatio", quae nomine ipso uitiosa declarari uidetur) – omnes eae sunt genere quattuor, partibus plures, (i) aegritudo, (ii) formido, (iii) libido, (iv) quamque Stoici communi nomine corporis et animi *hēdonēn* appellant, ego malo laetitiam appellare, quasi gestientis animi elationem uoluptariam. perturbationes autem nulla naturae ui commouentur, omniaque ea sunt opiniones ac iudicia leuitatis. itaque his sapiens semper uacabit.

Support from general consensus

[XI] 36. Omne autem quod honestum sit id esse propter se expetendum, commune nobis est cum multorum aliorum philosophorum sententiis. praeter enim tres disciplinas quae uirtutem a summo bono excludunt, ceteris omnibus philosophis haec est tuenda sententia, maxime tamen his qui nihil aliud in bonorum numero nisi honestum esse uoluerunt. sed haec quidem est perfacilis et expedita defensio. quis est enim aut quis umquam fuit aut auaritia tam ardenti aut tam effrenatis cupiditatibus, ut eandem illam rem quam adipisci scelere quouis uelit non multis partibus malit ad sese etiam omni impunitate proposita sine facinore quam illo modo peruenire?

Wisdom and courage are esteemed for their own sake

37. Quam uero utilitatem aut quem fructum petentes scire cupimus illa quae occulta nobis sunt – quomodo moueantur quibusque de causis ea quae uersantur in caelo? quis autem tam agrestibus institutis uiuit aut quis contra studia naturae tam uehementer

34. This good we think of and name as good not by any increase or addition to other things or comparison with them, but on account of its own inherent force.[139] Just as honey,[140] although the sweetest thing there is, is thought sweet because of its own characteristic taste, and not as the result of a comparison with others, so this good which we are discussing is of course to be valued above all else, but this is a value judgment of kind, not of quantity. For since value (the translation of *axia*) is counted neither as a good nor again as an evil, however much you add to it it will stay in its own kind. There is therefore another type of value belonging to virtue alone,[141] the worth of which lies not in increase but in kind.

35. There are also mental disturbances,[142] which make the lives of the unphilosophic unhappy and bitter (the Greek term is *pathē*, and in translating I could call them "diseases",[143] but this would not be suitable in all cases, for who would call pity or even anger a disease? still, the Greek word is *pathos*, so let us say "disturbance", where the very name clearly reveals the weakness) – these are all subdivisions of four main classes,[144] (i) grief, (ii) fear, (iii) improper desire and (iv) what the Stoics term *hēdonē* for both body or mind, which I prefer to call "delight", the pleasant excitement of a mind aroused.[145] Nevertheless these disturbances are not caused by any natural impulse, but they are all fancies and sentiments of an unstable character.[146] The wise man will therefore always be free of them.[147]

[XI] 36. We share the assumption that all that is right is desirable for its own sake with the systems of many other philosophers. Apart from the three schools[148] which remove virtue altogether from the supreme good, the assumption has to be a tenet of all remaining philosophies, and especially of the Stoics,[149] who were determined to include nothing except what is right in the class of goods. This position can be defended in a simple and straightforward manner. For who is there now, or was ever in the past, of such intense greed and with such unrestrained lusts, who would not prefer many times over, even if willing to commit any crime to achieve his end, and without any threat of punishment at all, to gain his object blamelessly[150] rather than by criminal means?

37. Further, what advantage or profit can we be aiming at when we are anxious to find out the secrets of natural science[151] – the movements of the heavenly bodies and the explanations for them? Who lives in such a backward society, who has set himself so

obduruit ut a rebus cognitione dignis abhorreat easque sine
uoluptate aut utilitate aliqua non requirat et pro nihilo putet? aut
quis est qui maiorum aut Africanorum aut eius quem tu in ore
semper habes, proaui mei ceterorumque uirorum fortium atque
omni uirtute praestantium facta, dicta, consilia cognoscens nulla
animo afficiatur uoluptate?

What is wrong is intrinsically repulsive

38. Quis autem honesta in familia institutus et educatus ingenue
non ipsa turpitudine, etiamsi eum laesura non sit, offenditur? quis
animo aequo uidet eum quem impure ac flagitiose putet uiuere?
quis non odit sordidos, uanos, leues, futiles? quid autem dici
poterit, si turpitudinem non ipsam per se fugiendam esse statuemus,
quo minus homines tenebras et solitudinem nacti nullo dedecore se
abstineat, nisi eos per se foeditate sua turpitudo ipsa deterreat?
innumerabilia dici possunt in hanc sententiam; sed non necesse est.
nihil est enim de quo minus dubitari possit quam et honesta
expetenda per se et eodem modo turpia per se fugienda.

The consequences of wrong conduct

39. Constituto autem illo de quo ante diximus, quod honestum esset
id esse solum bonum, intellegi necesse est pluris id quod honestum
sit aestimandum esse quam illa media quae ex eo comparentur.
stultitiam autem et timiditatem et iniustitiam et intemperantiam
cum dicimus esse fugienda propter eas res quae ex ipsis eueniant,
non ita dicimus ut cum illo quod positum est, solum id esse malum
quod turpe sit, haec pugnare uideatur oratio, propterea quod ea
non ad corporis incommodum referuntur sed ad turpes actiones
quae oriuntur ex uitiis (quas enim *kakias* Graeci appellant, uitia
malo quam malitias nominare).'

The Latinising of philosophy

[XII] **40.** 'Ne tu' inquam 'Cato, uerbis illustribus et id quod uis
declarantibus! itaque mihi uideris Latine docere philosophiam et ei
quasi ciuitatem dare; quae quidem adhuc peregrinari Romae
uidebatur nec offerre sese nostris sermonibus, et ista maxime
propter limatam quandam et rerum et uerborum tenuitatem. (scio
enim esse quosdam qui quauis lingua philosophari possit; nullis
enim partitionibus, nullis definitionibus utuntur, ipsique dicunt ea
se modo probare quibus natura tacita assentiatur; itaque in rebus
minime obscuris non multus est apud eos disserandi labor.) quaere

obstinately against the study of nature that he finds subjects that deserve consideration repulsive, rejecting and despising them, unless they bring some pleasure or profit?[152] Who is there who feels no pleasure at heart[153] when he learns of the actions and words and wisdom of our ancestors, of the Africani,[154] of my great-grandfather,[155] whom you mention continually, and all the other heroes excelling in every virtue?

38. On the other hand, what man of noble family and proper education[156] is not shocked by what is wrong on its own account, and even if it will not harm him? Who can look calmly on one he thinks to be leading a dissolute and criminal life? Who does not hate the mean, the trivial, the frivolous and the useless? And if we do not come to the conclusion that what is wrong is to be avoided on its own account, what could be said to keep a man back from any dishonourable act in private, under cover of darkness, unless the wrongness, by its very ugliness, acts as a deterrent?[157] Numerous arguments can be put forward in support of this stand; but they are not necessary. For nothing is less to be questioned[158] than that what is right is to be desired for its own sake, and what is wrong is for its own sake to be avoided.

39. Once the conclusion which we have been discussing, that only what is right is good, has been established, it has to be understood that what is right must be valued more highly than those neutral effects which result from it.[159] And when we say that folly, cowardice,[160] injustice and lack of temperance are to be avoided[161] because of the results following from them we do not mean that this way of speaking appears to contradict the principle already established, that only what is wrong is bad. This is because the results do not apply to bodily harm,[162] but to the wrong actions which arise from vices (which the Greeks call *kakiai*, but which I translate by "vices" rather than "evils").[163]

[XII] **40.** 'How clear[164] your terminology is, Cato;' I said, 'it gives your meaning precisely! Indeed, you seem to me to be teaching philosophy to speak Latin, and, as it were, giving her Roman citizenship;[165] until now she seemed to be an alien in Rome and did not speak our language, Stoic philosophy especially,[166] because of a certain sophistication and economy in thought and expression. (I know there are some[167] who could do philosophy in any language; without bothering about classifications and definitions[168] they claim to be commending only that which has the unspoken approval of nature; and that is why they do not put a great deal of effort into

attendo te studiose et quaecumque rebus iis de quibus hic sermo est nomina imponis memoria mando; mihi enim erit iisdem istis fortasse iam utendum. uirtutibus igitur rectissime mihi uideris et ad consuetudinem nostrae orationis uitia posuisse contraria. quod enim uituperabile est per se ipsum, id eo ipso uitium nominatum puto, uel etiam a uitio dictum uituperari. sin *kakian* malitiam dixisses, ad aliud nos unum certum uitium consuetudo Latina traduceret. nunc omni uirtuti uitium contrario nomine opponitur.'

Crucial disagreement with the Peripatetics

41. Tum ille: 'His igitur ita positis,' inquit, 'sequitur magna contentio, quam tractatam a Peripateticis mollius (est enim eorum consuetudo dicendi non satis acuta propter ignorationem dialecticae), Carneades tuus egregia quadam exercitatione in dialecticis summaque eloquentia rem in summum discrimen adduxit, propterea quod pugnare non destitit in omni hac quaestione, quae de bonis et malis appelletur, non esse rerum Stoicis cum Peripateticis controuersiam sed nominum. mihi autem nihil tam perspicuum uidetur quam has sententias eorum philosophorum re inter se magis quam uerbis dissidere; maiorem multo inter Stoicos et Peripateticos rerum esse aio discrepantiam quam uerborum, quippe cum Peripatetici omnia quae ipsi bona appellant pertinere dicant ad beate uiuendum, nostri non ex omni quod aestimatione aliqua dignum sit compleri uitam beatam putent.

Differences on the length and degree of happiness

[XIII] 42. An uero certius quicquam potest esse quam illorum ratione qui dolorem in malis ponunt non posse esse sapientem beatum esse cum eculeo torqueatur? eorum autem qui dolorem in malis non habent ratio certe cogit ut in omnibus tormentis conseruetur beata uita sapienti. etenim si dolores eosdem tolerabilius patiuntur qui excipiunt eos pro patria quam qui leuiore de causa, opinio facit, non natura, uim doloris aut maiorem aut minorem. **43.** ne illud quidem est consentaneum, ut, si cum tria genera bonorum sint (quae sententia est Peripateticorum) eo beatior quisque sit, quo sit corporis aut externis bonis plenior, ut hoc idem approbandum sit nobis, ut qui plura habeat ea quae in corpore magni aestimantur sit beatior. illi enim corporis commodis compleri uitam beatam putant, nostri nihil minus. nam cum ita placeat, ne eorum quidem bonorum, quae nos bona uere appellemus, frequentia beatiorem uitam fieri aut magis expetendam aut pluris

arguing for what is quite obvious.) So I am paying careful attention
to you and committing to memory all the terms which you are
using for the concepts under discussion; for possibly I shall soon
have to use[169] the same terminology myself. I think then that your
translation of the opposite of virtues as vices is correct and
consistent with our use of language. For what is vicious on its own
account is I think termed vice, or else "to be vicious" is derived
from "vice". If you had translated *kakia* as "malitia", Latin usage
could have indicated one particular vice (namely "malice"). As it
is, the word "vice" is opposed to virtue in general.'

41. Then Cato resumed: 'Once these principles are so established, a
major disagreement follows, which the Peripatetics treated with less
severity (their arguments are not sharp enough because of their
ignorance of logic),[170] but your Carneades,[171] with his distinction for
proficiency in logic as well as his great eloquence, made it a key
issue.[172] On the whole question of the problem of good and evil
Carneades never gave up the fight for his claim that the
disagreement between the Stoics and the Peripatetics was not about
facts but terminology.[173] But in my opinion it is most clearly
evident that these philosophers' tenets differ in substance more than
in words. I maintain that the distinction between the Stoics and the
Peripatetics is much more substantial than verbal,[174] especially in
the light of the Peripatetic claim that all which they call goods
contribute to happiness, whereas we do not think that what is of
some value is needed to make the happy life complete.

[XIII] **42.** Can anything really be more certain than that on the
philosophy of those[175] who count pain an evil[176] the wise man
cannot be happy while he is being tortured on the rack?[177] On the
other hand, the reasoning of those who do not include pains among
evils compels the conclusion that the wise man's happiness is
secure[178] whatever the torments. If those who suffer for their
country find the same pains more bearable than those who endure
them for a more trivial cause, it is surely the mental attitude[179] and
not the intensity of the pain itself which makes the impact more or
less severe. **43.** Further, from the assumption that, if there are
three classes of goods[180] (which is the Peripatetic view), a man will
be happier[181] the more physical and material goods he has, it does
not then follow that we allow the conclusion that the man who has
more of what is of positive value in the body is the happier. They
think that the happy life includes physical assets, but we deny it.
For since we consider that not even an abundance of what *we* truly
call goods[182] makes a life happier or more desirable or of greater

aestimandum, certe minus ad beatam uitam pertinet multitudo corporis commodorum.

There is no good but virtue

44. Etenim si et sapere expetendum sit et ualere, coniunctum utrumque magis expetendum sit quam sapere solum, neque tamen, si utrumque sit aestimatione dignum, pluris sit coniunctum quam sapere ipsum separatim. nam qui ualetudinem aestimatione aliqua dignam iudicamus neque eam tamen in bonis ponimus, iidem censemus nullam esse tantam aestimationem ut ea uirtuti anteponatur; quod idem Peripatetici non tenent, quibus dicendum est: quae et honesta actio sit et sine dolore, eam magis esse expetendum quam si esset eadem actio cum dolore. nobis aliter uidetur, recte secusne, postea; sed potestne rerum maior esse dissensio?

[XIV] **45.** Vt enim obscuratur et offunditur luce solis lumen lucernae, et ut interit in magnitudine maris Aegaei stilla mellis, et ut in diuitiis Croesi teruncii accessio et gradus unus in ea uia, quae est hinc in Indiam, sic, cum sit is bonorum finis, quem Stoici dicunt, omnis ista rerum corporearum aestimatio splendore uirtutis et magnitudine obscuretur et obruatur atque intereat necesse est.

Appropriateness is in the limit

Et quem ad modum "opportunitas" (sic enim appellemus *eukairian*) non fit maior productione temporis (habent enim suum modum quae opportuna dicuntur), sic recta effectio (*katorthōsin* enim ita appello, quoniam recte factum *katorthōma*) – recta igitur effectio, item conuenientia, denique ipsum bonum, quod in eo positum est ut naturae consentiat, crescendi accessionem nullam habet.

46. Vt enim opportunitas illa, sic haec, de quibus dixi, non fiunt temporis productione maiora, ob eamque causam Stoicis non uidetur optabilior nec magis expetenda beata uita, si sit longa, quam si breuis, utunturque simili: ut, si cothurni laus illa esset, ad pedem apte conuenire, neque multi cothurni paucis anteponerentur nec maiores minoribus, sic, quorum omne bonum conuenientia atque opportunitate finitur, nec plura paucioribus nec lonqinquiora breuioribus anteponentur. **47.** nec uero satis acute dicunt: si bona ualetudo pluris aestimanda sit longa quam breuis, sapientiae quoque usus longissimus quisque sit plurimi. non intellegunt ualetudinis aestimationem spatio iudicari, uirtutis opportunitate, ut uideantur

value, even less relevant to the happy life would be a large number of physical assets.

44. Now if both wisdom and health are desirable,[183] a combination of the two is more desirable than wisdom alone; however, if both were of value the two together would not be worth more than wisdom on its own. We put a certain value on health,[184] but we do not include it as a good nor do we think that there is any value great enough to be preferred to virtue. This is not the Peripatetics' case, for they say that right action without pain[185] is more desirable than the same action accompanied by pain. We think otherwise, whether justifiably or not we shall see later; but could there be a more substantial difference?

[XIV] 45. Just as the light of a lamp[186] is dimmed and swamped by the light of the sun, just as a drop of honey is lost in the vastness of the Aegean sea, as a penny added to the wealth of Croesus, as a step on the road from here to India, so, given that the ultimate good is as the Stoics claim, all the value of what belongs to the body[187] is inevitably dimmed and overwhelmed and lost in the dazzling greatness of virtue.

In the way in which suitability[188] (our translation of *eukairia*) is not improved by prolongation (for what is called suitable has its own limit) so right conduct (i.e. *katorthōsis, katorthōma* is an individual right act), right conduct[189] then and similarly harmony, and in sum that very good which rests in agreement with nature, admit of no additional increase.

46. Like suitability, these qualities of which I have spoken are not improved by length of time,[190] and that is why the Stoics do not think that if the happy life is a long one it is more attractive or more to be desired than a short one. They make the following comparison: if the chief merit of a shoe[191] is to fit the foot exactly, many shoes would not be preferable[192] to few, nor a larger size to a smaller, so, where the good is defined solely by harmony and appropriateness, a greater is not preferable to a less, nor a longer to a shorter. **47.** Some people, rather obtusely, put forward this argument: if good health is of more value if of long rather than short duration, then the most prolonged enjoyment of wisdom would also be the most highly prized. They do not realise that the value of health is judged by its length, but that of virtue by its appropriateness, so that the people who argue on these lines would

qui illud dicant iidem hoc esse dicturi, bonam mortem et bonum partum meliorem longum esse quam breuem. non uident alia breuitate pluris aestimari, alia diuturnitate.

There are no degrees of virtue

48. Itaque consentaneum est his, quae dicta sunt, ratione illorum, qui illum bonorum finem (quod appellamus extremum, quod ultimum) crescere putent posse – iisdem placere esse alium alio etiam sapientiorem itemque alium magis alio peccare uel rect~ facere; quod nobis non licet dicere, qui crescere bonorum finem non putamus. ut enim qui demersi sunt in aqua nihilo magis respirare possunt, si non longe absunt a summo, ut iam iamque possint emergere, quam si etiam tum essent in profundo, nec catulus ille, qui iam appropinquat ut uideat, plus cernit quam is, qui modo est natus, item qui processit aliquantum ad uirtutis habitum nihilo minus in miseria est quam ille, qui nihil processit.

The 'extension' of virtue and vice

[XV] Haec mirabilia uideri intellego, sed cum certe superiora firma ac uera sint, his autem ea consentanea et consequentia, ne de horum quidem est ueritate dubitandum; sed quamquam negant nec uirtutes nec uitia crescere, tamen utrumque eorum fundi quodam modo et quasi dilatari putant.

Digression on wealth and virtue

(**49.** Diuitias autem Diogenes censet eam modo uim habere, ut quasi duces sint ad uoluptatem et ad ualetudinem bonam, sed etiam uti ea contineant, non idem facere eas in uirtute neque in ceteris artibus, ad quas esse dux pecunia potest, continere autem non potest. itaque, si uoluptas aut si bona ualitudo sit in bonis, diuitias quoque in bonis esse ponendas, at, si sapientia bonum sit, non sequi ut etiam diuitias bonum esse dicamus. neque ab ulla re, quae non sit in bonis, id, quod sit in bonis, contineri potest, ob eamque causam, quia cognitiones comprehensionesque rerum, e quibus efficiuntur artes, appetitionem mouent, cum diuitiae non sint in bonis, nulla ars diuitiis contineri potest. **50.** quod si de artibus concedamus, uirtutis tamen non sit eadem ratio, propterea quod haec plurimae commentationis et exercitationis indigeat, quod idem in artibus non sit, et quod uirtus stabilitatem, firmitatem, constantiam totius uitae complectatur, nec haec eadem in artibus esse uideamus.)

seem ready to say that a good death and a good childbirth are better if long than short. They fail to recognise[193] that brevity adds to the value in some cases, and length of time in others.

48. It is consistent then with what has gone before that those who suppose that the greatest good (which we call the highest and final) is capable of increase must, according to their theory,[194] believe that one man is wiser than another, and similarly that one man can act rightly or wrongly to a greater degree[195] than another; but we who maintain that the chief good does not admit of increase cannot agree. Just as drowning men[196] can no more breathe when they are so close to the surface as to be on the very point of emerging than if they were even then at the bottom, and just as a puppy[197] who is about to open his eyes[198] is as blind as one newly born, so a man who has made some progress towards the state of virtue[199] is in a condition no less wretched than he who has made none.

[XV] I realise that this seems strange, but since our previous conclusions are undoubtedly well-founded and true, and this agrees with them and follows from them, then there can be no equivocation about the truth of this argument either; nevertheless, although the Stoics deny that virtue and vice admit of increase, they do believe that in a sense both can be expanded and extended.[200]

(**49.** Diogenes[201] thinks that wealth[202] merely has the power of leading us to pleasure and health; but, even granting[203] that it is essential for them, it has not the same effect regarding virtue and the other skills, to which wealth may act as a guide,[204] but for which it cannot be a necessary accompaniment. If pleasure or health are classed as goods, wealth too must then be included as a good, but if wisdom is a good,[205] it does not follow that we must say that wealth too is a good. What is counted as a good cannot be intrinsically bound up with anything which is not a good. Because of this, since cognitions and comprehensions[206] of what is in the world, which form the basis of the skills, awaken desire, no skill can necessarily be tied to wealth, for wealth is not a good. **50.** And even if we grant[207] that it can be so tied as far as the arts are concerned, the same argument would still not hold for virtue. This is because virtue requires deep meditation and long practice, which is not the case with the arts, and because it involves steadfastness, strength and perserverance through the whole of life, which again we see is not true of the different crafts.)

The theory of 'difference'

Deinceps explicatur differentia rerum, quam si non ullam esse diceremus, confunderetur omnis uita, ut ab Aristone; neque ullum sapientiae munus aut opus inueniretur, cum inter res eas, quae ad uitam degendam pertinerent, nihil omnino interesset, neque ullum dilectum adhiberi oporteret. itaque cum esset satis constitutum id solum esse bonum, quod esset honestum, et id malum solum, quod turpe, tum inter illa, quae nihil ualerent ad beate misereue uiuendum, aliquid tamen, quod differret, esse uoluerunt, ut essent eorum alia aestimabilia, alia contra, alia neutrum.

Examples of 'difference'

51. Quae autem aestimanda essent, eorum in aliis satis esse causae, quam ob rem quibusdam anteponerentur, ut in ualetudine, ut in integritate sensuum, ut in doloris uacuitate, ut gloriae, diuitiarum, similium rerum, alia autem non esse eius modi, itemque eorum quae nulla aestimatione digna essent, partim satis habere causae, quam ob rem reicerentur, ut dolorem, morbum, sensuum amissionem, paupertatem, ignominiam, similia horum, partim non item. hinc est illud exortum, quod Zeno *proēgmenon*, contraque quod *apoproēgmenon* nominauit, cum uteretur in lingua copiosa factis tamen nominibus ac nouis, quod nobis in hac inopi lingua non conceditur, quamquam tu hanc copiosiorem etiam soles dicere. sed non alienum est, quo facilius uis uerbi intellegatur, rationem huius uerbi faciendi Zenonis exponere.

The king and courtiers

[XVI] **52.** Vt enim, inquit, nemo dicit in regia regem ipsum quasi "productum" esse "ad dignitatem" (id est enim *proēgmenon*), sed eos, qui in aliquo honore sunt, quorum ordo proxime accedit, ut secundus sit, ad regium principatum, sic in uita non ea, quae primo loco sunt, sed ea, quae secundum locum optinent, *proēgmena*, (id est "producta") nominentur; quae uel ita appellemus (id erit uerbum e uerbo) uel "promota" et "remota" uel, ut dudum diximus, "praeposita" uel "praecipua", et illa "reiecta". re enim intellecta in uerborum usu faciles esse debemus.

53. Quoniam autem omne quod est bonum primum locum tenere dicimus, necesse est nec bonum esse nec malum hoc, quod "praepositum" uel "praecipuum" nominamus – idque ita definimus: quod sit "indifferens cum aestimatione mediocri" (quod enim illi *adiaphoron* dicunt, id mihi ita occurrit, ut "indifferens" dicerem). neque enim illud fieri poterat ullo modo, ut nihil relinqueretur in mediis, quod aut secundum naturam esset aut contra, nec, cum id

Next follows an explanation of 'difference' in the world. If we said that there was no such thing, then the whole of life would be turned into chaos, as it was by Aristo;[208] and as long as there is no distinction at all in what relates to the conduct of life no function or task is to be found for wisdom to perform,[209] and no obligation to make any choice.[210] That is why, once it was established that only what is right is good, and only what is wrong is evil, the Stoics were then ready to agree that a distinction does exist[211] in all that is of no importance for a life of happiness or misery, giving to some things a plus value, to some a minus, and to some neither.[212]

51. Among things to be given a plus value[213] are those which have adequate grounds for being preferred in certain cases, health for example, sharp senses, freedom from pain, fame, wealth and the like, while there are others not of this kind.[214] And similarly those which are of minus value[215] have at times adequate cause for their rejection, as pain, loss of sensation, poverty, disgrace and the like, and there are others which do not. From this comes Zeno's distinction[216] between *proēgmenon* and *apoproēgmenon*. Although his own language was rich he still coined new words,[217] which our impoverished vocabulary does not admit, though you often go so far as to say that Latin is the richer. Still, to understand more easily the meaning of this terminology, it is not out of place to explain Zeno's principle in constructing it.

[XVI] 52. In a royal court,[218] Zeno claims, no one says of the king himself that he is "promoted to honour" (the meaning of *proēgmenos*), but of those who have some state office,[219] and whose rank brings them very near to but not on a level with royal authority. Similarly in life the term *proēgmena* (i.e. "promoted") is applied not to what takes first place[220] but to all that has second position. We can call these "promoted"[221] (a literal translation), or "advanced" and "degraded", or, as we said just now, "preferred" or "superior", and the opposite "rejected". As long as the meaning is clear the terminology need not be precise.

53. Now, since we maintain that all which is good has the first place, what we call "preferred" or "superior" cannot be either good or evil – we define it as "indifferent, but with some value".[222] (I have just thought of using "indifferent" for the Stoic *adiaphoron*.) It would have been impossible for there to be nothing left in the neutral class that was not either according to or contrary to nature, then, when there was this residue,[223] not to include in it what has

relinqueretur, nihil in his poni, quod satis aestimabile esset, nec
hoc posito non aliqua esse "praeposita".

The illustration of the dice

54. Recte igitur haec facta distinctio est, atque etiam ab iis, quo
facilius res perspici possit, hoc simile ponitur: ut enim, inquiunt, si
hoc fingamus esse quasi finem et ultimum, ita iacere talum, ut
rectus assistat – qui ita talus erit iactus ut cadat rectus praepositum
quiddam habebit ad finem, qui aliter, contra, neque tamen illa
praepositio tali ad eum, quem dixi, finem pertinebit, sic ea, quae
sunt praeposita, referuntur illa quidem ad finem, sed ad eius uim
naturamque nihil pertinent.

Ends and means

55. Sequitur illa diuisio, ut bonorum (i) alia sint ad illud ultimum
"pertinentia" (sic enim appello, quae *telika* dicuntur; nam hoc
ipsum instituamus, ut placuit, pluribus uerbis dicere quod uno non
poterimus, ut res intellegatur), (ii) alia autem efficientia (quae
Graeci *poiētika*), (iii) alia utrumque. de pertinentibus nihil est
bonum praeter actiones honestas, de efficientibus nihil praeter
amicum, sed et pertinentem et efficientem sapientiam uolunt esse.
nam quia sapientia est conueniens actio, est in illo pertinenti
genere, quod dixi; quod autem honestas actiones affert et efficit, id
efficiens dici potest.

The sub-divisions of the class of things preferred

[XVII] **56.** Haec, quae "praeposita" dicimus, (i) partim sunt per
se ipsa praeposita, (ii) partim quod aliquid efficiunt, (iii) partim
utrumque, – (i) per se, ut quidem habitus oris et uultus, ut status,
ut motus, in quibus sunt et praeponenda quaedam et reicienda; (ii)
alia ob eam rem praeposita dicentur, quod ex se aliquid efficiant,
ut pecunia; (iii) alia autem ob utramque rem, ut integri sensus, ut
bona ualetudo.

The classification of reputation

57. De bona autem fama (quam enim appellant *eudoxian*, aptius
est "bonam famam" hoc loco appellare quam "gloriam") Chrysippus
quidem et Diogenes detracta utilitate ne digitum quidem eius causa
porrigendum esse dicebant; quibus ego uehementer assentior. qui
autem post eos fuerunt, cum Carneadem sustinere non possent,
hanc, quam dixi, bonam famam ipsam propter se praepositam et
sumendam esse dixerunt, esseque hominis ingenui et liberaliter

some value, and having settled this not to have some things "preferred".

54. Therefore the distinction is correctly drawn, and, to make it more easily understood, they introduce the following illustration: suppose we imagine it to be a kind of end or aim to throw a dice[224] so that it stands upright – anyone who throws the dice so that it falls upright[225] will have made some advance towards his aim, and one who throws otherwise the reverse, but that advance on the part of the dice will not be essentially related to the end indicated; similarly[226] "things preferred" are so called with reference to the end, but have no bearing on its essential nature.

55. Next comes the division of goods[227] into (i) those which are "essentially related" to that end (my rendering of *telika*[228] – we can put into practice our agreement to use several terms for bringing out the meaning where one does not suffice), (ii) those which are the means to the end (the Greek *poiētika*[229]) and (iii) those which are both.[230] Of what is essentially related to the end nothing is good except right actions, and of means the only example is a friend. Wisdom they claim is both essentially related[231] to the end and a means to it. In being harmony of conduct wisdom is essentially related to the end, as I have explained; and in bringing right actions with it and in being productive of them it can be called a means.

[XVII] 56. The class of what we call "things preferred" divides into three: things preferred (i) on their own account,[232] (ii) for their effects,[233] (iii) for themselves and their effects.[234] Under (i) are for example a certain style of feature and expression, stance and deportment, some being preferable and others to be rejected; under (ii) are other things which are called preferred because they produce certain effects from themselves, for example money; others again are under (iii) – preferred for both reasons, for example sound senses and good health.

57. On the question of a good reputation[235] (the Stoic term is *eudoxia* which is more suitably translated here by "good reputation" than "glory") Chrysippus and Diogenes maintained that apart from its utility[236] it is not worth stretching out a finger for;[237] and I definitely agree with them. However, since the Stoics who came after them[238] could not withstand Carneades, they claimed that the good reputation I spoke of should be preferred and adopted for its own sake,[239] and that a man free-born, and brought up to be a

educati uelle bene audire a parentibus, a propinquis, a bonis etiam
uiris, idque propter rem ipsam, non propter usum, dicuntque, ut
liberis consultum uelimus, etiamsi postumi futuri sint, propter
ipsos, sic futurae post mortem famae tamen esse propter rem,
etiam detracto usu, consulendum.

Appropriate actions

58. Sed cum, quod honestum sit, id solum bonum esse dicamus,
consentaneum tamen est fungi officio, cum id officium nec in bonis
ponamus nec in malis. est enim aliquid in his rebus probabile, et
quidem ita, ut eius ratio reddi possit, ergo ut etiam probabiliter
acti ratio reddi possit. est autem officium, quod ita factum est, ut
eius facti probabilis ratio reddi possit. ex quo intellegitur officium
medium quiddam esse quod neque in bonis ponatur neque in
contrariis.

(Quoniamque in iis rebus quae neque in uirtutibus sunt neque in
uitiis, est tamen quiddam quod usui possit esse, tollendum id non
est. est autem eius generis actio quoque quaedam, et quidem talis
ut ratio postulet agere aliquid et facere eorum; quod autem ratione
actum est, id officium appellamus; est igitur officium eius generis,
quod nec in bonis ponatur nec in contrariis.)

Appropriate action is common to all

[XVIII] **59.** Atque perspicuum etiam illud est, in istis rebus mediis
aliquid agere sapientem; iudicat igitur, cum agit, "officium" illud
esse. quod quoniam numquam fallitur in iudicando, erit in mediis
rebus officium. quod efficitur hac etiam conclusione rationis:
quoniam enim uidemus esse quiddam quod recte factum
appellemus, id autem est perfectum officium, erit etiam incohatum
– ut, si iuste depositum reddere in recte factis sit, in officiis
ponatur depositum reddere; illo enim addito "iuste" fit recte
factum, per se autem hoc ipsum reddere in officio ponitur.

Quoniamque non dubium est quin in iis quae media dicimus sit
aliud sumendum, aliud reiciendum, quicquid ita fit aut dicitur omne
"officio" continetur. ex quo intellegitur, quoniam se ipsi omnes
natura diligant, tam insipientem quam sapientem sumpturum quae
secundum naturam sint, reiecturumque contraria. ita est quoddam
commune officium sapientis et insipientis, ex quo efficitur uersari

gentleman, would want his parents and relatives and all good men to hear well of him, and not for the advantage it brings but for its own sake. They assert that, just as we are anxious to look to the interests of our children[240] for their own sake, even should they be posthumous, so we should take thought for the reputation we shall still have[241] after death for its own sake, even though it has no advantage.

58. Now, while we say that only what is right is good, it is still consistent to perform appropriate action,[242] although such an action is classed as neither good nor evil. Approval can be given on this neutral level[243] to some extent, in that it is possible for a rational explanation to be given of it, and so too it is possible to give a rational explanation of the performance[244] which merits approval. It can be seen from this that an appropriate action so defined is neutral, being included with what is neither good nor evil.

(Since in such actions which are neither virtuous nor vicious there is still the possibility of advantage, it should not be disregarded. And this class covers the sort of action where the the performance or production of something is as reason dictates. And what is carried out according to reason is called appropriate action, and so appropriate action belongs in the category of what is neither good nor evil.)[245]

[XVIII] **59.** It is also clear that the wise man sometimes acts on this neutral level;[246] when he does so he judges that this is "appropriate action". Since he is never mistaken in his judgment there will be appropriate action on this neutral level. This is shown too from the following argument: since we recognise that there is something called right action, and that this is appropriate action perfectly performed, there will also be action imperfectly performed[247] – for example, if to restore in justice something given on trust is a right act, to restore what is given on trust is an appropriate act; the addition of "in justice" makes the action right, but in itself the restoration is (merely) appropriate.

Since there is no doubt that on what we call the neutral level some things are to be adopted and others rejected, anything done or described on this level comes under the heading "appropriate action". From this[248] it can be seen that, since all men by nature have self-love, the unwise and wise alike will adopt what is according to nature and reject the opposite. Appropriate action is therefore common to the wise and the unwise, and this shows that

in iis, quae media dicamus.

Suicide

60. Sed cum ab his omnia proficiscantur officia, non sine causa dicitur ad ea referri omnes nostras cogitationes, in his et excessum e uita et in uita mansionem. in quo enim plura sunt quae secundum naturam sunt, huius officium est in uita manere; in quo autem aut sunt plura contraria aut fore uidentur, huius officium est e uita excedere. ex quo apparet et sapientis esse aliquando officium excedere e uita, cum beatus sit, et stulti manere in uita, cum sit miser. **61.** nam bonum illud et malum, quod saepe iam dictum est, postea consequitur; prima autem illa naturae siue secunda siue contraria sub iudicium sapientis et dilectum cadunt, estque illa subiecta quasi materia sapientiae. itaque et manendi in uita et migrandi ratio omnis iis rebus, quas supra dixi, metienda; nam neque uirtute retinetur ille in uita, nec iis, qui sine uirtute sunt, mors est oppetenda. et saepe officium est sapientis desciscere a uita cum sit beatissimus, si id opportune facere possit (quod est conuenienter naturae), sic enim censent, opportunitatis esse beate uiuere. itaque a sapientia praecipitur se ipsam, si usus sit, sapiens ut reliquat.

Quam ob rem cum uitiorum ista uis non sit, ut causam afferant mortis uoluntariae, perspicuum est etiam stultorum (qui iidem miseri sint) officium esse manere in uita, si sint in maiore parte rerum earum, quas "secundum naturam" esse dicimus; et quoniam excedens e uita et manens aeque miser est, nec diuturnitas magis ei uitam fugiendam facit, non sine causa dicitur iis, qui pluribus naturalibus frui possint, esse in uita manendum.

Parental love as the natural basis for social relations

[XIX] **62.** Pertinere autem ad rem arbitrantur intellegi natura fieri ut liberi a parentibus amentur. a quo initio profectam communem humani generis societatem persequimur. quod primum intellegi debet figura membrisque corporum, quae ipsa declarant procreandi a natura habitam esse rationem. neque uero haec inter se congruere possent, ut natura et procreari uellet et diligi procreatos non curaret. atque etiam in bestiis uis naturae perspici potest, quarum in fetu et in educatione laborem cum cernimus, naturae ipsius

it belongs on what we call the neutral level.[249]

60. While all appropriate action starts from things indifferent, there is reason for saying that all our deliberations, including the question of leaving life[250] or staying in it, are concerned with them. When a man's condition is for the most part according to nature, the appropriate action is to stay alive,[251] but the appropriate action for a man whose condition is for the most part contrary to nature or seems likely to be so[252] is to leave life. It is clear from this that it is sometimes an appropriate action for a wise man to leave life even though he is happy, and for an unwise man to stay alive although wretched,[253] **61.** The good and evil, as has often been said, are later results, whereas the primary objects – those according to nature and those contrary – come within the wise man's range of decision and choice, and make up as it were wisdom's subject matter.[254] That is why all deliberation about staying in life or leaving it has as its yardstick the objects just mentioned; for it is not because of virtue that a man stays alive,[255] nor need those without virtue bring death on themselves. Often it is the appropriate action for a wise man to abandon life while enjoying the greatest happiness if he can make a suitable exit (i.e. in accordance with nature),[256] for the Stoics maintain that the happy life is a question of suitability. So it is wisdom which bids the wise man leave her when the need arises.

And since therefore vice is not able to provide a motive for suicide, it is clearly an appropriate action even for the unwise (who are also the unhappy) to stay alive if their condition is for the most part what we call "according to nature"; and since whether he leaves life or stays in it he is equally unhappy, and length of time does not increase his obligation to flee from life, there is reason for saying that those who for the most part enjoy a natural condition ought to stay alive.[257]

[XIX] 62. The Stoics maintain that it is important to realise that the love of parents for their children[258] is due to nature. It is the source from which we trace the origin of men living together[259] in communities. This should be understood in the first place from the structure and parts of our bodies[260] which of themselves indicate that having children is a design of nature. Yet it would of course be inconsistent for nature to desire the procreation of children and then make no provision[261] for the children to be cared for. Even in animals[262] the natural impulse is clearly seen – when we observe the distress animals suffer in giving birth to and rearing their young we

uocem uidemur audire. quare ut perspicuum est natura nos a dolore abhorrere, sic appar⸗t a natura ipsa ut eos, quos genuerimus, amemus impelli. **63.** ex hoc nascitur ut etiam communis hominum inter homines naturalis sit commmendatio, ut oporteat hominem ab homine ob id ipsum, quod homo sit, non alienum uideri.

Comparative usefulness of bodily parts
(18.   Iam membrorum, id est partium corporis, alia uidentur propter eorum usum a natura esse donata, ut manus, crura, pedes, ut ea quae sunt intus in corpore, quorum utilitas quanta sit a medicis etiam disputatur, alia autem nullam ob utilitatem quasi ad quendam ornatum, ut cauda pauoni, plumae uersicolores columbis, uiris mammae atque barba.)

Examples from the animal world
Vt enim in membris alia sunt tamquam sibi nata, ut oculi, ut aures, alia etiam ceterorum membrorum usum adiuuant, ut crura, ut manus. sic immanes quaedam bestiae sibi solum natae sunt, at illa, quae in concha patula "pina" dicitur, isque, qui enat e concha, (qui quod eam custodit, "pinoteres" uocatur) in eandemque cum se recepit includitur, ut uideatur monuisse ut caueret; itemque formicae, apes, ciconiae aliorum etiam causa quaedam faciunt. multo haec coniunctius homines. itaque natura sumus apti ad coetus, concilia, ciuitates.

The cosmopolis and related duties
64. Mundum autem censent regi numine deorum – eumque esse quasi communem urbem et ciuitatem hominum et deorum, et unum quemque nostrum eius mundi esse partem; ex quo illud natura consequi, ut communem utilitatem nostrae anteponamus. ut enim leges omnium salutem singulorum saluti anteponunt, sic uir bonus et sapiens et legibus parens et ciuilis officii non ignarus utilitati omnium plus quam unius alicuius aut suae consulit. nec magis est uituperandus proditor patriae quam communis utilitatis aut salutis desertor propter suam utilitatem aut salutem. ex quo fit, ut laudandus is sit, qui mortem oppetat pro re publica, quod deceat cariorem nobis esse patriam quam nosmet ipsos.

Quoniamque illa uox inhumana et scelerata ducitur eorum, qui negant se recusare quo minus ipsis mortuis terrarum omnium deflagratio consequatur (quod uulgari quodam uersu Graeco

seem to hear the very cry of nature. While clearly it is natural for us to recoil from pain, it is equally obvious that it is natural to love those whom we have brought into being. 63. From this arises the mutual attraction men have naturally for one another, so that, because of their common humanity, no man should be seen as a stranger to another.[263]

(18. Now some of the limbs,[264] that is the parts of the body, have been given by nature because they are intrinsically useful. These include hands, legs and feet,[265] and the body's internal organs, even if there is disagreement among doctors as to how useful they are. Other parts however have no use but are a kind of decoration,[266] like the peacock's tail, doves' feathers of changing colours, and a man's breasts and beard.)[267]

Some limbs, for example eyes and ears, have been produced for themselves,[268] and others, such as legs and hands, are at the service of the rest of the body. Similarly some large animals are born for themselves, but the mussel called the "pina"[269] which lives in a broad shell, and the small crab (which because it watches over the pina is called the "pinotores") swims out of the shell and is shut in again on its return so that it seems to have given a look-out warning; similarly ants, bees and storks[270] act on occasion for the sake of others. Much closer is the bond[271] between men. And so we are fitted by nature to come together in groups, communities and states.

64. The Stoics maintain that the universe is governed by divine will[272] – it is a kind of city or state belonging jointly to gods and men,[273] each one of us being a part of the universe; and the natural result of this is that we put the general interest before our own. As laws set the welfare of the citizen body above that of individuals, so the man who is wise and good, obedient to the laws and conscious of his duty as a citizen, looks to the general interest[274] rather than that of any one individual or even his own. He who betrays his country[275] is not more reprehensible than one who abandons the advantage and welfare of all for personal interest or security. That is why, seeing that our country is fittingly more precious[276] to us than our own selves, a man who suffers death for his community[277] does indeed deserve to be praised.

Since the saying attributed to those who assert that they do not care if on their death a universal conflagration results is against humanity and criminal (the saying is usually quoted in the form of

pronuntiari solet), certe uerum est etiam iis, qui aliquando futuri sint, esse propter ipsos consulendum.

The duty of material and intellectual bequests

[XX]   65. Ex hac animorum affectione testamenta commendationesque morientium natae sunt. quodque nemo in summa solitudine uitam agere uelit ne cum infinita quidem uoluptatum abundantia, facile intellegitur nos ad coniunctionem congregationemque hominum et ad naturalem communitatem esse natos. impellimur autem natura, ut prodesse uelimus quam plurimis in primisque docendo rationibusque prudentiae tradendis. 66. itaque non facile est inuenire qui quod sciat ipse non tradat alteri; ita non solum ad discendum propensi sumus, uerum etiam ad docendum.

The duty to protect the weak

Atque ut tauris natura datum est ut pro uitulis contra leones summa ui impetuque contendant, sic ii, qui ualent opibus atque id facere possunt, ut de Hercule et de Libero accepimus, ad seruandum genus hominum natura incitantur. atque etiam Iouem cum Optimum et Maximum dicimus, cumque eundem Salutarem, Hospitalem, Statorem, hoc intellegi uolumus, salutem hominum in eius esse tutela. minime autem conuenit, cum ipsi inter nos uiles neglectique simus, postulare ut dis immortalibus cari simus et ab iis diligamur. quem ad modum igitur membris utimur priusquam didicimus cuius ea causa utilitatis habeamus, sic inter nos natura ad ciuilem communitatem coniuncti et consociati sumus. quod ni ita se haberet nec iustitiae ullus esset nec bonitate locus.

Man has no duty towards animals

67. Et quo modo hominum inter homines iuris esse uincula putant, sic homini nihil iuris esse cum bestiis. praeclare enim Chrysippus: cetera nata esse hominum causa et deorum, eos autem communitatis et societati suae, ut bestiis homines uti ad utilitatem suam possint sine iniuria.

Private property is justified

Quoniamque ea natura esset hominis, ut ei cum genere humano quasi ciuile ius intercederet, qui id conseruaret, eum iustum, qui migraret, iniustum fore. sed quem ad modum theatrum cum commune sit, recte tamen dici potest eius esse eum locum quem

a familiar line of Greek verse),[278] it is undoubtedly true that we should take thought also for those who will come after us, for their own sakes.[279]

[XX] 65. This attitude of mind is the explanation for men at the hour of death making wills[280] and appointing trustees. Because no one would wish to spend his life in complete isolation,[281] even if attended by countless pleasures, it is easy to see that we are born to combine and associate with our fellowmen, and to form a community according to nature.[282] Further, we have a natural instinct to wish to benefit as many people as possible, in particular by instructing them and by handing on the principles of practical wisdom.[283] 66. That is why it is difficult to discover anyone who does not hand on to another what he himself knows; so we have an inclination not only to learn, but also to teach.[284]

As it is the natural condition of bulls to fight[285] with all energy and force against lions in defence of their calves, so men of exceptional gifts and great ability, such as we hear of in the legends of Hercules[286] and Liber,[287] have a natural impulse to protect the human race. When we give to Jupiter the titles "Optimus" and "Maximus",[288] and address him as saviour, and as patron of guest-friendship and of steadfastness in battle,[289] we mean that the security of the human race depends on his guardian care.[290] But it is quite inconsistent to expect that we should be dear to the immortal gods and favoured by them when we despise and have no concern for one another.[291] And so, just as we set the different parts of our bodies to work before we have learnt the purpose and advantage of having them, so by nature we come together[292] and form an alliance in the common society of the state. If this were not the case there would be no scope for justice or benevolence.[293]

67. Although the Stoics maintain that man is united to man by the bond of law, they do not think that law unites men and animals.[294] Chrysippus put this clearly[295]: everything else has been generated to serve men and gods, but they are born for mutual companionship and association, so that men may make use of animals for their own advantage[296] without acting wrongly.

Since the nature of man is such that an individual is connected to the whole human race by a kind of civil law, he who supports that law will be just, and he who deviates from it unjust.[297] Nevertheless, in the same way as the theatre[298] is a public building, but an individual can correctly claim that the seat which he occupies is

quisque occuparit, sic in urbe mundoue communi non aduersatur
ius, quo minus suum quidque cuiusque sit.

Political and personal duties

68. Cum autem ad tuendos conseruandosque homines hominem
natum esse uideamus, consentaneum est huic naturae, ut sapiens
uelit gerere et administrare rem publicam, atque, ut e natura uiuat,
uxorem adiungere et uelle ex ea liberos. ne amores quidem sanctos
a sapiente alienos esse arbitrantur. Cynicorum autem rationem
atque uitam alii cadere in sapientem dicunt, si qui eius modi forte
casus inciderit ut id faciendum sit, alii nullo modo.

Benefits and injuries

[XXI]   69. Vt uero conseruetur omnis homini erga hominem
societas, coniunctio, caritas, et "emolumenta" et "detrimenta" (quae
ōphelēmata et blammata appellant) communia esse uoluerunt –
quorum altera prosunt, nocent altera. neque solum ea communia,
uerum etiam paria esse dixerunt. "incommoda" autem et
"commoda" (ita enim euchrēstēmata et duschrēstēmata appello)
communia esse uoluerunt, paria noluerunt. illa enim, quae prosunt
aut quae nocent, aut bona sunt aut mala, quae sint paria necesse
est. commoda autem et incommoda in eo genere sunt, quae
"praeposita" et "reiecta" diximus; ea possunt paria non esse. sed
emolumenta communia esse dicuntur, recte autem facta et peccata
non habentur communia.

Friendship

70. Amicitiam autem adhibendam esse censent, quia sit ex eo
genere quae prosunt. quamquam autem in amicitia alii dicant aeque
caram esse sapienti rationem amici ac suam, alii autem sibi cuique
cariorem suam, tamen hi quoque posteriores fatentur alienum esse
a iustitia (ad quam nati esse uideamur) detrahere quid de aliquo
quod sibi assumat. minime uero probatur huic disclipinae de qua
loquor aut iustitiam aut amicitiam propter utilitates ascisci aut
probari; eaedem enim utilitates poterunt eas labefactare atque
peruertere. etenim nec iustitia nec amicitia esse omnino poterunt,
nisi ipsae per se expetuntur.

Law

71. Ius autem, quod ita dici appellarique possit, id esse natura,
alienumque esse a sapiente non modo iniuriam cui facere, uerum
etiam nocere. nec uero rectum est cum amicis aut bene meritis

his, so in the city or in the universe, which are common to all, the law does not oppose individual possession of private property.[299]

68. Now since we have seen that the individual is born to protect and safeguard his fellow men, it is consistent with this natural instinct that the wise man should be ready to take part in politics and government,[300] and also to live according to nature by taking a wife,[301] and being willing to have children by her. The Stoics do not think that even homosexual love, if pure,[302] is ill-suited to the philosophic character. Some moreover say that the Cynic principles and way of life[303] are suitable for the wise man, if he should chance to meet with circumstances which indicate such a course of action, whereas others completely deny this.[304]

[XXI] 69. To maintain the fellowship, companionship and affection which unites every man to his fellow men, the Stoics claim that "benefits" and "injuries"[305] (their terms are *ōphelēmata* and *blammata*) are universal – the one class being beneficial, the other harmful. And they have said that these are not only universal but of equal value.[306] But "disadvantages" and "advantages"[307] (my translation of *euchrēstēmata* and *duschrēstēmata*) they held to be universal, but not of equal value. Acts which are beneficial and harmful are respectively good and evil, and so must be of equal value. But advantages and disadvantages come under our headings of "preferred" and "rejected", and these can be of unequal value.[308] Benefits are said to be universal; right and wrong acts are not considered universal.[309]

70. The Stoics maintain that friendship should be cultivated,[310] since it comes under the heading of "things beneficial". Now although on the question of friendship some assert that the affairs of his friend are as dear to the wise man as his own,[311] others say that each man has his own interests more at heart, yet even this latter class admit that it is abhorrent to justice (to which we are clearly naturally inclined) to rob another in order to enrich oneself. The school of which I am speaking rejects emphatically the theory that either justice or friendship is adopted or preferred with a view to personal advantage;[312] for that same advantage will be able to undermine and overthrow them. Indeed neither justice nor friendship will even be possible, unless they are pursued for their own sakes.[313]

71. Law moreover, in its accurate use and name, exists by nature,[314] and it is abhorrent to the wise man not only to do wrong but even to hurt anyone.[315] Nor is it right to associate or conspire[316]

consociare aut coniungere iniuriam, grauissimeque et uerissime defenditur numquam aequitatem ab utilitate posset seiungi, et quicquid aequum iustumque esset id etiam honestum; uicissimque quicquid esset honestum id iustum atque aequum fore.

Logic
72. Ad easque uirtutes, de quibus disputatum est, dialecticam etiam adiungunt et physicam; easque ambas uirtutum nomine appellant, alteram, quod habeat rationem, ne cui falso assentiamur neue umquam captiosa probabilitate fallamur, eaque, quae de bonis et malis didicerimus, ut tenere tuerique possimus. nam sine hac arte quemuis arbitrantur a uero abduci fallique posse. recte igitur, si omnibus in rebus temeritas ignoratioque uitiosa est, ars ea quae tollit haec uirtus nominata est.

Natural science
[XXII] 73. Physicae quoque non sine causa tributus idem est honos, propterea quod, qui conuenienter naturae uicturus sit, ei proficiscendum est ab omni mundo atque ab eius procuratione. nec uero potest quisquam de bonis et malis uere iudicare nisi omni cognita ratione naturae et uitae etiam deorum, et utrum conueniat necne natura hominis cum uniuersa. quaeque sunt uetera praecepta sapientium, qui iubent "tempori parere" et "sequi deum" et "se noscere" et "nihil nimis", haec sine physicis quam uim habeant – et habent maximam – uidere nemo potest. atque etiam ad iustitiam colendam, ad tuendas amicitias et reliquas caritates quid natura ualeat, haec una cognitio potest tradere. nec uero pietas aduersus deos nec quanta iis gratia debeatur sine explicatione naturae intellegi potest.

The beauty of Stoic philosophy
74. Sed iam sentio me esse longius prouectum quam proposita ratio postularet. uerum admirabilis compositio disciplinae incredibilisque rerum me traxit ordo; quem, per deos immortales! nonne miraris? quid enim aut in natura (qua nihil est aptius nihil descriptius) aut in operibus manu factis tam compositum, tamque compactum et coagmentatum inueniri potest? quid posterius priori non conuenit? quid sequitur, quod non respondeat superiori? quid non sic aliud ex alio nectitur, ut, si ullam litteram moueris, labent omnia? nec tamen quicquam est quod moueri possit.

with friends or benefactors to inflict injury, and with great
seriousness and truth it is maintained that equity can never be
divorced from advantage[317] and that whatever is fair and just will
always be right; conversely, whatever is right will also be just and
fair.

72. To the virtues already discussed the Stoics add dialectic[318] and
natural science; they call both of these virtues, the first because it
establishes principles which guard against assenting to what is false
or ever being tricked by any deceptive plausibility, and enables us
to uphold and defend what we have learned about good and evil.
For the Stoics think that without this skill anyone can be tempted
away from truth and fall into error. So, if in all matters rashness
and ignorance count as vice, then the skill which removes them is
correctly called virtue.[319]

[XXII]   73. Natural science[320] too has with justification been
similarly honoured, in particular on the grounds that a man who
intends to live in harmony with nature must start from the universe
and its government. No one surely can make a true assessment of
good and evil unless he has grasped the principles of both nature
and divine life,[321] and understands whether or not the nature of
man accords with that of the cosmos. Moreover, without natural
science no one can appreciate the full meaning – a meaning most
significant – of the maxims propounded of old[322] by wise men,
which bid us "yield to the times", "follow god", "know thyself" and
"nothing in excess". In addition this knowledge alone reveals the
power nature wields[323] in cultivating justice, and in maintaining
friendships and the other ties of affection. And lastly, reverence to
the gods[324] and the debt of gratitude owed to them cannot be
understood until the workings of nature are revealed.

74. Now however I realise that I have been carried further than the
programme laid down requires. But the wonderful system in Stoic
philosophy and the amazing sequence of its subject matter[325] drew
me on. Tell me seriously, do you not admire it? What can be
found either in nature (which surpasses all in symmetry and
exactness) or in the craftsmen's products that is so well ordered,
constructed and welded?[326] What conclusion does not follow from
its premise? What later argument is not consistent with the earlier?
Where is the interlocking not so tight that, if you were to alter a
single letter, the whole would topple?[327] and yet there is nothing
which can be altered.

Panegyric of the wise man

75. Quam grauis uero, quam magnifica, quam constans conficitur persona sapientis! qui, cum ratio docuerit, quod honestum esset, id esse solum bonum, semper sit necesse est beatus uereque omnia ista nomina possideat, quae irrideri ab imperitis solent. rectius enim appellabitur rex quam Tarquinius, qui nec se nec suos regere potuit, rectius magister populi (is enim est dictator) quam Sulla, qui trium pestiferorum uitiorum – luxuriae, auaritiae, crudelitatis – magister fuit, rectius diues quam Crassus, qui nisi eguisset, numquam Euphraten nulla belli causa transire uoluisset. **76.** recte eius omnia dicentur, qui scit uti solus omnibus, recte etiam pulcher appellabitur (animi enim liniamenta sunt pulchriora quam corporis), recte solus liber nec dominationi cuiusquam parens nec oboediens cupiditati, recte inuictus, cuius etiamsi corpus constringatur, animo tamen uincula inici nulla possint. nec exspectet ullum tempus aetatis, uti tum denique iudicetur beatusne fuerit, cum extremum uitae diem morte confecerit, quod ille unus e septem sapientibus non sapienter Croesum monuit; nam si beatus umquam fuisset, beatam uitam usque ad illum a Cyro exstructum rogum pertulisset. quod si ita est, ut neque quisquam nisi bonus uir et omnes boni beati sint, quid philosophia magis colendum aut quid est uirtute diuinius?'

75. Then how dignified, how splendid,[328] how unwavering a character is the wise man's shown to be! He whom reason has taught that only what is right is good must always be happy,[329] and indeed possess all those titles which are usually scoffed at by the ignorant. He will be called king more truly than Tarquin,[330] who could govern neither himself nor his people, more truly master of the people (for such is a dictator) than Sulla,[331] who was master of three pernicious vices – excessive self-indulgence, greed and cruelty, more truly rich than Crassus,[332] who, if he had not been in want, would never have agreed to cross the Euphrates when there was no need to fight. **76.** Truly only the one who knows how to make use of all things will be said to own them, truly he will be called handsome[333] (for the features of the soul are more beautiful than those of the body), truly will he alone be a free man,[334] bowing to no tyranny nor yielding to any passion, truly unconquerable, for although his body might be fettered, no bonds can restrict his spirit. He does not need to wait a while, to be judged finally happy or not, only when he has rounded off his life's last day in death, as one of the seven wise men unwisely warned Croesus;[335] for if he had ever been happy he would have carried his happiness to that pyre built by Cyrus. If it is the case that all the good and only the good are happy, what is more to be encouraged than philosophy?[336] what is more godlike than virtue?'[337]

PARADOXA STOICORUM

M. TULLI CICERONIS

Paradoxa Stoicorum

PROOEMIUM

1. Animaduerti, Brute, saepe Catonem, auunculum tuum, cum in senatu sententiam diceret, locos graues ex philosophia tractare, abhorrentes ab hoc usu forensi et publico, sed dicendo consequi tamen ut illa etiam populo probabilia uiderentur. **2.** quod eo maius est illi quam aut tibi aut nobis, quia nos ea philosophia plus utimur quae peperit dicendi copiam, et in qua dicuntur ea quae non multum discrepant ab opinione populari. Cato autem, perfectus mea sententia Stoicus, et ea sentit, quae non sane probantur in uulgus, et in ea est haeresi, quae nullum sequitur florem orationis neque dilatat argumentum; minutis inter-rogatiunculis, quasi punctis, quod proposuit efficit.

3. Sed nihil est tam incredibile quod non dicendo fiat probabile, nihil tam horridum, tam incultum, quod non splendescat oratione et tamquam excolatur. quod cum ita putarem, feci etiam audacius quam ille ipse de quo loquor. Cato enim dumtaxat de magnitudine animi, de continentia, de morte, de omni laude uirtutis, de diis immortalibus, de caritate patriae Stoice solet oratoriis ornamentis adhibitis dicere. ego tibi illa ipsa quae uix in gymnasiis et in otio Stoici probant ludens conieci in communes locos. **4.** quae quia sunt admirabilia contraque opinionem (ab ipsis etiam *paradoxa* appellantur) temptare uolui possentne proferri in lucem – id est in forum – et ita dici ut probarentur, an alia quaedam esset erudita, alia popularis oratio: eoque locos scripsi libentius, quod mihi ista *paradoxa* quae appellant maxime uidentur esse Socratica longeque uerissima.

5. Accipies igitur hoc paruum opusculum, lucubratum his iam contractioribus noctibus, quoniam illud maiorum uigiliarum munus in tuo nomine apparuit, et degustabis genus exercitationum earum

M. TULLIUS CICERO

Stoic Paradoxes

PREFACE

1. I have often noticed, Brutus, that when your uncle Cato was speaking to a motion in the senate, he used to introduce weighty philosophical topics. They were unsuitable for the forum and assembly, but nonetheless his oratory made them acceptable even to ordinary people. **2.** This is a greater achievement for him than for you or me, because we generally favour a philosophy that encourages fluency in speaking and the expression of ideas which are not very different from common sentiment. But Cato, in my opinion a model Stoic, holds theories which are unacceptable to the masses, and belongs to a school which rejects rhetorical ornament and extended argument; it achieves its end by little tiny syllogisms like pinpricks.

3. Yet there is nothing so unbelievable that persuasive speech cannot make acceptable, nothing so rough and uncouth that does not glow once oratory has given it a polish. Since this is what I think, I have acted even more boldly than the very man I refer to. For Cato adopts the Stoic practice of adding rhetorical flourishes only when he is speaking on such subjects as greatness of soul, self-mastery, death, a general panegyric on virtue, the immortal gods or love of country, whereas I have amused myself by popularising for you those doctrines which the Stoics find difficult to propound even in the seclusion of their schools. **4.** Because these doctrines are amazing and run counter to common opinion (even the Stoics call them 'paradoxes') I want to find out whether it is possible to bring them into the light, that is into the forum, and to expound them in a way which would make them acceptable, or whether there is one kind of eloquence for the intelligentsia and another for ordinary people. And I have written on these topics with all the more pleasure because what the Stoics call 'paradoxes' seem to me to be very much in the style of Socrates, and are far and away the truest.

5. So you will be receiving this little work, written by lamplight as the nights get shorter, for the labour of the longer night hours has already appeared with a dedication to you, and you will sample a

quibus uti consueui, cum ea, quae dicuntur in scholis *thetika*, ad nostrum hoc oratorium transfero dicendi genus. hoc tamen opus in acceptum ut referas, nihil postulo, non enim est tale ut in arce poni possit quasi illa Minerua Phidiae, sed tamen ut ex eadem officina exisse appareat.

PARADOXON I

Quod honestum sit, id solum bonum esse.

[I] 6. Vereor ne cui uestrum ex Stoicorum hominum disputationibus, non ex meo sensu deprompta haec uideatur oratio; dicam quod sentio tamen, et dicam breuius quam res tanta dici poscit.

Numquam me hercule ego neque pecunias istorum neque tecta magnifica neque opes neque imperia neque eas quibus maxime astricti sunt uoluptates in bonis rebus aut expetendis esse duxi, quippe cum uiderem rebus his circumfluentes ea tamen desiderare maxime quibus abundarent. neque enim umquam expletur, nec satiatur cupiditatis sitis, neque solum ea qui habent libidine augendi cruciantur, sed etiam amittendi metu.

7. In quo equidem continentissimorum hominum maiorum nostrorum saepe requiro prudentiam, qui haec imbecilla et commutabilia pecuniae membra uerbo bona putauerunt appellanda, cum re ac factis longe aliter iudicauissent. potestne bonum cuiquam malo esse? aut potest quisquam in abundantia bonorum ipse esse non bonus? atqui ista omnia talia uidemus ut etiam improbi habeant et absint probis. 8. quam ob rem licet irrideat, si qui uult; plus apud me tamen uera ratio ualebit quam uulgi opinio, neque ego umquam bona perdidisse dicam si qui pecus aut supellectilem amiserit. neque non saepe laudabo sapientem illum

type of essay-writing which I usually adopt when I am translating what are called 'propositions' in the schools into my own oratorical style. I am not however asking you to put this to my credit, for it is not the sort of thing that should be set up in the citadel like Phidias's Minerva, but that could at least be recognised as coming from the same workshop.

PARADOX I

Only what is right is good.

[I] 6. I am afraid that some of you may think that this essay is based on the discussions of the Stoics and not on my own ideas; still, I shall say what I think, and speak more briefly than such an important topic warrants.

I have never supposed, for heaven's sake, that other people's money or splendid homes or possessions or high positions or the pleasures that so tightly restrict them count as goods or are to be desired, especially when I see that, although these people are swamped by such things, they still crave what they have so much of. For lust's thirst is never quenched or sated, and they are doubly tortured, not only by their craving for more, but also by the terror of losing what they already have.

7. In this context, I often miss the practical wisdom of our ancestors, those masters of self-restraint, for they thought that these feeble and unstable units of wealth could nominally be called goods, but in deed and action they had come to quite the opposite conclusion. Can what is good be for anyone an evil? Can a man who is surrounded by what is good not be good himself? yet we see that all these things are owned by scroundels and missing from the just. 8. That is why anyone may laugh at me if he likes, but true reason weighs more with me than public opinion, and I shall never agree that those who have lost animals or furniture have lost what is good. And I frequently speak with approval of that wise man,

Biantem, ut opinor, qui numeratur in septem; cuius cum patriam Prienam cepisset hostis, ceterique ita fugerent ut multa de suis rebus secum asportarent, cum esset admonitus a quodam ut idem ipse faceret, 'Ego uero' inquit 'facio; nam omnia mecum porto mea'. **9.** Ille haec ludibria fortunae ne sua quidem putauit, quae nos appellamus etiam bona. 'Quid est igitur' quaeret aliquis, 'bonum?' Si quid recte fit et honeste et cum uirtute, id bene fieri uere dicitur, et, quod rectum et honestum et cum uirtute est, id solum opinor bonum.

[II] **10.** Sed haec uideri possunt obscuriora, cum lentius disputantur. uita atque factis illustranda sunt summorum uirorum haec quae uerbis subtilius quam satis est disputari uidentur. quaero enim a uobis – num ullam cogitationem habuisse uideantur ii qui hanc rempublicam tam praeclare fundatam nobis reliquerunt, et argenti ad auaritiam, aut amoenitatum ad delectationem, aut supellectilis ad delicias, aut epularum ad uoluptates? **11.** ponite ante oculos unum quemque – regum uultis a Romulo? uultis post liberam ciuitatem ab iis ipsis, qui liberauerunt eam? quibus tandem gradibus Romulus escendit in caelum? iisne, quae isti bona appellant, an rebus gestis atque uirtutibus? quid? a Numa Pompilio minusne gratas diis immortalibus capudines ac fictiles urnulas fuisse quam filicatas aliorum pateras arbitramur? omitto reliquos: sunt enim omnes pares inter se praeter Superbum.

12. Brutum si quis roget quid egerit in patria liberanda, si quis item reliquos eiusdem consilii socios quid spectauerint, quid secuti sint, num quis exsistat cui uoluptas, cui diuitiae, cui denique praeter officium fortis et magni uiri quidquam aliud propositum fuisse uideatur? quae res ad necem Porsennae C. Mucium impulit sine ulla spe salutis suae? quae uis Coclitem contra omnes hostium copias tenuit in ponte solum? quae patrem Decium, quae filium deuotauit atque immisit in armatas hostium copias? quid continentia C. Fabrici, quid tenuitas uictus M'. Curi sequebatur? quid duo propugnacula belli Punici, Cn. et P. Scipiones, qui Carthaginiensium aduentum corporibus suis intercludendum putauerunt? quid Africanus maior? quid minor? quid inter horum aetates interiectus Cato? quid innumerabiles alii (nam domesticis

Bias I think his name was, who was one of the Seven. The enemy had seized his country Priene, and the rest of the people were trying to carry away a lot of their possessions in their flight, and when someone suggested that he should do the same, he replied 'but I am indeed doing so, for everything I own I carry with me'. **9.** He did not think that these trifles of fortune which we call goods even belonged to him. 'What then *is* good?' someone will ask. If an action is performed morally, rightly and with virtue, it is truly said to be performed in a good way, and only what is moral, right and virtuous is, I think, good.

[II] **10.** But when these ideas are discussed quite coolly, they seem rather far-fetched. They need to be illuminated by the life and actions of great men - words by themselves make a discussion more recondite than need be. I put the question to you - do those who founded our republic in glory and passed it on to us appear to have had any thoughts of silver to satisfy their greed, gardens for their delight, furniture for their comfort or banquets for their pleasure? **11.** Pass them before your eyes in turn - do you want to start with Romulus and the kings? Do you want to start after the liberation of the state with its very liberators? What were the steps which led Romulus to heaven? Was it by means of those so-called goods or by his achievements and virtues? Well then, do you think that the gods were less pleased with the bowls and clay pots of Numa Pompilius than with the finely-wrought dishes of others? I leave out the rest of the kings, for they are all on the same level, apart from the arrogant Tarquin.

12. If anyone were to ask Brutus what his aim was in liberating the state, and similarly were to question his allies in that same *coup* about their intentions and goals, would one be found who would appear to have been motivated by pleasure, riches or anything else except the action appropriate to a brave hero? What spurred Gaius Mucius to kill Porsenna without any hope of his own survival? What force kept Cocles on the bridge, one man against the whole enemy army? What inspired the Decii, father and son, to offer themselves as living sacrifices and throw themselves at the armed enemy ranks? What was the purpose behind the self-restraint of Gaius Fabricius and the meagre diet of Manius Curius? What drove those two bulwarks of the Punic war, Gnaeus and Publius Scipio, to think it their duty to block the advance of the Carthaginians with their own bodies? What about the older Africanus? and the younger? What about Cato, between the two in age? and the countless others (for we have models of our own in abundance) -

exemplis abundamus) – cogitasse quidquam in uita sibi expetendum, nisi quod laudabile esset et praeclarum uidentur?

[III] 13. Veniant igitur isti irrisores huius orationis ac sententiae, et iam uel ipsi iudicent utrum se horum alicuius, qui marmoreis tectis ebore et auro fulgentibus, qui signis, qui tabulis, qui caelato auro et argento, qui Corinthiis operibus abundant, an C. Fabrici, qui nihil eorum habuit, nihil habere uoluit, se similes esse malint? 14. atque haec quidem, quae modo huc modo illuc transferuntur, facile adduci solent ut in rebus bonis esse negent; illud arte tenent accurateque defendunt uoluptatem esse summum bonum.   quae quidem mihi uox pecudum uidetur esse, non hominum. tu, cum tibi siue deus siue mater, ut ita dicam, rerum omnium natura dederit animum, quo nihil est praestantius neque diuinius, sic te ipse abicies atque prosternes ut nihil inter te atque quadripedem aliquam putes interesse? quicquam bonum est, quod non eum qui id possidet meliorem facit?

15. Vt enim est quisque est maxime boni particeps, ita et laudabilis maxime, neque est ullum bonum de quo non is qui id habeat honeste possit gloriari. quid autem est horum in uoluptate? melioremne efficit aut laudabiliorem uirum? an quisquam in potiendis uoluptatibus gloriando se et praedicatione effert? atqui si uoluptas, quae plurimorum patrociniis defenditur, in rebus bonis habenda non est, eaque quo est maior eo magis mentem e sua sede et statu demouet, profecto nihil est aliud bene et beate uiuere, nisi honeste et recte uiuere.

PARADOXON II

In quo uirtus sit, ei nihil deesse ad beate uiuendum.

16. Nec uero ego M. Regulum aerumnosum nec infelicem nec miserum umquam putaui; non enim magnitudo animi eius cruciabatur a Poenis, non grauitas, non fides, non constantia, non ulla uirtus, non denique animus ipse, qui, tot uirtutum praesidio

did they think that they should desire anything in life except what would win praise and renown?

[III] 13. So let those who laugh at this style of speech and way of thinking step forward and give their decision in person on whether they would like to model themselves either on one of those people who are swamped by marble houses ablaze with ivory and gold, and have more than enough of statues and paintings and decorated gold and silver plate and Corinthian works of art, or rather on Gaius Fabricius, who neither possessed nor wished for any of these things? 14. Although these scoffers can easily be persuaded that such possessions as pass easily from hand to hand cannot count as good, they still assiduously maintain and scrupulously defend their claim that pleasure is the ultimate good. This seems to me to be like cattle speaking, not men. When god or, if I may say so, universal mother nature has given you a mind, pre-eminent over all and most god-like, will you so humiliate and degrade yourself that you suppose that there is no difference between you and a four-footed animal? Is anything good which does not improve the one who has it?

15. A man who is most committed to good merits most praise, and there is no good of which he who has it may not justifiably be proud. But how much of this is found in pleasure? Does it improve a man or make him more deserving of praise? Is anyone elated because of pride in his possession of pleasures and the publication of them? Yet if pleasure, which has the greatest number of advocates, is not to be included in the class of goods, and if the more intense it is the more it shakes the mind from its secure station, surely the only way to live a good and happy life is to live morally and rightly.

PARADOX II

The life of virtue is the completely happy life.

16. I have never thought of Marcus Regulus as distressed, unfortunate or unhappy, for the Carthaginians did not torture his greatness of soul, nor his serious demeanour nor his honesty nor steadfastness nor any other virtue of his, and above all they did not touch his mind. This had so strong a defence of virtues and so many in attendance that, although his body could be taken

tantoque comitatu, cum corpus eius caperetur, capi certe ipse non potuit. C. uero Marium uidimus, qui mihi secundis rebus unus ex fortunatis hominibus, aduersis unus ex summis uiris uidebatur, quo beatius esse mortali nihil potest.

17. Nescis, insane, nescis, quantas uires uirtus habeat; nomen tantum uirtutis usurpas; quid ipsa ualeat, ignoras. nemo potest non beatissimus esse qui est totus aptus ex sese, quique in se uno sua ponit omnia. cui spes omnis et ratio et cogitatio pendet ex fortuna, huic nihil potest esse certi, nihil quod exploratum habeat permansurum sibi unum diem. eum tu hominem terreto, si quem eris nactus, istis mortis aut exili minis; mihi uero quidquid acciderit in tam ingrata ciuitate, ne recusanti quidem euenerit, non modo non repugnanti. quid enim ego laboraui, aut quid egi, aut in quo euigilauerunt curae et cogitationes meae, si quidem nihil peperi tale, nihil consecutus sum ut eo statu essem quem neque fortunae temeritas neque inimicorum labefactaret iniuria?

18. Mortemne mihi minitaris, ut omnino ab hominibus, an exilium ut ab improbis demigrandum sit? mors terribilis est iis quorum cum uita omnia exstinguuntur, non iis quorum laus emori non potest; exilium autem illis quibus quasi circumscriptus est habitandi locus, non iis qui omnem orbem terrarum unam urbem esse ducunt. te miseriae, te aerumnae premunt omnes, qui te beatum, qui florentem putas. tuae libidines te torquent, tu dies noctesque cruciaris, cui nec sat est quod est, et id ipsum ne non sit diuturnum times. te conscientiae stimulant maleficiorum tuorum; te metus exanimant iudiciorum atque legum: quocumque aspexisti, ut furiae sic tuae tibi occurrunt iniuriae, quae te suspirare non sinunt.

19. Quam ob rem ut improbo et stulto et inerti nemini bene esse potest, sic bonus uir et fortis et sapiens miser esse nemo potest. nec uero, cuius uirtus moresque laudandi sunt, eius non laudanda uita est; neque porro fugienda uita, quae laudanda est; esset autem fugienda, si esset misera. quam ob rem quidquid est laudabile, idem et beatum et florens et expetendum uideri debet.

prisoner, his mind certainly could not. We have indeed looked on Gaius Marius, who in my opinion was in prosperity one of the men fortune favours, and in adversity one of our greatest heroes, and no mortal can be happier than that.

17. You have no idea at all, you fool, of virtue's mighty powers. You merely use the name of virtue without understanding what it means in itself. No one who is totally self-reliant, and contains within himself all that he owns, can fail to be completely happy. A man whose every hope and thought and plan depends on luck has nothing secure, nothing that he can be sure of keeping for a single day. If you find a man like that, he is the one to terrify with those threats of death or exile, but in my case I shall not only not resist but not even protest at whatever happens to me in this city of such ingratitude. For what is the result of my efforts, what have I achieved, what was the purpose of those sleepless nights of worry and deliberation if indeed I have produced nothing, gained nothing, to secure myself a position that neither the caprice of fortune nor the injustice of my enemies can undermine?

18. Do you threaten me with death, to make me leave the whole human race, or with exile, to leave just the wicked? Death is frightening for those who lose everything with their life, not for those whose fame is undying; exile is frightening for those who live in a place fenced in by a boundary, not for those who think of the whole world as one city. You consider yourself happy and prosperous, but you are oppressed by unhappiness and every affliction. Your lusts rack you, you are tormented day and night, since what you have is not enough and you fear even that may not last long. A guilty conscience stings you, law-courts and sentences make you faint with terror; wherever you look your crimes face you like furies, and do not let you breathe freely.

19. That is why no one who is wicked, foolish and idle can any more enjoy a good life than a good, brave and wise man can be unhappy. One whose virtue and character are to be praised lives a life to be praised, and the life to be praised is not one to be shunned; but if the life is unhappy that life is to be shunned. So whatever merits praise must be considered happy, prosperous and to be desired.

PARADOXON III

Aequalia esse peccata et recte facta.

[I] 20. 'Parua' inquis, 'res est'. At magna culpa, nec enim peccata rerum euentu, sed uitiis hominum metienda sunt. in quo peccatur, id potest aliud alio maius esse aut minus, ipsum quidem illud peccare, quoquo uerteris, unum est. auri nauem euertat gubernator an paleae – in re aliquantulum, in gubernatoris inscientia nihil interest. lapsa est libido in muliere ignota – dolor ad pauciores pertinet quam si petulans fuisset in aliqua generosa ac nobili uirgine; peccauit uero nihilo minus, si quidem est peccare tamquam transilire lineas, quod cum feceris, culpa commissa est. quam longe progrediare cum semel transieris, ad augendam culpam nihil pertinet. peccare certe licet nemini. quod autem non licet, id hoc uno tenetur, si arguitur non licere; id si nec maius nec minus umquam fieri potest (quoniam in eo est peccatum, si non licuit, quod semper unum et idem est), quae ex eo peccata nascuntur aequalia sint oportet.

21. Quod si uirtutes pares sunt inter se, paria esse etiam uitia necesse est. atqui pares esse uirtutes, nec bono uiro meliorem nec temperante temperantiorem nec forti fortiorem nec sapiente sapientiorem posse fieri facillime potest perspici. an uirum bonum dices, qui depositum nullo teste, cum lucrari impune posset auri pondo decem, reddiderit, si idem in decem milibus pondo non idem fecerit? aut temperantem eum, qui se in aliqua libidine continuerit, in aliqua effuderit? 22. una uirtus est consentiens cum ratione et perpetua constantia. nihil huic addi potest quo magis uirtus sit, nihil demi ut uirtutis nomen relinquatur. etenim si bene facta recte facta sunt, et nihil recto rectius, certe ne bono quidem melius quicquam inueniri potest. sequitur igitur ut etiam uitia sint paria, si quidem prauitates animi recte uitia dicuntur. atqui quoniam pares uirtutes sunt, recte facta, quando a uirtutibus proficiscuntur, paria esse debent; itemque peccata, quoniam ex uitiis manant, sint aequalia necesse est.

[II] 23. 'A philosophis' inquis 'ista sumis'. Metuebam ne 'a lenonibus' diceres. 'Socrates disputabat isto modo'. bene hercule

PARADOX III

Wrong acts are all equal, as are moral ones.

[I] 20. 'It's a small matter' you say, but the offence is great. For
wrong acts are gauged not in their consequences but by the vices of
the human agents. The wrong action may be more serious in one
context and less in another, but the actual committing of the fault,
however you prevaricate, is one and the same. A pilot wrecks a
ship with a cargo of gold, or of straw - a slight difference in the
result but none in the pilot's incompetence. A man gives way to
passion and has sex with an unknown woman - fewer people are
offended than if he had lost control with a virgin of high birth
from the nobility; he had acted wrongly nonetheless, since acting
wrongly is like crossing a boundary, and once you have done that
an offence has been committed. How much further you go when
once you have crossed over makes no difference to the gravity of
the offence. Of course wrong acts are not allowed, but the veto
only holds where the veto is demonstrated; if this admits of no
increase or decrease (since the wrongness of the act lies in
transgressing the veto, which always stays one and the same) the
wrong acts that arise from it have to be equal.

21. If virtues are alike, then vices too must be alike. But it can
very easily be seen that virtues are alike, and that it is not possible
to be better than a good man or more self-controlled than a
self-controlled man, or braver than a brave one or wiser than a
wise. Will you call a man good who returns a deposit of ten
pounds' worth of gold when he could have kept it for himself with
impunity as there was no witness, but does not return it when the
sum is ten thousand pounds? Will you call a man self-controlled
who restrains one of his lusts, but gives another full rein? 22.
Virtue in harmony with reason and continuous steadfastness is one
whole. Nothing can be added to virtue to increase it, nothing taken
away and still leave the name of virtue. If good acts are moral
acts, and nothing is more moral than morality, certainly nothing
better than what is good can be found. So it follows that vices too
are alike (if deformities of the mind are properly called vices).
Now since virtues are alike, moral acts too must be alike as they
proceed from virtues; so wrong acts similarly are necessarily equal
as they stem from vices.

[II] 23. 'You take your proposals from philosophers' you claim. I
was afraid you were going to say 'from pimps'. 'Socrates used to

narras. nam istum doctum et sapientem uirum fuisse memoriae traditum est. sed tamen quaero ex te (quando uerbis inter nos contendimus, non pugnis) utrum de bonis est quaerendum quid baioli atque operarii an quid homines doctissimi senserint? praesertim cum hac sententia non modo uerior sed ne utilio quidem hominum uitae reperiri ulla possit? quae uis enim est quae magis arceat homines ab improbitate omni quam si senserint, nullum in delictis esse discrimen? aeque peccare se, si priuatis ac si magistratibus manus afferant, quamcumque in domum stuprum intulerint, eandem esse labem libidinis?

24. 'Nihilne igitur interest' (nam hoc dicet aliquis) 'patrem quis necet, an seruum?' Nuda ista si ponas, iudicari qualia sint non facile possunt. patrem uita priuare si per se scelus est, Saguntini, qui parentes suos liberos emori quam seruos uiuere maluerunt, parricidae fuerunt. ergo et parenti non numquam adimi uita sine scelere potest, et seruo saepe sine iniuria non potest. causa igitur haec non natura distinguit; quae quando utro accessit, id fit propensius; si utroque adiuncta est, paria fiant necesse est.

25. Illud tamen interest, quod in seruo necando, si id fit iniuria, semel peccatur; in patris uita uiolanda multa peccantur. uiolatur is qui procreauit, is qui aluit, is qui erudiuit, is qui in sede ac domo atque in republica collocauit; multitudine peccatorum praestat, eoque poena maiore dignus est. sed nos in uita non quae cuique peccato poena sit sed quantum cuique liceat spectare debemus. quidquid non oportet scelus esse, quidquid non licet nefas putare debemus. 'Etiamne in minimis rebus?' Etiam, si quidem rerum modum fingere non possumus, animorum modum tenere possumus.

26. Histrio si paulum se mouit extra numerum, aut si uersus pronuntiatus est syllaba una breuior aut longior, exsibilatur et exploditur: tu in uita – quae omni gestu moderatior, omni uersu aptior esse debet – in syllaba te peccare dices? poetam non audio

argue like you.' You are right of course; tradition has it that he was clever and wise. But still I put this question to you (since we are competing in a war of words, not coming to blows): in a discussion about what is good, should we find out the opinions of porters and labourers, or those of learned men, especially since no judgment truer or more useful in human life can be found? For what power is there which can hold men back more effectively from all wickedness than the conviction that there are no differences among crimes? The offences are equally wrong, whether one lays hands on a private individual or on a man of high station; yielding to lust is the same, no matter whose house the adulterer invades.

24. 'Is there then no difference' (someone is sure to ask this) 'between killing one's father and killing a slave?' When you put it so baldly it is not easy to make a judgment on these examples. If it is a crime in itself to take a father's life, then the citizens of Saguntum, who preferred their parents to die as free men rather than live as slaves, were parricides. So sometimes it may not be a crime to take a father's life, whereas it can often be unjust to take a slave's. It is the motive therefore, not the type of action, which makes the difference; if the motive is an additional factor in one of the two acts, it makes that one more serious; if in both, they both necessarily are made equal.

25. There is however a distinction in that the killing of a slave, if it is done without due cause, is only one wrong action, but many wrongs are involved in the violent murder of a father. There is the violence to the man who gave us life, who brought us up and educated us, and secured us a place in home and family and state; the parricide is the most notable for the great number of his wrong actions, and so deserves the severer penalty. But in our lives we should not be concerned about the penalty that attaches to each wrong action, but about the limit of what is allowed to us all. We must consider what custom forbids as a crime, but what law forbids as sacrilege. 'Even in little things?' Yes, since we may not of course be able to shape the way things are, but we can control our own minds.

26. If an actor makes the slightest movement out of step, or recites a metric line that is too short or too long by a single syllable, he is hissed and booed off the stage. In *your* role in life - which should be more controlled than any stage gesture, more regulated than any metre - will you plead that you were only a syllable wrong? I do

in nugis, in uitae societate audiam ciuem digitis peccata dimetientem sua? 'Si uisa sint breuiora, leuiora uideantur?' Qui possint uideri cum, quidquid peccatur, perturbatione peccetur rationis atque ordinis, perturbata autem semel ratione et ordine, nihil possit addi quo magis peccari posse uideatur?

PARADOXON IV

Omnem stultum insanire.

[I] 27. Ego uero te non stultum, ut saepe, non improbum, ut semper, sed dementem ... sapientis animus magnitudine consili, tolerantia rerum humanarum, contemptione fortunae, uirtutibus denique omnibus ut moenibus saeptus, uincetur et expugnabitur, qui ne ciuitate quidem pelli potest? quae est enim ciuitas? omnisne conuentus etiam ferorum et immanium? omnisne etiam fugitiuorum ac latronum congregata unum in locum multitudo? certe negabis. non igitur erat illa tum ciuitas, cum leges in ea nihil ualebant, cum iudicia iacebant, cum mos patrius occiderat, cum, ferro pulsis magistratibus, senatus nomen in republica non erat. praedonum ille concursus et, te duce, latrocinium in foro constitutum et reliquiae coniurationis a Catilinae furiis ad tuum scelus furoremque conuersae non ciuitas erat.

28. Itaque pulsus ego ciuitate non sum quae nulla erat; arcessitus in ciuitatem sum, cum esset in republica consul qui tum nullus fuerat, esset senatus, qui tum occiderat, esset consensus populi liberi, esset iuris et aequitatis, quae uincula sunt ciuitatis, repetita memoria. ac uide quam ista tui latrocinii tela contempserim. iactam et immissam a te nefariam in me iniuriam semper duxi, peruenisse ad me numquam putaui, nisi forte cum parietes disturbabas, aut cum tectis sceleratas faces inferebas, meorum aliquid ruere aut deflagrare arbitrabare.

29. Nihil neque meum est neque cuiusquam quod auferri, quod eripi, quod amitti potest. si mihi eripuisses diuinam animi mei

not listen to a minstrel who is only slightly out of tune, shall I pay attention to a citizen who, in life's associations, measures his wrong acts by the length of his fingers? 'If they look smaller, aren't they that much lighter?' How could they look so, when every wrong action throws reason and order into confusion, and once reason and order are in confusion, nothing can be added to make the wrong action look more wrong?

PARADOX IV

Every fool is mad.

[I] 27. I shall not demonstrate here that you (Clodius) are foolish, as often, or wicked, as always, but that you are actually mad ... will the mind of a wise man that is defended by the ramparts of high purpose, by endurance of man's lot, by disregard for fortune, and by all the virtues, be defeated and stormed when it cannot even be exiled from the city? For what is a city? any horde of wild savages? any band of thugs and runaways brought together in one place? 'Of course not' you'll say. So that was not a city then, when laws in it had no force, the courts were suspended and ancestral custom overthrown, when the magistrates had been driven out at sword-point, and 'senate' was a name unknown in the state. That gang of crooks and bandits collected in the forum under your leadership, along with the remnants of Catiline's conspiracy who had been converted from his ravings to your lunatic villainy - that was no city.

28. So I was not banished from a city that did not exist. But I was called to the city when the state had a consul where previously there had been none, when there was a senate (reestablished) which has previously collapsed, where there was the verdict of a free people and the memory restored of that law and justice which bind a city. See how I despised the missiles of your thugs. I always understood that you had aimed and hurled vile injustice at me, but I do not think that it ever reached me, unless perhaps you were of the opinion that when you were pulling down my walls or viciously setting fire to the roofs your destruction and arson were directed against anything of mine.

29. Nothing of mine, or of anyone else, can be removed, stolen or lost. If you had stolen my godlike steadfastness of mind along with

constantiam meis curis, uigiliis, consiliis quibus respublica te inuitissimo stat, si huius aeterni beneficii immortalem memoriam deleuisses, multo etiam magis si illam mentem, unde haec consilia manarunt, mihi eripuisses, tum ego accepisse me confiterer iniuriam. sed si haec nec fecisti, nec facere potuisti, reditum mihi gloriosum iniuria tua dedit, non exitum calamitosum. ergo ego semper ciuis, et tum maxime, cum meam salutem senatus exteris nationibus ut ciuis optimi commendabat – tu ne nunc quidem, nisi forte idem esse hostis et ciuis potest. an tu ciuem ab hoste natura ac loco, non animo factisque distinguis?

[II] **30.** Caedem in foro fecisti, armatis latronibus templa tenuisti, priuatorum domos, aedes sacras incendisti. cur hostis Spartacus, si tu ciuis? potes autem tu esse ciuis, propter quem aliquando ciuitas non fuit? et me tuo nomine appellas, cum omnes meo discessu exsulasse rempublicam putent? numquamne, homo amentissime, te circumspicies? numquam nec quid facis considerabis, nec quid loquare? nescis exilium scelerum esse poenam, meum illud iter ob praeclarissimas res a me gestas esse susceptum? **31.** omnes scelerati atque impii, quorum tu te ducem esse profiteris, quos leges exilio affici uolunt, exules sunt, etiam si solum non mutarunt. an cum omnes leges te exulem esse iubeant, non appelletur inimicus 'qui cum telo fuerit'? ante senatum tua sica deprehensa est; 'qui hominem occiderit'? tu plurimos occidisti; 'qui incendium fecerit'? aedes Nympharum manu tua deflagrauit; 'qui templa occupauerit'? in foro castra posuisti.

32. Sed quid ego communes leges profero, quibus omnibus es exsul? familiarissimus tuus de te priuilegium tulit ut, si in opertum Bonae Deae accessisses, exulares. at te id fecisse, etiam gloriari soles. quo modo igitur, tot legibus in exilium eiectus, nomen exulis non perhorrescis? 'Romae sum', inquis; et quidem in operto fuisti. non igitur, ubi quisque erit, eius loci ius tenebit, si ibi eum legibus esse non oportebit.

my ever-watchful concern and counsel which (very much to your chagrin) were keeping the state stable, if you had obliterated the deathless memory of this unending public service, and even more so if you had stolen the intellect that was the source of these counsels, then I would admit to having been wronged. But if you did not and could not have done so, your injustice caused my glorious return, not a ruinous departure. So I have always been a citizen, and especially then when the senate recommended me as one of high standing to foreign nations, whereas you are not a citizen even now, unless of course the same man can be both citizen and public enemy; or do you distinguish citizen from enemy by family and domicile, not character and action?

[II] 30. You carried out a massacre in the forum, you occupied the temples with armed thugs, you set fire to private houses and sacred buildings. Why was Spartacus a public enemy if you were a citizen? Could *you* be a citizen when, because of you, there was a time when there was no city? Do you call *me* by the name that belongs to you, when everyone thought that, when I departed, the state had been sent into exile? Will you never look around you, you lunatic? Will you never reflect on what you are doing, what you are saying? Don't you understand that exile is a punishment for crime, whereas that journey of mine was taken up because of the glorious deeds I had done? 31. All criminals and blasphemers (and you claim to be their leader) under sentence of punishment from the laws are exiles, even if they have not left the country. Since all the laws condemn you to exile, will there not be the name of enemy for one 'found in possession of a weapon'? - your dagger was seized in front of the senate-house; 'who murdered a man'? - you have committed very many murders; 'who has been guilty of arson'? - with your own hand you set fire to the house of the Nymphs; 'who has taken over temples'? - you set up camp in the forum.

32. But why do I quote the individual laws of the community when you are an exile on all counts? Your closest friend passed a special measure about you, decreeing that you would be exiled if you entered the inner shrine of the Good Goddess - and you did that very thing, and even went around boasting of it. When so many laws have cast you into exile how is it then that you do not shudder at the name of exile? 'I am at Rome' you say; and you were also in that shrine. Wherever a man is, the rights of that place do not protect him, if according to its laws he should not be there.

PARADOXON V

Solum sapientem esse liberum et omnem stultum seruum.

[I] **33.** Laudetur uero hic imperator aut etiam appelletur aut hoc nomine dignus putetur – imperator quo modo? aut cui tandem hic libero imperabit, qui non potest cupiditatibus suis imperare? refrenet primum libidines, spernat uoluptates, iracundiam teneat, coerceat auaritiam, ceteras animi labes repellat – tum incipiat aliis imperare, cum ipse improbissimis dominis, dedecori ac turpitudini, parere desierit. dum quidem his obediet, non modo imperator, sed liber habendus omnino non erit. praeclare enim est hoc usurpatum a doctissimis – quorum ego auctoritate non uterer, si mihi apud aliquos agrestes haec habenda esset oratio; cum uero apud prudentissimos loquar, quibus haec inaudita non sunt, cur ego simulem me, si quid in his studiis operae posuerim, perdidisse? – dictum est igitur ab eruditissimis uiris, nisi sapientem, liberum esse neminem.

34. Quid est enim libertas? potestas uiuendi, ut uelis. quis igitur uiuit ut uult, nisi qui recta sequitur, qui gaudet officio, cui uiuendi uia considerata atque prouisa est? qui ne legibus quidem propter metum paret, sed eas sequitur atque colit, quia id salutare maxime esse iudicat, qui nihil dicit, nihil facit, nihil cogitat denique nisi libenter ac libere? cuius omnia consilia resque omnes quas gerit ab ipso proficiscuntur, eodemque referuntur, nec est ulla res, quae plus apud eum polleat quam ipsius uoluntas atque iudicium, cui quidem etiam quae uim habere maximam dicitur fortuna ipsa cedit, si, ut sapiens poeta dixit, suis ea cuique fingitur moribus. soli igitur hoc contingit sapienti, ut nihil faciat inuitus, nihil dolens, nihil coactus.

35. Quod etsi ita esse pluribus uerbis disserendum est, illud tamen et breue et confitendum est: nisi qui ita sit affectus, liberum esse neminem. serui igitur omnes improbi, serui. nec hoc tam re est, quam dictu inopinatum atque mirabile, non enim ita dicunt eos esse seruos ut mancipia, quae sunt dominorum facta nexu aut aliquo iure ciuili, sed si seruitus sit – sicut est – obedientia fracti

PARADOX V

Only the wise man is free and every fool is a slave.

[I] 33. A man may indeed be saluted as commanding-officer or named by this rank or thought worthy of it - but commanding officer in what sense? Will there be a free man he can command when he cannot command his own desire? Let him first curb his lusts, despise pleasures, control his temper, restrain his greed and remove the other stains of character - then let him begin to command others when he has himself stopped being at the beck and call of those unprincipled masters, dishonour and depravity. As long as he serves them he will not only not be considered a commanding officer but not even a free man. For there is a saying adopted by the learned - I would not introduce their authority here if I were addressing country bumpkins, but since I am speaking to a very intelligent audience who are not strangers to my theme, why should I pretend that I have wasted my time if I have given some attention to these studies? - it is said then by the highly educated that no one is free unless he is wise.

34. What is freedom? the ability to live as you wish. So does anyone live as he wishes, except the man who follows what is right, who enjoys doing what he should, who has considered and worked out his way of life in advance? who does not so much obey the laws out of fear as follow and respect them because he concludes that that is what best promotes one's well-being, and whose words and actions and even thoughts come freely, a product of his own free will? All his deliberations and achievements are self-determined from beginning to end. Nothing has more influence with him than his own will and judgment, to whom even fortune herself submits (and she is said to have the greatest power, if, as the wise poet says, a man's fortune is shaped by his character). It is therefore true only of the wise man that he does nothing against his will, nothing to grieve at, nothing under compulsion.

35. Although this is a topic which should be discussed at length, the following brief proposition is surely admitted: only a man with this kind of character is free. Slaves then are all the wicked, slaves. This is not in fact as unexpected and strange as it sounds, for the Stoics do not mean that the wicked are slaves in the sense of bondsmen who have come into the possession of their masters as surety for debt or by some act of civil law, but, if slavery means - as it does - the submission of a spirit that has been broken and

animi atque abiecti et arbitrio carentis suo, quis neget omnes leues, omnes cupidos, omnes denique improbos esse seruos?

[II] **36.** An ille mihi liber, cui mulier imperat? cui leges imponit, praescribit, iubet, uetat quod uidetur? qui nihil imperanti negare potest, nihil recusare audet? poscit, dandum est; uocat, ueniendum; eiicit, abeundum; minatur, extimescendum. ego uero istum non modo seruum, sed nequissimum seruum, etiam si in amplissima familia natus sit, appellandum puto. atque ut in magna familia sunt seruorm alii lautiores – ut sibi uidentur – serui, sed tamen serui, atrienses ac topiarii, pari stultitia sunt, quos signa, quos tabulae, quos caelatum argentum, quos Corinthia opera, quos aedificia magnifica nimio opere delectant. 'At sumus' inquiunt 'ciuitatis principes'. uos uero ne conseruorum quidem uestrorum principes estis. **37.** sed ut in familia, qui tractant ista – qui tergunt, qui ungunt, qui uerrunt, qui spargunt – non honestissimum locum seruitutis tenent, sic in ciuitate, qui se istarum rerum cupiditatibus dediderunt, ipsius seruitutis locum paene infimum obtinent. 'Magna' inquit 'bella gessi, magnis imperiis et prouinciis praefui.' Gere igitur animum laude dignum. Aetionis tabula te stupidum detinet aut signum aliquod Polycleti. mitto unde sustuleris, et quo modo habeas – intuentem te, admirantem, clamores tollentem cum uideo, seruum te esse ineptiarum omnium iudico.

38. Nonne igitur sunt ista festiua? sint. nam nos quoque oculos eruditos habemus. sed, obsecro te, ita uenusta habeantur ista, non ut uincula uirorum sint, sed ut oblectamenta puerorum. quid enim censes? si L. Mummius aliquem istorum uideret, matellionem Corinthium cupidissime tractantem, cum ipse totam Corthinthum contempsisset, utrum illum ciuem excellentem, an atriensem diligentem putaret? reuiuiscat M'. Curius aut eorum aliquis quorum in uilla ac domo nihil splendidum, nihil ornatum fuit praeter ipsos, et uideat aliquem, summis populi beneficiis usum, barbatulos mullos exceptantem de piscina et pertractantem et muraenarum copia gloriantem – nonne hunc hominem ita seruum iudicet ut ne in familia quidem dignum maiore aliquo negotio putet?

humiliated and has no will of its own, who could deny that the capricious, the envious, in fact all the wicked are slaves?

[II] 36. Do I think a man is free whom a woman commands? who imposes on him rules and regulations, orders and prohibitions as she thinks fit? and the man cannot object to her commands, and dare refuse her nothing? She demands, he must give; she calls, he must come; she dismisses, he must leave; she threatens, he trembles perforce. I think a man like that should be called not only a slave but the most miserable of slaves, even if he was born into one of the noblest houses. Now in a great house some slaves are grander - they suppose - than others, the butler for example or the landscape gardner, but they are still slaves. Even so they are not more foolish than those who are led astray by extravagant delight in statues, paintings, embossed silver, Corinthian bric-à-brac and sumptuous buildings. 'But we are prominent citizens' they object; you are not even prominent among your fellow-slaves. 37. Just as those who handle such objects in a house - wiping, dusting, polishing and spraying them - are not in the highest order of slaves, so those in the state who surrender to a desire for them occupy about the lowest place in real slavery. 'I have managed great wars' you object, 'I have held great commands and governed provinces'. Then manage a soul worthy of credit. A painting by Aetion or a statue by Polyclitus holds you spellbound. To say nothing about where you got them from or how they are in your possession - when I see you gazing admiringly and uttering little cries, I take you to be a slave of every silliness.

38. But surely such works of art are a sheer delight? Of course; my eyes too have been trained to appreciate them. Still, I beg you, let their attractions be thought of as children's amusements, not bonds to tie down grown men. Tell me, what do you think of this case? Suppose Lucius Mummius saw someone like you eagerly handling a little Corinthian pot whereas he had despised the entire city of Corinth, would he think him a fine citizen - or an attentive butler. Bring back Manius Curius or one of those whose town or country house contained nothing glittering, no adornment other than themselves, and let him see the recipient of the people's highest favours taking mullet (with little beards!) out of his fish-tank and studying them, or boasting of his supply of lamprey - wouldn't he suppose that here was a man so servile that he could not be made responsible even for a household task of any importance?

39. An eorum seruitus dubia est, qui cupiditate peculi nullam conditionem recusant durissimae seruitutis? hereditatis spes – quid iniquitatis in seruiendo non suscipit? quem nutum locupletis orbi senis non obseruat? loquitur ad uoluntatem, quidquid denunciatum est facit, assectatur, assidet, muneratur. quid horum est liberi? quid denique non serui inertis?

[III] **40.** Quid? iam illa cupiditas quae uidetur esse liberalior, honoris, imperii, prouinciarum, quam dura est domina, quam imperiosa, quam uehemens! Cethego, homini non probatissimo, seruire coegit eos qui sibi esse amplissimi uidebantur – munera mittere, noctu uenire domum ad eum, Praeciae denique supplicare. quae seruitus est, si haec libertas existimari potest? quid? cum cupiditatum dominatus excessit, et alius est dominus exortus ex conscientia peccatorum – timor. quam est illa misera, quam dura seruitus! adolescentibus paulo loquacioribus est seruiendum; omnes qui aliquid scire uidentur tamquam domini timentur. iudex uero quantum habet dominatum, quo timore nocentes afficit! an non est omnis metus seruitus?

41. Quid ualet igitur illa eloquentissimi uiri, L. Crassi, copiosa magis quam sapiens oratio? 'Eripite nos ex seruitute!' Quae est ista seruitus tam claro homini tamque nobili? omnis animi debilitati et humilis et fracti timiditas seruitus est. 'Nolite sinere nos cuiquam seruire.' In libertatem uindicari uult? minime; quid enim adiungit? 'nisi uobis uniuersis' – dominum mutare, non liber esse uult – 'quibus et possumus et debemus.' Nos uero, siquidem animo excelso et alto et uirtutibus exaggerato sumus, nec debemus nec possumus. tu posse te dicito, quoniam quidem potes, debere ne dixeris; quoniam nihil quisquam debet, nisi quod est turpe non reddere.

Sed haec hactenus. ille uideat, quomodo imperator esse possit, cum eum ne liberum quidem esse ratio et ueritas ipsa conuincat.

39. Again, is there any doubt about the slavery of those who do not shrink from any condition of the harshest service because of their avarice? The hope of a legacy - what injustice does it not drive a man to tolerate in its service? what nod from a dotard, rich and childless, does he not jump to? He speaks when the old man wishes, runs on his errands, walks with him, sits by him, gives him presents. Which of these activities belongs to the free man? which does not belong to the spineless slave?

[III] **40.** What then? The desire which does seem to belong more to a free man - for political office, military command and provincial government, how harsh a mistress is that, how domineering, how tyrannical! She compelled those who thought themselves very distinguished to minister to that disreputable character Cethegus - to send him presents, to go to his house at night and even to grovel to his moll Praecia. What *is* slavery, if this can be thought freedom? What then? once the tyranny wielded by desires has left, still another tyrant emerges from a guilty conscience - that of fear. How pitiable, how harsh is the servitude it imposes. Young men a little too ready to talk have to be appeased; anyone who seems to know anything is treated like a fearsome tyrant. And a judge - how much power he has, with what terror he strikes the guilty! Doesn't being afraid always mean being a slave?

41. What is the force then of the address delivered - with more eloquence than wisdom - by that splendid speaker Lucius Crassus? 'Deliver us from slavery!' What slavery does this mean for a man so well-known, so distinguished? Slavery is all the nervousness of a spirit weakened, degraded and broken. 'Let us not serve any individual!' Does he really want to claim his rights as a free man? no; for what does he add? 'but only you, the whole citizen body' - he wants to change masters, not to be free - 'whom we can and should serve'. Yet we neither should nor can, if we have a spirit noble, sublime, held aloft by virtue. Say you can, since of course you can, but don't say you should, since no one *should* do anything except what it is wrong not to do.

But enough of this. Let that man we started with work out how he can be a commanding-officer, when reason and very truth prove decisively that he is not even free.

PARADOXON VI

Solum sapientem esse diuitem.

[I] **42.** Quae est ista in commemoranda pecunia tua tam insolens ostentatio? solusne tu diues? pro di immortales! egone me audiuisse aliquid et didicisse non gaudeam? solusne diues? quid, si ne diues quidem? quid, si pauper etiam? quem enim intelligimus diuitem, aut hoc uerbum in quo homine ponimus? opinor in eo cui tanta possessio est ut ad liberaliter uiuendum facile contentus sit, qui nihil quaerat, nihil appetat, nihil optet amplius.

43. animus oportet tuus se iudicet diuitem, non hominum sermo, neque possessiones tuae. nihil sibi deesse putat, nihil curat amplius, satiatus est aut contentus etiam pecunia? concedo, diues es. sin autem propter auiditatem pecuniae nullum quaestum turpem putas (cum isti ordini ne honestus quidem possit esse ullus), si cotidie fraudas, decipis, poscis, pacisceris, aufers, eripis, si socios spolias, aerarium expilas, si testamenta amicorum exspectas, aut ne exspectas quidem, atque ipse supponis – haec utrum abundantis, an egentis signa sunt?

44. Animus hominis diues, non arca appellari solet; quamuis illa sit plena, dum te inanem uidebo, diuitem non putabo. etenim ex eo, quantum cuique satis est, metiuntur homines diuitiarum modum. filiam quis habet? pecunia est opus; duas? maiore; plures? maiore etiam; si, ut aiunt Danao, quinquaginta sint filiae, tot dotes magnam quaerunt pecuniam. quantum enim cuique opus est ad id accommodatur, ut ante dixi, diuitiarum modus. qui igitur non filias plures, sed innumerabiles cupiditates habet, quae breui tempore maximas copias exhaurire possint – hunc quo modo ego appellabo diuitem, cum ipse etiam egere se sentiat? **45.** Multi ex te audierunt, cum diceres neminem esse diuitem, nisi qui exercitum alere posset suis fructibus, quod populus Romanus tantis uectigalibus iam pridem uix potest. ergo, hoc proposito, numquam eris diues ante quam tibi ex tuis possessionibus tantum reficietur ut eo tueri sex legiones et magna equitum ac peditum auxilia possis.

PARADOX VI

Only the wise man is rich.

[I]   42. What is this high-and-mighty display every time you mention your money? Are you the only rich man? Heavens above! am I not glad to have been a student and learned something? Are you the only rich man? Suppose you are not rich after all? suppose you are even poor? What do we mean by 'a rich man'? to whom do we give this title? to the one, I suppose, who has so much that he is tolerably content to lead a decent life, with no further striving, who aims at nothing, desires nothing more.

43.   Your own soul should decide that you are rich, not other people's talk, or your belongings. Does your soul think that it needs nothing, has no further worries, is satisfied or at least content with the money that you have? I admit it then - you are a rich man. But if, in your greed for money, you think no profitable deal wrong (when for someone of your standing none could be right), if your days are full of deceits and tricks and demands and bargains and thefts and extortions, if you rob your colleagues and plunder the treasury, if you wait for your friends' wills (or don't even wait for them but substitute forged ones yourself) - are these the signs of one who has more than enough, or of one who is in need?

44. A man's mind is usually called well-endowed, not his safe. That may be full, but as long as I see that there is nothing in you, I shall not think you rich. In fact people calculate the limit of wealth at the point at which a man has enough. Does so-and-so have a daughter? he needs money; two daughters? more money; more than two? even more. And if, as they say of Danaus, he has fifty daughters, he needs a great deal of money for that many dowries. For, as I said before, the limit of wealth is set at what the individual needs. So a man who does not have many daughters but does have innumerable desires which are capable of draining vast resources in a short time - how can I call him rich, when he himself still feels that he is in need? 45. Many people have heard you say that no one is rich who cannot maintain an army from his personal estate, something which the Roman republic with all its great resources has for a long time only just about managed to do. So on these terms you will never be rich until you generate enough income from your capital to maintain six legions and large auxiliary forces of cavalry and infantry. And so you admit now that you are

iam fateris igitur non esse te diuitem, cui tantum desit ut expleas id quod exoptas. itaque istam paupertatem uel potius egestatem ac mendicitatem tuam numquam obscure tulisti.

[II] 46. Nam ut iis, qui honeste rem quaerunt mercaturis faciendis, operis dandis, publicis sumendis, intelligimus opus esse quaesito, sic, qui uidet domi tuae pariter accusatorum atque indicum consociatos greges, qui nocentes et pecuniosos reos – eodem te auctore – corruptelam iudici molientes, qui tuas mercedum pactiones in patrociniis, intercessiones pecuniarum in coitionibus candidatorum, dimissiones libertorum ad fenerandas diripiendasque prouincias, qui expulsiones uicinorum, qui latrocinia in agris, qui cum seruis, cum libertis, cum clientibus societates, qui possessiones uacuas, qui proscriptiones locupletium, qui caedes municipiorum, qui illam Sullani temporis messem recordetur, qui testamenta subiecta, qui sublatos tot homines, qui denique omnia uenalia, delectum decretum, alienam suam sententiam, forum domum, uocem silentium, quis hunc non putet confiteri sibi quaesito opus esse? cui autem quaesito opus sit, quis umquam hunc uere dixerit diuitem?

47. Etenim diuitiarum est fructus in copia. copiam autem declarat satietas rerum atque abundantia; quam tu, quoniam numquam assequere, numquam omnino es futurus diues. meam autem quoniam pecuniam contemnis (et recte, est enim ad uulgi opinionem mediocris, ad tuam nulla, ad meam modica), de me silebo, de re loquar. 48. si censenda nobis atque aestimanda res sit, utrum tandem pluris aestimemus pecuniam Pyrrhi quam Fabricio dabat, an continentiam Fabricii, qui illam pecuniam repudiabat? utrum aurum Samnitum, an responsum M'. Curii? hereditatem L. Paulli, an liberalitatem Africani, qui eius hereditatis Q. Maximo fratri partem suam concessit? haec profecto, quae sunt summarum uirtutum, pluris aestimanda sunt quam illa, quae sunt pecuniae. quis igitur (si quidem, ut quisque quod plurimi sit possideat, ita diuitissimus habendus sit) dubitet quin in uirtute diuitiae sint, quoniam nulla possessio, nulla uis auri et argenti pluris quam uirtus aestimanda est.

[III] 49. O di immortales! non intelligunt homines, quam magnum uectigal sit parsimonia. uenio enim iam ad sumptuosos, relinquo istum quaestuosum. capit ille ex suis praediis sescenta

not rich, since you need so much to fulfil your longings; and that is why you have never made a secret of your poverty - or rather your state of beggarly indigence.

[II] 46. We realise that those who try to make an honest penny by commerce, construction-works or tax-collecting need some income, so look at the evidence in your case - gangs of professional prosecutors and informers gathered together at your house, guilty and wealthy plaintiffs conspiring (at your suggestion) to corrupt the jury, profitable contracts in chambers, bribery at election swindles, instructions to freedmen to fleece and plunder the provinces, eviction of neighbours, land seizures, unholy alliances with slaves, freedmen and clients, properties emptied, proscriptions of the rich, massacres in the Italian townships, the memory of that terrible harvest in the time of Sulla, the forged wills, the disappearance of so many men, and finally the evidence of everything for sale - military conscription, senatorial decrees, votes (other people's as well as one's own!), public and private affairs, speaking up and staying silent. Wouldn't anyone think that a person like that was admitting the need for income? But who could ever have called someone so in need of income truly a rich man?

47. The benefit of riches is in the supply of it; the supply is publicised when what one has is enough and more than enough, and since you will never reach this point you will never ever be a rich man. But as you despise *my* income (and rightly so, for most people think it insignificant, you non-existent and I moderate enough) I shall say nothing about myself but address the question of wealth. 48. If we are to assess and evaluate wealth shall we value more highly the money of Pyrrhus, used to bribe Fabricius, or the self-restraint of Fabricius in refusing it? the gold of the Samnites or the answer of Manius Curius? the bequest of Lucius Paullus or the generosity of Africanus who gave his share of that bequest to his brother Quintus Maximus? Surely the latter alternatives, the possession of the greatest virtues, are to be valued more highly than the former, that of money? Who then could doubt (on the assumption that a man is to be considered the richest in proportion to his having the most valuable possessions) that riches rest in virtue, since no possession, no amount of gold and silver, can be thought more valuable than virtue?

[III] 49. Heavens above! don't people understand how much money thrift produces? For now I leave aside the money-makers, and come to the extravagant spenders. That man makes 600

sestertia, ego centena ex meis; illi aurata tecta in uillis et sola marmorea facienti, et signa, tabulas, supellectilem et uestem infinite concupiscenti, non modo ad sumptum ille est fructus, sed etiam ad fenus exiguus; ex meo tenui uectigali, detractis sumptibus cupiditatis, aliquid etiam redundabit. uter igitur est diuitior – cui deest, an cui superat? qui eget, an qui abundat? cuius possessio quo est maior eo plus requirit ad se tuendam, an quae suis se uiribus sustinet?

50. Sed quid ego de me loquor, qui morum ac temporum uitio aliquantum etiam ipse fortasse in huius saeculi errore uerser? M'. Manilius patrum nostrorum memoria – ne semper Curios et Luscinos loquamur – pauper tandem fuit? habuit enim aediculas in Carinis et fundum in Labicano; nos igitur diuitiores, qui plura habemus? utinam quidem! sed non aestimatione census, uerum uictu atque cultu terminatur pecuniae modus. **51.** non esse cupidum pecunia est, non esse emacem uectigal est. contentum uero suis rebus esse maximae sunt certissimaeque diuitiae. etenim si isti callidi rerum aestimatores prata et areas quasdam magno aestimant quod ei generi possessionum minime quasi noceri potest, quanti est aestimanda uirtus, quae nec eripi, nec surripi potest umquam, neque naufragio nec incendio amittitur, nec ui tempestatum nec temporum perturbatione mutatur!

Qua praediti qui sunt, soli sunt diuites. **52.** soli enim possident res et fructuosas et sempiternas, solique – quod est proprium diuitiarum – contenti sunt rebus suis, satis esse putant quod est; nihil appetunt, nulla re egent, nihil sibi deesse sentiunt, nihil requirunt. improbi autem et auari, quoniam incertas atque in casu positas possessiones habent, et plus semper appetunt, nec eorum quisquam adhuc inuentus est cui quod haberet esset satis, non modo non copiosi ac diuites, sed etiam inopes ac pauperes existimandi sunt.

sestertia from his property, I make 100 from mine, but since he has gilded ceilings and marble floors in his houses, and never stops wanting statues, pictures, furniture and drapery, there is but a small return to pay not only for his expenditure but even for the interest on his debts; from my slender income on the other hand there is even a little in credit once the expenses for what I want have been paid. So which of us is the richer - the one with a deficit or the one in credit? the one in need or the one with more than he needs? the one who is always looking for more to maintain an ever-expanding estate or the one who is self-sufficient?

50. But why do I speak of myself, who, because of the fault of our way of life and the times we live in, have been perhaps personally caught up in the wrongs of this generation? Within our fathers' memory was Manius Manilius - to avoid the standard citations from the Curii and Luscini - a poor man, do you think? for he had only a little house in the Keels district and a small-holding in Labicanum. Are we who have more than that therefore richer? I wish we were, but the amount of one's wealth is not to be gauged by the census ratings, but by one's way of life and general standards. **51.** Not to be greedy is riches, not to be a compulsive buyer brings in an income. Indeed, to be content with what one has is the greatest and most secure wealth. Now if your skilled valuers put a high price on some piece of town or country real estate because it is the kind least liable to depreciation, how great a value should be given to virtue, of which one can never be robbed or cheated, which is never lost through shipwreck or fire, nor affected by violent storms or revolutions?

Those endowed with virtue are the only ones who are rich. **52.** For they alone own what is profitable and permanent, they alone are content with what they have - the mark of true wealth. They think their possessions enough, they aim for nothing more, need nothing, are aware that they want for nothing, look for nothing. The wicked and greedy on the other hand, since what they have is uncertain and depends on chance, are always aiming for more, and not one of them has yet been found who is satisfied with what he has - they are to be judged not only *not* well-provided for and rich, but even as without resources and poor men.

APPENDIX

PRO MURENA 61–63

PRO MURENA 61-63

61. Et quoniam non est nobis haec oratio habenda apud imperitam multitudinem aut in aliquo conuentu agrestium, audacius paulo de studiis humanitatis, quae et mihi et uobis nota et iucunda sunt, disputabo. in M. Catone, iudices, haec bona, quae uidimus diuina et egregia, ipsius scitote esse propria; quae nonnumquam requirimus, ea sunt omnia non a natura, uerum a magistro.

Fuit enim quidam summo ingenio uir, Zeno, cuius inuentorum aemuli Stoici nominantur. huius sententiae sunt et praecepta huius modi: sapientem gratia numquam moueri, numquam cuiusquam delicto ignoscere; neminem misericordem esse nisi stultum et leuem; uiri non esse nec exorari neque placari; solos sapientes esse, si distortissimi sint, formosos, si mendicissimi, diuites, si seruitutem seruiant, reges; nos autem, qui sapientes non sumus, fugitiuos, exsules, hostes, insanos denique esse dicunt; omnia peccata esse paria, omne delictum scelus esse nefarium, nec minus delinquere eum, qui gallum gallinaceum, cum opus non fuerit, quam eum qui patrem suffocauerit; sapientem nihil opinari, nullius rei paenitere, nulla in re falli, sententiam mutare numquam.

62. haec homo ingeniosissimus, M. Cato, auctoribus eruditissimis inductus arripuit, neque disputandi causa, ut magna pars, sed ita uiuendi. petunt aliquid publicani - 'caue quidquam habeat momenti gratia'. supplices aliqui ueniunt miseri et calamitosi - 'sceleratus et nefarius fueris, si quicquam misericordia adductus feceris'. fatetur aliquis se peccasse et eius delicti ueniam petit - 'nefarium est facinus ignoscere'; at leue delictum est - 'omnia peccata sunt paria'. dixisti - 'quippe iam fixum et statutum est'; non re ductus es, sed opinione - 'sapiens nihil opinatur'. errasti aliqua in re - maledici putat. hac ex disciplina nobis illa sunt: 'dixi in senatu me nomen consularis candidati delaturum'. iratus dixisti - 'numquam' inquit 'sapiens irascitur'. at temporis causa - 'hominis est mendacio fallere, mutare sententiam turpe est, exoriari scelus, misereri flagitium.

IN DEFENCE OF MURENA 61-63

61. Since I am not delivering this speech before an uneducated crowd or at some gathering of peasants, I shall speak a little more boldly about those liberal studies which we are all well-versed in and enjoy. Know, gentlemen, that in Marcus Cato those good qualities which we recognise as godlike and most excellent are the products of his own character; it is because of his schooling, not his nature, that others are sometimes missing.

For there was once a very talented man, Zeno, and those who follow his teaching are called Stoics. His principles and precepts are as follows: the wise man is never influenced by favour, he never forgives anyone's transgression; no one is compassionate except the foolish and flippant; it is not appropriate for a citizen to give way to entreaty or to be appeased; only the wise are handsome even if they are deformed, rich even if beggars, kings even if serving as slaves. The Stoics say that we however who are not wise are runaways, exiles, public enemies and in fact mad; all sins are equal, every transgression a wicked crime. The man who wrings the neck of a cock when there was no need sins no less than one who strangles his father; the wise man never hazards an opinion, regrets nothing, makes no mistakes and never changes his mind.

62. The highly intelligent Marcus Cato was led astray by learned teachers and adopted these principles, not, as most people do, to argue about them, but to live by them. The tax-collectors submit a petition - 'take care that favour carries no weight with you'. Some poor unfortunates plead for help - 'you will be a wicked criminal if you act out of pity'. Someone else confesses that he has done wrong and asks pardon for his transgression - 'it is criminal to forgive a wrong', but it was only a slight transgression - 'all sins are equal'. You spoke - 'yes, and it is now an unalterable pronouncement', but as a result of an opinion, not because of what really happened - 'the wise man never offers an opinion'. You made a mistake in some matter - he thinks he is being insulted. These are some of the consequences of this dogma: 'I said in the senate that I would prosecute the consular candidate'. You spoke in anger - 'the wise man' he says 'is never angry'; you spoke for the moment - 'to deceive with a lie' he says 'is the sign of a scoundrel, to change one's mind is wrong, to give way to entreaty wicked and to show compassion a crime'.

63. Nostri autem illi - fatebor enim, Cato, me quoque in adulescentia diffisum ingenio meo quaesisse adiumenta doctrinae - nostri, inquam, illi a Platone et Aristotele, moderati homines et temperati, aiunt apud sapientem ualere aliquando gratiam, uiri boni esse misereri, distincta genera esse delictorum et dispares poenas, esse apud hominem constantem ignoscendi locum, ipsum sapientem saepe aliquid opinari, irasci nonnumquam, exorari eundem et placari, quod dixerit interdum, si ita rectius sit, mutare, de sententia decedere aliquando; omnes uirtutes mediocritate quadam esse moderatas.

63. Now our teachers - for I will admit that I too in my youth mistrusted my natural character and looked for support from philosophy - our teachers, I claim, the successors of Plato and Aristotle, moderate men not given to extremes, maintain that a wise man does give some weight to favour, that it is appropriate for a good man to show compassion, that there are different grades of wrong-doing and so different penalties, that a resolute man has room for pardon, that even the wise man often offers an opinion, is sometimes angry, gives way to entreaty and is won over, that occasionally he corrects what he has said if it is for the better, and from time to time changes his mind; all the virtues are tempered by moderation.

COMMENTARY
De Finibus Bonorum et Malorum III

The title
'Finis' translates the Greek *telos*, which means the end or purpose of the structure and function of a living organism; περὶ τέλους (*On the end*) was the title of a work by Epicurus and in its plural form by Chrysippus. 'Finis bonorum', lit. 'the end of goods', is the goal of *human* striving, and, like 'summum bonum', refers to the greatest or supreme good available to men, and at which they aim; its opposite is 'finis malorum', the worst of evils, and that which is to be avoided above all. There was general consensus that possession of the greatest good would bring happiness, and of the greatest evil misery, but the differences about the content of these terms were often irreconcilable. The title therefore means something like 'Concerning (different opinions on) the greatest of goods and the worst of evils' or 'A debate on supreme good and evil'. Cicero had emphasised the difficulty of the topic, and its central role in philosophy, at *Fin* 1. 11 and 12.

I. 1 - 2 *Pleasure has been eliminated as a good*
   1   Pleasure: 'uoluptas' (Gk. *hēdonē*), the opening word of book 3, was the main subject of the dialogue of the previous two books. Torquatus first expounded Epicurean ethics, in which pleasure was claimed to be all important as the primary instinct, the persisting criterion and the final aim of human life; his position was then criticised by Cicero in his own person in book 2, esp. 18-21, 31-35. The personification of pleasure in this initial paragraph, with the sustained metaphor of her contest with *uirtus* and ultimate defeat and dismissal, shows that Cicero's criticisms were more on moral than logical grounds. There may be a reminiscence here of the famous allegory of the 'Choice of Hercules', with the hero faced with a decision between the two females, lascivious Pleasure and serious Virtue, cf. Xenophon *Mem* 2.1.21-33, where authorship is attributed to the sophist Prodicus, and Cicero's use of the *topos* at *Fin* 2.12, *Ac* 2.138 and *Off* 1.117-8.
   2   such determined defenders: Despite official disapproval Epicureanism had a strong following at Rome, which included Cicero's close friend Atticus as well as Torquatus and Lucullus, cf. notes 9 and 26.
   3   virtue: 'uirtus'. The Greek equivalent, *aretē*, was originally the overall quality of human excellence, shown on the Homeric

battlefield in heroic prowess and courage, later, in the context of the state, in sound political leadership, and in private life in the successful management of one's affairs; moral aspects of the term came to the fore in the fifth century, in sophistic and Socratic ethical debates. In Roman times the Latin word tended to keep its connotations of courage, and connected more positively with morality in general. It was the key concept in Stoic ethics, and the great rival to pleasure as the source of happiness. What was actually meant by the term will become clearer from Cato's exposition, which starts at ch.V.

4 what is right: 'honesta', Cicero's standard term for what is unequivocally morally good; 'bona', like its English translation, is ambiguous between moral and material 'goods', cf. n.50 and Glossary.

5 what is agreeable ... physical gratification ... feeling of delight: technical terms in Epicurean hedonism. 'What is agreeable' ('iucunda') corresponds to the general range of pleasures, comparable to 'honesta' above, the general range of moral acts; 'physical gratification' ('dulcedo corporis') refers to the 'kinetic' pleasure of enjoyable stimulus after the removal of pain, whereas 'the feeling of delight' ('laetitia', Gk. *chara*) is the positive sense of contentment achieved over a period of time when the body is free from pain and has enjoyments in moderation, and the mind has no anxieties but is pleasurably active.

6 a sense of responsibility and tenacity of purpose: Stoic ideals (and typically Roman) to be set against the attractions of hedonism. 'Grauitas animi' and 'constantia' are enduring attributes of mind and character against which it is futile for the ephemeral physical charms of pleasure to struggle.

7 supreme good: 'summum bonum', a synonym for 'finis bonorum', is the *telos* or aim of human life; cf. on the title above. If it is not pleasure that will make us happy, then what will? The question is of universal concern.

8 absence of pain: a candidate for the supreme good set up by Hieronymus in the third century b.c., a former Peripatetic who founded his own school, but with few adherents; cf. below on ch.IX, where the main alternative views on the supreme good are listed.

I. 2 contd. - 3 *No subtle argument was needed*

9 Torquatus: L. Manilius Torquatus was from one of the most distinguished families in Rome, which had reputedly acquired its cognomen from an ancestor in the fourth century, who had stripped a necklace ('torques') from a Celt defeated in single combat. A main point Cicero makes against Torquatus (whose coming praetorship in 50 b.c. fixes the dramatic date of the first two books of *Fin*) is that so distinguished a statesman would surely not practice the Epicureanism he preaches. In his inaugural address, in which he will be expected to give the guidelines for the administration of justice during his year of office, would he really proclaim that he intends to run his praetorship according to the dictates of pleasure? cf. *Fin* 2.74.

10 not skilled in debate: It was a standard charge against the Epicureans that they had no interest in logic and rules of argument. The charge has some foundation in Epicurus' deliberately provocative rejection of pedantry, and his insistence on philosophy's practical relevance (cf. 'Vain are the words of that philosopher who offers no relief for human suffering', Porphyry *Marc* 31), but fragments surviving from Epicurus' *On Nature* and from Philodemus show expertise in a range of problems and arguments. Cicero's attitude tends to be one of wilful ignorance, cf. *Fin* 1.22: 'in logic Epicurus is, it seems to me, completely unarmed and unprotected' ('inermis ac nudus', i.e. unable to attack or defend).

11 the verdict depends on the senses: cf. Sextus *Math* 8.63: 'Epicurus used to say that all objects of sensation (*aisthēta*) are true and that every impression (*phantasia*) results from what actually exists and is like that which stimulates the sense'. This is the first and most basic 'criterion' of truth for the Epicureans. They countered the sceptics' claim that, on the contrary, any sensation was no more true than false with the 'self-refuting' argument ('you will not have a standard to judge even those of them you say are mistaken' *KD* 23), and attributed *apparent* errors in perceptions to opinions formed by the mind on them, cf. Lucretius 4.353-86. The Epicureans maintained that what is immediately self-evident to the senses, and therefore true, is that a pleasant sensation is good and so desirable, and a painful one bad and to be avoided. The axiom is taken as obvious; we are clearly aware of it, and it would be absurd to require it to be proved.

12 my delivery was straightforward: In book 2 Cicero answered Torquatus' defence of Epicurus in his own person. He started 'dialectice' with Socratic-type questions and answers, and then, from ch. 6 onwards, proceded 'rhetorice', on the grounds that an 'oratio' is suitable for philosophers as well as rhetoricians. There may be a reference to a technical 'plain' style for his speech in 'dilucida' - 'clear and straight-forward'; on the content of the criticism, cf. *Intr*. VI.

I. 3 contd. - 4 *The Stoics' discourse uses a sophisticated terminology*

13 sophisticated or 'spiky': The importance of rationality as the specific characteristic of human nature meant that logic, and dialectic in particular, played a key role in Stoic ethics; cf. sect.72, where it is said that the wise man must be proficient in dialectic to be able to defend the truth and not be tricked into error. Most of Stoic work on logic derives from Chrysippus, notorious for subtleties of argument and style.

14 match new terms to new discoveries: Cicero, like Lucretius, tends to refer to the problems of putting Greek philosophy in Latin when a particularly difficult argument is ahead of him, cf. sect.5.

15 esoteric jargon: Individual professions and trades all have their own technical terms, making their conversations and books incomprehensible to the layman. Even oratory, which in its end product aims at public persuasion and so must be intelligible to all, has its specific terminology and trade secrets. Cicero himself wrote on the subject in *De Inventione*, *De Oratore*, *Brutus*, *Orator* and the more technical *Partitiones Oratoriae* and *Topica*.

II. 4 contd. - 5 *Problems in Latinising Greek philosophy*

16 agriculture: probably a reference to *Rerum rusticarum libri III*, one of the most famous of nearly 500 works by Cicero's friend, the polymath Varro.

17 art of life: The philosopher's quest for a *technē* for living ('ars uitae' or 'uiuendi') goes back to Socrates. Plato shows him searching for a set of principles with practical application for living that would be comparable to the expertise of professionals and craftsmen. On the Stoic 'ars uitae', cf. ch.VII.

18 Zeno their founder was not so much the inventor of new ideas as of new words: Zeno of Citium (in Cyprus, which had strong links with Phoenicia), was born in 335 b.c., and came to Athens in his early 20s. He studied there in the old Academy under Philemon, then with the Megarians Diodorus and Stilpo; he followed Crates the Cynic for a time and was later attracted back to Socrates by Xenophon's *Memorabilia* and the teaching of Antisthenes. At about the time that Theophrastus was organising the Peripatetic school Zeno began work on the details of his own Stoic philosophy, so called from his first lectures in the decorated public colonnade (*Stoa Poikilē*). Cicero repeats the claim of Antiochus – which shows little respect for the subtleties of Stoicism – that Zeno's system of ethics was merely a rewording of Aristotle's, cf. *Fin* 4.20 and 60, *Leg* 1.38, 55; at *Fin* 5.74 the

Stoics are compared to thieves changing the marks on Peripatetic goods. Diogenes (7.108) reports that Zeno invented at least the term *kathēkon* (translated by Cicero as 'officium', cf. n.71); for further 'new words' cf. n.51 and Glossary.

19 tackle the discipline for the first time: Cicero's silence on the work of Lucretius in Latinising Greek philosophy (when he had seen at least parts of *De Rerum Natura*) can perhaps be attributed to their different interests as well as to Cicero's sense of his own wider-ranging achievement in making the ethical systems of all the major schools available in Latin. Cicero's problems of translating individual technical Greek terms were not the same as those of putting a treatise on atomic physics into Latin hexameters, but the sense of pioneer pride is comparable, cf. Lucr 1.922-50, 4.1-25, and *Fin* 5.57 where the 'devotees of learning' may well include Lucretius.

20 even surpass them: Roman *literati* tended either towards the snobbery of speaking and writing in Greek (cf. *Intr.* V) or the patriotism of producing works in Latin that would rival those of the corresponding Greek *genre*. There had already been early Roman comedy and tragedy, Catullus and his circle had recently been experimenting with different types of lyric and elegiac poetry, and epic was continually developing, to reach its climax in the Roman answer to the Homeric poems, Vergil's *Aeneid*. The 'locus classicus' for the comparison of the two literatures is Quintilian, 10.1. In translating and adapting Greek, Latin was constantly at a disadvantage in its lack of such basic grammatical tools as a definite article, an active past participle and a range of subtly distinct particles, cf. notes 50 and 217, and also Cicero's complaints at *Tusc* 2.7 and 35, *ND* 1.8.

21 all their words which we traditionally treat as Latin: the naturalisation of the vocabulary of Greek education and culture shows how thoroughly 'conquered Greece had made her uncouth conqueror her captive' (cf. Horace *Ep* 2.1.156). 'Grammar' covers the range of linguistic competence, and 'music' refers to literature generally, but especially poetry.

II. 6 *The dedication to Brutus*

Cicero dedicated this work, the *Paradoxes*, *De Natura Deorum* and the *Tusculans* to Marcus Iunius Brutus, and also named a treatise on rhetoric, written a year or two earlier, after him. Brutus had joined the Pompeians, but was pardoned by Caesar after Pharsalus, who appointed him governor of Cisalpine Gaul, and then city praetor (44 b.c.). The decision to join the conspiracy in that year was a particularly hard one, and according to tradition, it was

Brutus' ingratitude to Caesar that made his blow the deadliest. As a writer Brutus had produced extensive works on history and oratory, on moral issues (referred to here as 'the most important field of philosophy)', composed poems, and kept up a correspondence with Cicero; on the shared interests in oratory and philosophy, and Cicero's hopes for a place for Brutus in public life suited to his talent cf. *Brut* 331-2, and on Brutus' distinction as a Latinising philosopher *Ac* 1.12, *Fin* 1.8. There was however a certain uneasiness in their friendship, because of their difference in age and status (Brutus was linked to the noblest Roman families, and his ancestor was said to have founded the Republic), their technical disagreements on the best style of public oratory, and especially because of the ambiguity of the attitudes of both to Caesar; on this cf. A.E. Douglas' introduction to his edition of *Brutus* (Oxford 1966), xvii-xxv, and in general on the complexities of the Brutus-Caesar relationship cf. Clarke *Noblest Roman* 22-33. The recipient of a dedication was expected to undertake some of the functions of editor, reviewer. and publisher, cf. Raymond Starr 'The Circulation of Literary Texts in the Roman World', *CQ* 37 (1987) 213-23.

II. 7 - 9 *The meeting with Marcus Cato*

22 Tusculum: a distinguished city 15 miles south-east of Rome, about 700 m. above sea-level; despite its name it does not seem to have had links with Etruria. It was the first of the Latin towns to be given Roman citizenship, and some of the highest Roman families (notably the Manilii and the Fulvii) came from there. It was a popular resort for the wealthy, and Cicero's splendid Tusculan villa was his favourite, where he wrote the eponymous five books of *Disputations* as well as most of his other philosophical works.

23 the young Lucullus: orphan son and heir of the famous Lucius Lucullus (cf. n.26), and ward of Cato, his mother's step-brother.

24 Marcus Cato: great-grandson of Cato the Censor, and in the family tradition of uncompromising severity and conservatism, which made him immediately sympathetic to Stoicism. He was born in 95 b.c., and brought up with the children of his mother's first marriage, who included Caepio (cf. n.27) and Servilia, Brutus' mother and Caesar's mistress. Cato was quaestor, tribune, and eventually (in 54 b.c.) praetor, but failed to win the consulship. He supported Cicero in the execution of the Catiline conspirators, then first opposed Pompey, but later joined him in the struggle against Caesar. He fought for the Pompeians in Sicily, Pharsalus and eventually Africa, where, rather than submit to Caesar after the defeat at Thapsus, he committed suicide in dramatic fashion. His death in 45 b.c. (a year before *De Finibus* was written) canonised his way of life, and made him almost the only Roman to be considered by the later Stoics as a possible 'Wise Man'. Cicero had mocked his Stoic extremism in his defence of Murena against Cato's prosecution (cf. Appendix), but generally respected him, and the two were firm friends. Caesar however hated him, and had just published his *AntiCato* to blacken his memory, but it only served to enhance Cato's standing as Republican martyr and Stoic hero.

25 a rare old time: 'helluari' or 'heluari', a colloquial word with comic tones of gluttony, here meaning something like 'gobbling up' books; the unfamiliar verb caused the scribes some problems – MS A has 'belluari', presumably 'to behave like a wild animal' ('belua')'; for the library cf. Plutarch *Luc* 42.

26 a credit to his father: Lucius Licinius Lucullus, the famous senator and general, was Sulla's right-hand man as quaestor, aedile and praetor, and eventually held the consulship in 74 b.c. He fought against Mithridates in Asia Minor and was one of many who attempted to subdue Parthia. He was an able soldier and administrator, but was out-manoevred in the politics of the late Republic by Pompey and then Caesar. He went into proverbially luxurious retirement after 59 b.c. (his mansion included the well-known 'gardens of Lucullus') and died some five years later. There is a certain irony in Cato defending Stoicism in the elegant house of the most famous Epicurean of the time. At the end of this section Cicero refers to his own admiration for Lucullus and close friendship with him.

27 to our friend Caepio ... his grandfather's memory: There is a problem with the relationships here, compounded by most MSS having 'Scipioni' for 'Caepioni'; it is best resolved by taking 'auus' ('grandfather') as a scribe's slip for 'auunculus' ('maternal uncle'). Quintus Caepio, grandfather to both Brutus and the young Lucullus, could not be meant, as he was killed in the Social War (after an active political life) when Cicero was only 16. His son however, of the same name, who was Cato's much admired step-brother and uncle to Brutus and Lucullus, had the promise of a brilliant career cut short by death in early manhood.

28 the trust of their children: From this interchange it seems that Cicero had an informal responsibility for the young Lucullus and an (unknown) child of Caepio, whereas Cato, because of the family relationship, had formal wardship of Lucullus. This preliminary discussion on the future of a young man of wealth and talent, with a public career ahead of him, is an appropriate introduction to a debate on the best way to live, and shows the strong ties of sympathy and friendship between Cicero and Cato, despite their philosophical disagreements.

III. 10 - 11 *Is Stoicism original only in terminology?*

29 some treatises of Aristotle: perhaps the *Politics*, since Cicero produced the *De Republica* a year later, in 51 b.c.

30 some time to myself: As Cicero had explained in sect.8, he took the opportunity to leave Rome during the games. which, like many cultured Romans, he disliked. Any leisure ('otium') that Cicero had, brief at the dramatic date of the dialogue but more extensive at the time of its composition, was given to philosophy, cf. Brutus' encouragement at *Tusc* 1.1 and *Off* 3.1. Leisure was traditionally considered essential for the pursuit of philosophy, cf. Aristotle *Met* 981b20-25, *Pol* 1329a1-2, and later Seneca *De Otio* 6.3-7.4.

31 nothing but virtue as a good: on 'uirtus' and 'honestum', cf. sect.1. The fundamental, strict and overriding tenet of Stoic ethics, which Cato will expound and argue for from ch. V onwards, is given its full form below, sect.11: nothing is good ('bonum') except what is morally right ('honestum' / 'uirtus'), and nothing is bad ('malum') except what is morally wrong ('turpe' / 'uitium').

32 new terms: cf. notes 13-15, and Carneades' specific charge (sect.41) that Stoics differed from Peripatetics only in terminology. Cicero suggests that more generally he and Cato share the same basic moral principles and methods of argument, and that their differences are merely verbal.

33 in fact demolish virtue: Cato claims that his disagreement with Cicero's moral position *is* one of substance, because of the exclusive stand taken by the Stoics on virtue. The consideration of anything else at all as a human objective and 'good' would destroy virtue's uniqueness and so the whole structure of Stoic ethics.

34 Pyrrho and Aristo: often mentioned together by Cicero, only to be immediately rejected, cf. *Fin* 2.35, 43, 4.49, 5.23, *Ac* 2.130, *Off* 1.6. Pyrrho of Elis (c.365-275 b.c.) was contemporary with Zeno and Epicurus and the acknowledged founder of scepticism, or at least 'he appears to have applied himself to scepticism more thoroughly and more conspicuously than his predecessors' (Sextus *Pyrr* 1.7). He was honoured by his own city and by Athens, and accompanied Alexander through Asia to India, where he met and was impressed by the Hindu ascetics, the Gymnosophistae or 'Naked Philosophers'. Like Pythagoras and Socrates he left no writings, and the opinions of his successors, the Pyrrhonians, were attributed back to him. According to Timon, his close disciple, 'Pyrrho states that things are equal and without differences, unstable and imperceptible, and consequently our perceptions and opinions are neither true nor false'. Every object 'no more is than is not *or* both is and is not *or* neither is nor is not', consequently one should be impassive and have no opinions, and the result will then be the optimum state of 'no disturbance' (*ataraxia*, also the Epicurean goal). Various anecdotes about the practical dangers for Pyrrho of his total indifference are told, but nonetheless he lived to be nearly 90. (The Timon passage is from Aristocles in Eusebeius *PE* 14.18.2-4, and is discussed by Annas and Barnes, p.11; cf. also DL 9.61-67).

Aristo(n) of Chios (c. 320-250 b.c.), known as 'The Bald' and 'The Siren', was a dissenting student of Zeno. He scorned logic and physics, and emphasised the complete indifference of everything except virtue; in effect he agreed with Pyrrho that 'there was no difference at all between the best of health and the most serious illness' (*Fin* 2.43). Aristo held that there were no distinguishable parts or aspects of virtue, and, together with his denial of Zeno's subtle classification of what was neither good nor bad, he rejected a role for practical wisdom and rules of conduct, so that 'indifference' became an end in itself. (Cf. DL 7.161-2, Sextus *Math* 11.64, and for Cicero's particular interest in refuting him *ND* 1.37, 3.77, *Fin* 4.40, 43, 47, 68-71, 5.73, and below, n.208.)

III. 11 contd. *The only good life is the life of virtue*

35 men in public life: Cato evades taking issue with Pyrrho and Aristo until pressed again by Cicero; the refutation then requires the complete exposition of Stoic theory which begins in ch. V. Here Cato adopts the well-known position that the Romans, and in particular Roman statesmen, were by character and education inclined to Stoicism. Such men had the necessary qualities of goodness (in a general sense, and used instead of the cardinal virtue of wisdom, which might not be so appropriate), courage, justice and temperance, and lived a Stoic type of life without any formal philosophical training. In many respects the Stoic 'doctrina' confirmed the Romans' traditional code of conduct, cf. Clarke *Roman Mind*, 32-33.

36 follow nature herself: To follow nature ('naturam sequi') and act in conformity with her ('uiuere congruenter naturae') were the all important goals of Stoic ethics. Their attainment brings rational humanity into harmony with the cosmos as a whole. In addition the ideals of individual integrity and public service fostered by the Romans made them sympathetic to the concept of citizenship of the 'ciuitas' of gods and men, cf. notes 78, 133 and

273.

37 the other schools of philosophy: These will be dealt with in detail later (cf. ch.IX). The better schools, according to Cato, are those which take virtue as one but not the only good, the worse (and in particular the Epicureans) discount it. Romans who are not going to follow the Stoic 'doctrina' would be less prone to corruption if they abandoned philosophy altogether, and kept to their own traditions.

38 or evil: For completeness the sentence should read 'aut (uitii expertem) in malis', but the sense is clear. Similarly the anacoluthon of 'ceterae disciplinae' picked up by the accusative 'eas' as subject of the infinitive 'adiuuare' would offend only the purists. There is however a problem with the second infinitive. The MS L and many editors read 'afferre' (which would be too weak after 'adiuuare'), the other MSS have 'affirmare'. Madvig suggests 'confirmare' or simply 'firmare' here, to give the required sense of 'strengthen' or 'support'.

39 if a wise man can be unhappy: That only the wise can achieve happiness (*eudaimonia*, which Cicero translates by 'beata uita') is a crucial tenet of Stoicism, which will be developed later, cf. especially sect.28 for the connotations.

40 *I* would not think: 'ne' (sometimes 'nae', transliterating the Greek equivalents) is an interjection, preceding a personal pronoun to emphasise it.

IV. 12 - 14 *Pyrrho and Aristo allow no exercise of choice*

41 The only good: cf. notes 7 and 31. 'Summum bonum' (the supreme good) is ambiguous between (a) the highest of a series of goods, and (b), as a translation of *telos agathōn*, the (one) final good. Cicero argues that, if Cato accepts (a), the Stoics can be assimilated to the Peripatetics, if (b) to Pyrrho and Aristo. Cato therefore replies with a complete exposition of the distinctiveness of the Stoic position.

42 all wise men are always happy: The argument in full is: (a) virtue is the only good, (b) the only good brings happiness, (c) all the wise always practise virtue, therefore (d) all the wise are always happy. Pyrrho, according to Timon (cf. above, n.34) appears to have based happiness on the correct attitude to the external world, but certainly Aristo and the Stoics would accept the moves from (a) to (d). The Stoics however would add that virtue includes the exercise of choice, and this would be denied by those who adopt the *ou mallon* principle of 'no more this than that'.

43 an essential property of virtue: Theoretical wisdom ('sapientia', the Greek *sophia*) needs to be put into practice as 'prudentia' (*phronēsis*) in the appropriate choice between what is according to nature and what is contrary. The primary and most urgent example of such a choice is whether to stay alive or not (cf. sects. 20 and 60). In this theory of the role of 'prudentia' there is a clear reference back to Aristotle *EN* VI (cf. 1144b30: 'it is not possible to be good in the strict sense without practical wisdom'). But the Stoics, especially in the Roman era, were less inclined to accept the superiority of theoretical over practical wisdom, or to recognise the subtleties of the distinction.

44 with no exercise of choice: *lit.* 'so that they use no choice' – the second purpose clause is dependent on the first. An alternative reading of 'ut in' for 'uti' encouraged some editors to write 'ut in nullam selectionem uerterentur'.

45 I leave them: The Stoics divided 'indifferent things' into those with plus value (which are according to nature), those with minus value (which are contrary to nature), and those that are really indifferent, falling into neither class. The distinction, with examples, is explained in sects. 50 and 51.

46 'How is that?' I asked: An alternative punctuation gives: 'How is that, I ask?', and does not involve a change of speaker.

47 right, moral, praiseworthy, fine: The list is not precise, and the opposites do not follow the same order. The English translation here aims to be consistent throughout, but cannot reproduce the exact nuances of meaning; the Greek equivalents are listed in the Glossary. The pairs are 'honestum' and 'inhonestum' ('right' and 'wrong'), 'decorum' and 'indecorum' ('fine' and 'disgraceful', with reference to inner beauty), the metaphorical 'rectum' and 'prauum' ('moral' and 'immoral' from 'straight' and 'crooked') and 'laudabile' and 'turpe' ('praiseworthy' and 'shameful', which indicate other people's estimates of one's conduct); 'criminal' and 'foul' are added to the second list gratuitously.

48 you know quite well: Cicero's feigned ignorance and the touch of Socratic banter mark the *rapport* between the two friends, despite the disagreements that will emerge.

IV. 15 - 16 *An exposition of Stoic ethics in Latin is required*

49 [strange]: There is a textual problem here. The MSS read 'rerum nouarum non uidebantur'. Madvig assumed a lacuna, and supplied 'noua erant, ferenda' before 'non'. The assumption of a lacuna seems unnecessary, and given the letters in context, the early Minutius reading of 'noua' for 'non' is acceptable. MSS B and E have 'uocarunt' for 'nouarum'; cf. Wright *LCM* 1990 'New wine in new bottles'.

50 what do you think will happen in Latin?: Cicero has already devoted the second chapter to the problems of expounding Greek philosophy in Latin, and he raises the question of mastering the vocabulary before the main exposition. Cicero's alternatives for dealing with Greek words are (a) to invent a word (such as 'beatitudo' at *ND* 1.95), (b) to cover the meaning with a number of near synonyms (as the lists above, sect. 14, for *agathon* and *kakon*, (c) to transliterate, or (d) to find a Latin equivalent (as below, n.163, when he wonders whether 'uitium' or 'malitia' is better for *kakia*, and chooses the former); cf. also on 'qualitas' as an 'inauditum uerbum' for *poiotēs*, *Ac* 1.24, and 'uoluptas' as an improvement on *hēdonē Fin* 2.12; cf. also sect.40, but Cicero is not being a mere translator, cf. *Off* 1.6.

51 some outlandish name: Stoic technical terms that Cicero will have to deal with include *katalēpsis* (n.61), *kathēkon* (n.71, for which 'officium ' causes particularly difficulties), *ennoia* (n.75), *homologia* (n.78), *katorthōma* (n.97) and *katorthōsis* (n.189), *epigennēmatikon* (n.100), *eukairia* (n.188) and *euchrestēmata* and their opposite (sect.69). Some, such as *pathos*, *telos* and *hēdonē* (disparaged as less accurate than 'uoluptas' for the Epicurean concept, *Fin* 2.12) belong to Greek philosophy generally.

52 fortune favours the brave: The form 'fortis' rather than 'fortes', as well as the absence of the verb, indicates the antiquity and popularity of the saying. It first appears in Terence (*Phormio* 1.4.26) as 'fortes fortuna adiuuat'. Cicero, at *Tusc* 2.11, says that he would prefer 'ratio' to 'fortuna' as the subject.

V. 16 contd. *The primary instinct is for self-preservation*

53 as soon as a living creature is born: εὐθὺς γενόμενος, the starting point for the 'cradle' argument. According to Plutarch (*Stoic rep.* 1038b) Chrysippus introduced this into all his physical and theoretical works, and cf. *Fin* 5.54 'everyone goes to the nursery'. The behaviour of new-born children and animals, both of whom are without reason (*alogoi*), provides evidence for the character of the first stimulus, the primary instinct (πρώτη ὁρμή – 'principium naturae') for basic and unperverted natural activity (cf. Brunschwig in Schofield *Norms* 112-44). The interest in studying infants and animals as a guide to the foundations for adult behaviour goes back to Aristotle, cf. *HA* 588a31 and *Pol* 1252b33; the Stoics however broke off kinship with the animal world when the child became rational, cf. sect.67.

54 it feels an attachment for itself: The context of this passage is an important source for the famous Stoic doctrine of *oikeiōsis*, according to which an animal or infant is attached and 'dear' to itself, and is consequently driven by its primary instinct to keep itself alive. (From the vast literature on this subject cf. especially the articles by Pembroke, Kerferd, Striker and White.) The adjective *oikeion* means 'of the same *oikos*' or family, and so 'one's own'. With the sense of belonging and kinship comes attachment, and the opposite is *allotrios* – 'belonging to another', 'alien'. In the related quotation from Chrysippus on this subject (at DL 7.85) the corresponding verb is used in the genitive absolute with *physis* as the subject – 'nature making the living creature at one with itself'. Elsewhere the verb tends to be middle – 'to make one's own'; Cicero's 'conciliari' probably covers this middle sense (a common poetic use of the Latin passive). The animal or infant is in the process of making itself belong to itself, not in the sense of manipulating two 'selves', or of engaging in a sophisticated search for personal identity, but simply of establishing its own existence.

55 The Stoics demonstrate this: The argument preserved here does not have an extant Greek equivalent; Cicero's version is in an abbreviated form which obscures its logic. Six stages are involved: (1) self-awareness, 'sensus sui', which leads to (2) self-love, 'sibi conciliari' / 'se diligere', reworded as (3) love of one's condition and estrangement from its destruction. There is therefore (4) a primary instinct, 'principium', to preserve oneself, 'commendari ad se conseruandum', and from this comes (5) the love of what will preserve that condition, resulting in (6) the movement towards what is condition-preserving, 'salutaria', and avoidance of the opposite. In sum the primary instinct is for self-preservation, derived from love of one's self and one's condition. Now stage (6) is observable and agreed on (the new-born babe's first movement is to reach for the breast, a rabbit scurries at a hint of danger) but those preceding it are disputable, and were in fact disputed. The Epicureans claimed that the primary instinct which led to the observed results was for pleasure, and others for the avoidance of pain (cf. the next section); some modern theories suggest that preservation of the species is primary. There is an additional Stoic argument for (2), used later in a slightly different context, which claims that nature would not alienate the living creature from itself, nor make it neither alien nor attached, and so (by elimination) it must be attached (*oikeion*) to itself (cf. DL 7.85 and below on sect.62). But even without the teleology implied here, the Stoics were basically sound in claiming that one's very existence has to be most primary, and that new-born animals and humans are instinctively aware of what will ensure the continuation of that existence and act accordingly; cf. the interesting illustrations *ND* 2.121-8.

There is a particular problem with stage (1): what does 'self-awareness' mean and why is it the necessary condition for the operation of the primary instinct? As common to the babe and animal 'sensus sui' would not involve intelligence, nor assent to any articulated proposition of the form 'I am myself' or even 'I exist'. The phrase refers rather to that primitive *perception* of being alive which necessarily precedes the motivation for staying in life. In Stoic physical terms it is to be interpreted as the combination of contact of the *pneuma* internally with the body and externally with the surrounding air as the living creature starts to breathe. Although the 'condition' of the animal and the relation of its *pneuma* to the body remain basically static throughout its growth, in the human child powers of reasoning, and possibly perfect reasoning, will eventually develop. The theory takes into account Aristotle's discussion of self-perception in *DA* 3, ch.2, and later interested Seneca, especially *Ep.* 121 on 'How does the animal perceive itself?'.

56 feared its destruction: The movements of the animal and babe, when not asleep, oscillate between reaching towards what is life-preserving and shrinking from what is life-threatening. Seneca, in the same *Ep* 121, connects the fear of death with 'sensus sui' in the example of the child being alone in the dark. The particular terror of this experience is that, in a situation where there is nothing to see or hear or any stimulus to the senses, the child starts to lose its self-awareness and consequently its hold on life itself. Modern experiments with deprivation of all sense-stimulus corroborate the Stoic theory.

V. 17 *The primary instinct is not for pleasure*

57 pleasure should not be included: The Epicureans made pleasure both the primary instinct and the greatest good, the *telos* (cf. note 1). The 'primary instinct' claim had been put forward by Torquatus: 'As soon as a living creature is born, it seeks pleasure and rejoices in it as the greatest good, but recoils from pain and drives it from itself as far as it can; it acts in this way when it is not yet perverted, and according to nature's own fair and honest verdict' (*Fin* 1.30, and cf. *Leg* 1.47). This was countered by Cicero at 2.31ff, mainly as impossible to reconcile with Epicurean hedonistic theory as a whole, and was replaced by the Stoics' own 'cradle' argument, cf. n.53. Further arguments against pleasure as primary will be brought in later in the book, in sect.65 on the unacceptability of an isolated life even with countless pleasures, and in 62 on the avoidance of pain being defeated by the stronger impulse to give birth to and rear the young; cf. also Seneca *Ep*

121.6-15 on the struggle to walk overcoming the toddler's aversion to pain.

58 numerous immoral consequences: The standard Stoic attack on pleasure as a good was that pleasure generally is *aischron* (shameful, immoral), and nothing *aischron* is good, cf. Chrysippus at DL 7.103, and also Cicero's elaboration in *Paradox* 1. Psychologically, following an instinct for pleasure and becoming a philhedonist results in the mind's loss of strength (*arrostēma*, cf. DL 7.115-7, and refs. in *SVF* Index Verborum s.v.), so the wise man will be 'austere' in dealing with pleasure. Rather than it being the primary impulse, the Stoics agreed with Aristotle that pleasure came later as a by-product – a 'bloom' – concomitant with the thriving of the natural condition (Chrysippus again at DL 7.86, but cf. also 'irrational elation' 7.114; Aristotle *EN* 1174b34; Plato has pleasure and pain as the child's first *aisthēsis*, *Laws* 653a). The Stoics however were ready to admit some 'worthy delight' into the life of the wise man, at the opposite extreme to the disgraceful pleasures of the vicious, cf. DL 7.116.

59 gained at nature's prompting: MSS B and E have the stronger and more personal 'asserta' ('arrogated', 'claimed') for 'ascita' ('brought in', 'gained'). 'natura' is ablative – 'by nature', i.e. at nature's prompting.

60 no one who ... would not prefer: An argument from general consensus is added to clinch the Stoic position, namely (1) a healthy body (i.e. with limbs well-formed and sound) is according to nature, (ii) all esteem their healthy bodies and would not want them maimed, so (iii) esteem for a healthy body is according to nature. In fact the continued possession of a healthy body is the welcome consequence of following from birth the instinct for self-preservation generated by self-love, cf. further on health as *proegmēnon*, n.213.

V. 17 – 18 *There is intrinsic merit in rational activity*

61 cognitions: i.e. *katalēpseis*. The manuscripts vary throughout in using Greek or Roman letters for Greek technical terms; on Cicero's alternatives for dealing with Greek words, including transliteration, cf. n.50. 'quas uel comprehensiones uel perceptiones', not found in some MSS, may be later suggestions for translations; 'perceptiones *uerae*' would be more accurate, but the two nouns here contain the sense of mental 'grasping' that is crucial to the Greek, and brought out at the end of the sentence as that which 'embraces truth and holds it fast'.

The theory is as follows: when there is a presentation (*phantasia*) to the senses or the mind which is clear and striking, and called then a 'cognitive' presentation, there is immediate assent to it, and cognition (*katalēpsis*) results. This may then be understood – although perhaps only by the wise man – as a piece of knowledge. Zeno's famous 'fist' illustration compared the presentation to open fingers, the assent to fingers partially closed, cognition to the clenched fist, and the knowledge thereby assimilated to the other hand clasping the fist, cf. *Ac* 2.145. All humans, because they have reason, can discriminate between perceptions, and give assent to those that are forceful and correspond with reality. The assent is free, 'up to us' (*eph' hēmīn*), and the accompanying conviction provides a criterion by which presentations that are not self-evident may be judged. Apparently confusing exceptions introduced by the sceptics, like wax pomegranates or Alcestis restored to life, only proved the general rule. For the debate on this criterion cf. further Sextus *Math* 7.177, 254-8, 402-29, 8.397, DL 7.46, 54, Cicero *Ac* 1.41, 2.31-60, 77-85, and on its importance in the history of epistemology Sandbach in Long, *Problems*, 9-21, and Long and Sedley ii.249-52.

62 taken up for their own sake: The desire for knowledge ('cupiditas cognoscendi' cf. *Tusc* 1.44), independent of utilitarian considerations, is above all the sign of humanity, expressed most famously by Aristotle at the outset of the *Metaphysics*: 'all men by nature yearn to know', and elaborated by him in its first two chapters; cf. for Cicero *Off* 1.11-13, and the Epicurean objection *Fin* 1.23. Cato, as the Stoic spokesman in book 3, uses 'we', 'they' and 'the Stoics' without distinction.

63 observed in children: The interest that children have in puzzles of all kinds and their delight in solving them irrespective of reward are signs of nascent reason, and their uninhibited wonder matures into the curiosity of the philosopher, cf. *Fin* 5.48-50, 57. Because children have the seed of reason, the early Stoics optimistically expected it would accompany the initiative towards right conduct, and that the child would grow to be both wise and virtuous if uncorrupted by externals. There was difficulty however with the observed fact that children are sometimes naughty, however well brought up, cf. Galen *Hipp Plat* 5.5.3-6 (SVF iii 229, Long and Sedley 65M).

64 the arts should be adopted: An 'art' ('ars', Gk *technē*) covers a range of skills in crafts and sciences which involve both the understanding of general principles and their practical application; the term includes pottery and metal-working as well as navigation and medicine. The arts are to be adopted because they contain what is worth adopting, not tautologically, but in that they derive from a set of cognitions (a 'system' of *katalēpseis*, Sextus

Math 2.10 and others SVF i.21, ii.93), and proceed by logical method; they therefore characterise and embellish the rational human life, cf. Aristotle *Met* 980b26-7: 'men live by *technē* and logical reasoning', and on the role of 'ratio' here, Cicero *Ac* 2.26, Sextus *Pyrrh* 3.241.

65 repelled by an assent to what is false: Children's behaviour would again be a pointer to what is according to nature, when their often embarrassing habit of blunt truth-telling looks forward to the adult's love of truth and rejection of what is false; in extreme cases these are characteristics of the heroic man, of Oedipus or Socrates for example.

The last sentence of sect.18 deals with the teleology of animal parts and is clearly out of place here; it has been transposed to the relevant discussion in sect.63, ch.XIX.

V. 19 *The style must suit the subject matter*

66 the ABC of nature: 'elementa' (*stoicheia*) is used for atoms or elements in scientific contexts, for letters of the alphabet and for first principles in general. Democritus had shown that the wide variety of phenomena could be derived from a few basics in a way similar to the Homeric poems being composed from the small number of alphabet letters – the structure in both is determined by the arrangement of units and spaces, cf. Lucr 1.824, 2.688-9, Horace *Sat* 1.1.25. Primary instincts and the formation of the cognitive processes are for the Stoics fundamental principles of nature comparable both to letters making up words and to the ground rules of an 'art'.

67 expresses himself plainly and clearly: for Cato's 'pin-pricking' style and rejection of detailed ornament, cf. the preface *Parad* 2. Cicero undertakes the *Paradoxes* partly to show that oratorical skill can make material even as intransigent as hard-core Stoic ethics persuasive and generally acceptable. Zeno, in another 'fist' illustration (cf. n.61) compared dialectic to the clenched fist, and rhetoric to the open palm (*Orat* 113). As Socrates insisted at his trial, speaking well really means speaking the truth, and for the Stoics this was best done with precise vocabulary, brevity and neatness, cf. Plato *Ap* 18a, Cicero *de Orat* 3.65, DL 7.59, Quintilian *Proem* v, and in general Arnold ch. 6 'Of reason and speech', and especially 148-50.

VI. 20 *The classification 'value plus' and 'value minus'*

68 fundamental classification: not 'one consequence' (as Long and Sedley translate) but the basic division, following from the functioning of the primary instinct, is into those things which promote the survival of the living creature (and so are according to nature) and those that threaten it (and so are contrary to nature). Later, in the discussion of ethics for the grown man, for whom virtue is the only good, vice the only evil and everything else indifferent, this division is used in the partition of indifferents into (i) what is according to nature, (ii) what is contrary, and (iii) what is completely indifferent. Then what is according to the nature of the mature human includes such qualities of mind and body and external advantages as enhance personal, social and political life, cf. below on sects. 50-54.

69 **"of plus value"**: 'aestimabilia' are according to nature and so to be adopted (*proēgmena*); they are non-moral, and the value they have is relative. Good, which alone is of absolute value, has yet to emerge. Such worth as *aestimabilia* have connects with nature directly as life-enhancing, or indirectly as intermediately productive of the enhanced life. As the human develops from the animal-like child to the rational adult, what accords with his developing nature becomes correspondingly more sophisticated, cf. further the sub-divisions of *aetimabilia* given in sect.56.

70 **"of minus value"**: the opposite category of 'inaestimabilia', contrary to nature and to be rejected (*apoproēgmena*). The term denotes not merely the absence of value, but an additional negation of it ('disvaluable' in Long and Sedley, 'sans valeur' in the Budé). To retain the three levels needed, this translation uses 'of plus value', 'of no value' and 'of minus value' for the divisions.

71 **"appropriate action"**: the Greek *kathēkon*, and another key problem word; it is sometimes translated 'duty', 'obligation' or (in Long and Sedley) 'proper function'. Cicero was not sure about using *officium* even for his famous treatise *De Officiis* (cf. *Att* 16.14). The main section dealing with 'appropriate action' is below at sect.58, again in the context of adult ethics, and particularly in connection with Stoic concepts of choice and progress (*prokopē*), but the principles of the theory are summarised here.

72 **choice conditioned by appropriate action**: Appropriate actions are initially the practical effects of the working of primary natural instinct in basic survival, shown in movements towards what is life-preserving and away from what is life-damaging; these first movements continually recur and eventually develop into a more positive 'holding fast' and 'driving off'. Both stages are common to all living creatures and are inherent – animals and young children cannot act otherwise than as they do. But with the growing of the human living creature conscious decisions begin to be made (refusal to eat, for example, is a common form of juvenile defiance), and actions that were previously spontaneous are now deliberately chosen or rejected. When all goes well in environment and education the rational choice is made for what is according to nature; when this choice becomes habitual, continually made in the light of reason, then life consistently according to nature results.

73 good begins to be apparent: There are five stages in all: (i) movement spontaneously towards what is according to nature (and away from what is not), (ii) holding fast to this (and driving off the opposite), (iii) consciously choosing to do so, (iv) making the choice a habit, and (v) living consistently in harmony with nature. At the end of these, the conditions are ready for the emergence of the good and the start of a moral life. Instinct gives the stimulus to reason and then reason controls instinct, cf. further on sects. 22-23. 'inesse' here means 'to be apparent', 'to be involved' rather than 'to be present', for to say that something *begins* to be present is odd, and the good is not gradually brought in from outside, but develops from within. For the Stoics man is born to be good rather than being, as in some doctrines, basically bad.

VI. 21 *Reason and conformity*

74 Man's first attraction: a reference back to the *oikeiōsis* theory of ch.V, with 'conciliatio' as the noun form of 'conciliari sibi'. The Latin tenses in this paragraph vary between present and past, and some MSS read a future 'aestimabit' for 'he regards'.

75 conceptual understanding: The child has repeated sensations that are stored in the memory, and constant use of memory applied to further sensation adds up to experience; the growing man (from about age 14) then uses reason to derive conclusions from experience, and this is conceptual understanding or abstract thought(s) (*ennoia / ennoiai*). Abstract thought is based on perception, then becomes independent of it, cf. *Leg* 1.30, *Tusc* 1.69-70 and (on the superiority of the life devoted to thought) 5.8-10. By its means we can survey the past and future as well as the present, trace the chain of cause and effect, and express the conclusions as propositions which may be assented to if true or rejected as false, cf. *Off* 1.11, (connecting possibly with the same source as Aetius 4.11.1-4), the obvious Aristotelian influences (e.g. *Met* 980b26-82a2, *MA* 701b17, *Mem* 449b30-450a10, *DA* 431b3-19) and the discussions by Sandbach in Long *Problems* ch. 2, and Engberg-Pederson in Schofield *Norms* 157.

76 at first: 'prima' here could be either adverbial 'at first' or taken with 'omnia' – 'all these primary things'; 'that' ('eam') refers to 'concordia', and the feminine noun is then picked up later (as often) with a neuter pronoun 'in *eo* collocatum'.

77 man's chief good ... rests here: All things thrive when they reach their end or *telos*. Man's essential humanity, which distinguishes him from other living creatures, lies in his reason, and in its highest functioning he achieves his *telos*. Through 'cognitio' and 'ratio' (the acquisition of knowledge and 'working things out') his understanding of himself advances from 'sensus sui' (cf. n.55) to a realisation of the potential of his truly human nature and its relation to the sum of things; his aim then correspondingly advances from self-preservation to order and harmony in action, cf. DL 7.89, Sextus *Math* 11.26.

78 *homologia*: the state of achievement of this 'chief good' in harmonious action – a consistent tenor of life, also expressed as 'to live harmoniously', cf. Epictetus 1.6, quoted and discussed by Long *Hellenistic Philosophy* 173-4, and also n.133.

79 right action and right itself: An action according to nature is 'appropriate' ('officium', *kathēkon*), and this is on the non-moral level, common from childhood to old age; action in relation to the good is 'officium perfectum' or 'honestum factum' (*katorthōma*), and belongs to man as moral agent. The continual performance of right actions shows the practical external functioning of the internal rational principle, as it maintain the *pneuma* in the soul in the correct tension and keeps in harmony with itself and with the cosmos, cf. sects. 31 and 55.

80 desirable for its own sake: Primary natural objects are *means* to the end, stages on the journey, and, in the terminology of sect.69, 'advantages' but not 'benefits'. Progress can be made in the adoption of them (as in the hierarchy of king and courtiers at sect.52) but the end is external to them, and such value as they have is in relation to this end, namely man's chief good – right itself.

VI. 22 *Moral action is according to nature*

81 appropriate actions arise from natural first impulses: What contributes to our bodily well-being has a certain positive value (as has been shown), and the appropriate action of adopting it, first instinctively and then by choice, is to be commended as long as morality (the good) is not involved; when it is involved it totally overrides all other considerations.

82 right action is not included: Appropriate action is concerned primarily with self-preservation, and then with what is according to nature for the adolescent, and for the adult in a non-moral context. Right action relates to the good, and is desired and chosen by the mature individual as he strives to reach his *telos* as a rational moral agent, cf. n.77.

83 stimulates our desire for itself: As the child matures reason takes over from instinct (being much more highly esteemed), and the desire for good which reason fosters is more forceful than that for self-preservation which was based on instinct. The seeds of virtue in the human baby develop into an innate urge to be good, which may however then be corrupted by environment and upbringing; cf. *Leg* 1.30 (virtue is attainable by all), 1.33 on reason, nature and morality, *Tusc* 3.2 ('semina innata uirtutum') and throughout *Fin*. e.g. 2.33-4, 4.14, 5.43, 60, also *DL* 7.107-9, Plutarch *adv Stoic* 1071a, *Virt Mor* 441c, Aurelius 3.1.4, and for the Socratic origins of the crucial awareness of *desire* for virtue, cf. Santas *Socrates* 189-94.

VI. 22 contd. *There is only one supreme good*
84 there are *two* supreme goods: i.e. things according to nature and right itself; the error connects with the charge that the difference between Stoic and Peripatetic theory on the good life was merely verbal, cf. n.18. The Stoics continually had to insist that things according to nature were preferable but not desirable, and had no value *per se*. *Fin* 3 has a number of illustrations to support the difference – the archer here, the puppy and the drowning man (sect.48), the king and courtiers (52), the dice (54), and the series beginning with the lamp and the sun (45).

85 not at all: 'etenim' is Schiche's emendation of the MSS 'ut enim', and 'sicut' is preferred here to the less well-attested 'sic'. 'Etenim si' 'introduces a particular instance in support of a general assertion' (*OLD*), here a general counter-assertion to the two-goods claim. Editors concur in deleting after 'd' imus' the repetition 'sic illi facere omnia, quae possit, ut conliniet'.

86 to aim with a spear or arrow: Aristotle, at the beginning of *EN* (1094a24) explains that men desire a *telos* for its own sake – like archers with an mark to aim at. Here there is the added refinement that aiming correctly is more important than hitting the bull's-eye. The analogy would hold with any sport where the old *ethos* prevails that the play is more important than the score – to win is preferable but not essential for a satisfying game.

87 *his* supreme good: shown in correct aiming and continued concentration. These are in the control of the archer, whereas the bull's-eye score may be a matter of chance. Similarly, in a moral context, virtue – the continuous state of psychic harmony – is the good, and this is in the individual's control, but things according to nature, which may determine a particular success, are not.

88 "to be chosen" and not "to be desired": As in archery hitting the target is preferable but not intrinsically essential for the sport, so in ethics the 'promoted' things, those according to nature, are preferable and have value in relation to the good, but are not desirable *per se*; they give direction to action without being objects of desire cf. sects. 21 and 37, and the discussion by Striker in Schofield, *Norms* 190-4.

VII. 23 *Wisdom begins from primary natural instincts*

89 appropriate actions start from primary natural instincts: The first appropriate action is to keep in one's natural condition (following the primary instinct for self-preservation), the second to hold fast to this, then, from about ages 7 to 14, to begin to understand how action follows instinct and to choose accordingly; then the habit of so choosing is formed, and conditions are now ripe for the emergence of wisdom and for action as a moral agent.

90 who is introduced to another: common in sexual contexts where attention is switched from the old to the new love, suitable here in that things according to nature mediate in the transition from instinct to wisdom, having a place both in the life of animal and child, and in the ordinary, non-moral life of the adult.

91 wisdom becomes dearer to us: This is because wisdom is the characteristic of our essentially *human* nature, and sets us on the scale of life above the functions of nutrition, growth and reproduction in plants, and of locomotion and perception in animals, cf. Plato *Laws* 653a7-54a5, Aristotle *DA* 3.9, *HA* 8.1, DL 7.86 and the analogy of the vine, *Fin* 4.38.

92 mind's instinctive desire: Instinctive desires, in addition to the primary impulses, include that for mental development towards knowledge. This is present from the start, but comes to function later in the increasing purposefulness of the older child and adolescent, as the *awareness* of self ('sensus sui') matures into an *understanding* of self ('sese agnoscere'), cf. *Fin* 5.24-26, 41, and sects. 20 and 22.

93 life with a particular design: The Stoics, following Aristotle in opposition to the mechanistic theories of the Epicureans, believed that everything in the world is adapted to fulfil an end appropriate to it, directed towards the best possible state of affairs, comparable to an acorn 'programmed' to grow into the best possible oak tree. We are therefore provided with limbs to act in a certain physical way (hands to work with, feet to walk on – cf. n.265 on the *telos* of bodily parts), instincts to act in a certain natural way (to adopt what preserves and enhances life and reject the opposite), and wisdom to act in a certain moral way, cf. the next section.

VII. 24 - 25, 32 *The 'art' of living*

94   As the actor is assigned gestures: The application of analogies from professional skills (and arts, crafts and sciences are subsumed under *technai*, 'artes') to ethics in the search for a *technē* of life as a whole ('ars uiuendi'), combining theoretical knowledge of a set of principles with its practical application in individual cases, goes back to Socrates and links with the Socratic testing of the hypothesis that virtue is knowledge, that being good depends on a combination of understanding and expertise. Socrates' most common examples include the sciences of mathematics, medicine and navigation, sports (running, boxing, horse-riding) and physical training, and such crafts as building, carpentry, cobbling and weaving. The comparison of life to a theatrical performance was proverbial (e.g. 'all the world's a stage' *AP* 10.72, and for the wise man as an actor playing a part, Aristo at DL 7.160); for varieties of dancing in the ancient world cf. *OCD* s.v. In the main, ancient dancing consisted (like ballet) of movements and gestures following a fixed pattern; ancient playwrights created the choreography as well as the music and words of the choral lyrics.

95   harmonious and consistent: cf. 'order and harmony in action', sect.21, and for reason shaping impulse 'like a craftsman' (*technitēs*) DL 7.86. Wisdom sets the pattern of harmony and consistency, and in acting accordingly the individual leads a virtuous life; a life 'at random' is irrational and so less than human. On Stoics and the sciences cf. the evidence and discussion in Long and Sedley sect. 42, and for the contribution of Antipater, Striker in Schofield *Norms*, 188-204.

96   exercise of the skill in itself: 'effectio' covers both the practice of a skill and a skill's end-product. Navigation and medicine have end-products (safe arrivals in port and successful cures) and the test of the skill is in these results rather than the travelling or treatment. In acting and dancing however the skill is in the actual performance, and there is no additional consequence comparable to a cure or a craftsman's pot or a shoe that marks its successful completion. So virtue is more like acting and dancing in that the skill is directed to the performance rather than to any consequence of it.

97   acts ... "rightly done": 'recte facta', synonymous with 'honeste facta' and 'perfecta officia' as translations of *katorthōmata*, cf. n.79.

98   involve every category of virtue: Despite the resemblance between virtue and acting or dancing in the skill being shown in performance, and according to pre-set patterns, (i) acting and dancing are not continuous in absolute terms, for the activity finishes at the end of the show but there is no intermission in right living, (ii) they need extraneous items such as composer/director, stage, audience and musical accompaniment, and (iii) all species are not necessarily included in one genus – tragic actors may not be experts at comedy, for example. Wisdom however is complete, self-sufficient and all-embracing, the other virtues being aspects of wisdom, in the application of knowledge to particular contexts. The founding discussion is at Plato *Protag* 329c-334c, and on the unity of virtue for the Stoics cf. the evidence and discussions at Zeller 241-50, *SVF* iii.63-74, de Vogel iii.151-3, Long and Sedley sect 61, and also Cicero *Off* 2.17.

99   high-mindedness, justice and that quality ... : The 'cardinal' virtues along with wisdom were usually justice, courage and self-control (cf. Plato *Protag* loc. cit. *Rep* passim, and Cicero *Fin* 1.42-54 and *Off* 1.15 Piety was sometimes included, and magnanimity was added notably by Aristotle (*EN* 4.3); the quality mentioned here, which means something like 'righteous pride' is new. The individual virtues were characterised by the Stoics as sub-divisions of wisdom in that justice involves understanding of what is due, magnanimity of the place of wealth, and 'righteous pride' of what is to be despised.

100   a chronological and logical result: *epigennēmatikon*, a medical term for the after-birth, used by the Stoics, and combined here by Cicero with 'artificiose', for the end-product of craft and science skills, which emerges at the completion of the exercise of the expertise, and is a consequence of it. But for virtue, as for the performing arts, the very beginning is part of the complete whole.

Sect.32 ch.IX, has been transposed to VIII.25 as relevant here rather than between technical discussions about the definition of good in sects. 31 and 33, cf. Madvig p.401, and Martha (Budé) on 32: 'ce développement ne semble pas à sa place'.

101   Treason, violence to parents and sacrilege: the three most heinous crimes in the ancient world, threatening the foundations of *polis*, family and religion.

102   fear, grief and lust: Emotions are mental failings, indicating a continuing state of psychic ill-health, which may or may not erupt in particular acts of violence, cf. on *pathē*, n.142. 'Delight' is usually added to these (cf. sect.35) to give the four basic wrong states, involving intellectual mistakes about what is good and bad in the present (delight and grief) and in the future (fear and lust).

103   similarly ... at its very adoption: Vicious deeds are eruptions from a consistently disordered soul, and right ones the outward manifestations of inner psychological harmony. The psychic state, which holds from the start of the moral life, is all important, and from it the morality of individual actions is to be judged.

VII. 25 contd. - 26 *Conclusion to V - VII*

104 between right and wrong: The most fundamental Stoic doctrine was that what is right is good and what is wrong is bad, so that the only difference is between right and wrong, with everything else to be classed as 'indifferent'. This will be developed in the following sections, and elaborated with a number of arguments and illustrations; cf. Cicero for Zeno here *Ac* 1.37-38, and at *Tusc* 5.34-36 he makes explicit the Socratic source of the doctrine, and supports the claim with Latin translations of Plato *Gorg* 470d-e and *Menex* 247e; for the general emphasis cf. sect.26, the arguments in sects. 27-30, and also *Paradox* 1.

105 with nature: Rightly ordered reason ('recta ratio' at *Tusc* 4.34) acting consistently (Chrysippus added 'with nature') achieves the *telos* of humanity in a life of conformity and harmony, cf. n.133, and for Cicero on the *telos* of animals and men cf. *Tusc* 5.37-39.

106 happiness, perfection and good fortune, without any restriction: Right living, i.e. the continuous life of virtue guided by reason in conformity with nature, has two main effects – (i) happiness, not the aim but the consequence of the life of virtue, and (ii) freedom, in that the individual is liberated from external possessions, dependencies and needs; cf. *Tusc* 5.40-42 for the happiness and self-sufficiency of the wise man, and *Paradox* V on his freedom.

107 in a rhetorical manner: 'rhetorice' is omitted in inferior MSS and by some editors. Cicero himself elaborates 'rhetorice' through Cato on the happiness of the wise man in sect.75, and in his own voice on various Stoic tenets in the *Paradoxes*, cf. the Preface to these, and also n.13 on the 'spiky' style of the Stoics.

VIII. 27 *The syllogism for 'what is good is right'*

108 are set out: The verb 'concludere' can be used specifically for syllogistic argument, cf. 'concludendi modus' *Top* 54. The failure of Stoic syllogisms to deal with practical moral problems is denounced at *Fin* 4.52-3.

109 the conclusion is valid: The syllogism is of the most common form, and valid in 'Barbara': major premiss – all 'bonum' is 'laudabile', minor premiss – all 'laudabile' is 'honestum', conclusion – all 'bonum' is 'honestum', cf. *Tusc* 5.49. The logical validity of the conclusion however is independent of the truth of the premisses.

110 it is not the case: Cato claims that the minor premiss would be generally accepted, but admits difficulties with the major – that all 'bonum' is 'laudabile', i.e. deserving public appreciation of merit. What is understood popularly to be a good may not be praiseworthy, and the Epicureans in particular would object, for whom pleasure is good, but not necessarily 'laudabile', cf. Aristotle *EN* 1.12, and especially 1101b26-30: 'Eudoxus thought that the fact of pleasure not being praised, although a good, is evidence that it is superior to the goods that are praised, as God and the Good are also, because they are the standards to which all other goods are referred' (trans. Thomson). For a list of philosophers who would not accept the premiss cf. *Fin* 4.48-50.

111 So it follows: To make the major premiss (all 'bonum' is 'laudabile') acceptable a *sorites* or chain argument is used, i.e. a series of syllogisms is set out with the conclusion of the first forming the major premiss of the next, the conclusion of that becoming the third major premiss and so on, but here, as often, in an elliptical form. Instead of one proposition combining two sharply distinguishable terms, a number are interposed, making the shift from one term to the other more gradual, so that it is almost impossible for the objector to mark off the unacceptable move. So between 'bonum' and laudabile' four further terms intervene – 'expetendum' (to be desired), 'placens' (agreeable), 'diligendum' (to be chosen) and 'probandum' (to be approved). In full the first syllogism would be: all 'bonum' is 'expetendum', all 'expetendum' is 'placens', therefore all 'bonum' is 'placens'; the second then starts: all 'bonum' is 'placens', and the pattern continues until the conclusion: all 'bonum' is 'laudabile' is reached. The argument from Chrysippus (ap. Plutarch *Stoic rep* 1039c) has a shorter *sorites* with the links *agathon* ('bonum') – *haireton* ('expetendum') – *areston* ('placens') – *epaineton* ('laudabile'); cf. also *Fin* 4.50..

VIII. 28 *The happy life is the good life*

112 a wretched or unhappy life: 'laus' is the external recognition by others of merit, whereas the aspect of 'gloria' in 'gloriatio' and the verb 'gloriari' here is the individual's inner awareness of that merit, which he may proclaim *to* others. It would be agreed that no one would connect *gloria* with an unhappy life, but the content of such a life is nonetheless debatable. Glossing 'misera uita' with 'non beata' confirms it as the equivalent of *kakodaimonia*$_2$ which has the same basic ambiguity between moral and material connotations as *eudaimonia* / 'beata uita'. Socrates notoriously played on this ambiguity in the Greek terms, cf. especially Plato *Meno* 77b-79e, which this present passage recalls.

(The ambiguity still holds in the English equivalents of 'living well' and 'the good life'.)

113 the happy life is the righteous life: the conclusion of another syllogism with major premiss: the happy life (1) is worthy of 'gloriatio' (2), and the minor: what is (truly) worthy of 'gloriatio' is the right/righteous life; the equivalent terms in Chrysippus' syllogism were *charton* (1), *semnon* (2) and *kalon* (3), cf. Plutarch *Stoic rep* 1039c, DL 7.127, Cicero *Tusc* 5.12, 48 and the evidence and discussion, Long and Sedley sect. 36.

VIII. 29 *The only evil is vice*

114 pain is not an evil: That pain was the greatest evil was the converse of the fundamental principle of the Cyrenaics and Epicureans that pleasure was the chief good; Hieronymus held that freedom from pain was the greatest good, and other philosophers, with the exception of Zeno, Aristo and Pyrrho, admitted pain as an evil, but not the worst of evils, cf. *Tusc* 2.14-15. In fact Cicero devoted the whole of book 2 of the *Tusculans* to the topic of pain, both as a philosophical problem, and with practical advice supported by a range of 'exempla'. In book 5 he faces the common-sense stand of his respondent: 'I just do not believe that being good is all that is needed to be happy ... when you look at the truth of the matter, one question is plain – *can* anyone be happy while he is being tortured?' (*Tusc* 5.12, 14). Being happy on the rack was taken as the extreme paradox (elaborated in gory detail in the challenge to Socrates in Plato *Rep* 361e).

115 impossible ... to despise what he has decided is evil: The argument is as follows: we are afraid of what we really think is evil and despise what we are indifferent to. If pain and death (which we all suffer) were truly evil we would all be afraid of them, and there would be no examples of courage, but there *are* men of courage who are indifferent to or despise pain and death, therefore pain and death are not evils.

116 the high-minded and courageous man: Both Stoics and Epicureans believed in the power of the mind to conquer pain, the Epicureans by finding distraction from present pain in memories of past pleasures and anticipations of future ones, the Stoics by confronting pain outright with 'fortitudo'. This struck a chord in the Romans' own tradition of courage and endurance, cf. notes 99 and 114. But the Stoics went further, considering not only pain and death but everything else in human life of no account, i.e. indifferent; cf. sects. 50, 51 and 56.

117 nothing is evil except vice: As 'bonum' (*agathon*) identifies with 'honestum (*kalon*) to the exclusion of all else, so do their opposites, 'malum' (*kakon*) with 'turpe' (*aischron*). Since the worst that can happen to the body has been shown not to be evil, then evil, like good, relates to the mind. It is to be explained as inner conflict and disturbed reason, and since this is a blighting of what is most essentially human, the result can only be unhappiness, cf. notes 142 and 157.

VIII. 29 contd. *No evil can befall the good man*

118 The object of our search: The discussion so far has concentrated on normal human physical and mental development from birth to maturity, where there is no impediment in environment or education to life in conformity with nature. Sections 28 and 29 have treated top human achievement in both Socratic and traditional Roman terms, and this is the broad basis for Cato's exposition in book 3. Now, with the introduction of the 'sapiens' (the official Stoic 'Wise Man'), the exemplum of rare but attainable heroic moral status shades into the almost impossible ideal, cf. sect. 75.

119 no evil can befall the wise man: The quotation, with the permissible Stoic substitute of 'wise' for 'good' is from the end of Socrates' address to the jury: 'You must be optimistic about death, and consider this one thing as true, that no evil befalls the good man either during his life-time or after his death' (Plato *Ap* 41c). Cf. Zeller's summary: 'Pain (the wise man) may feel, but as he does not consider it an evil, he will suffer no torture and know no fear. He may be slandered and abused, but he cannot be injured or degraded' (*Stoics* p. 237 with references). One of the most problematic possible causes of distress to the wise man (and rejected at length by Carneades) was the fall of his country, cf. *Tusc* 3.54.

120 the one lived virtuously: The adjectives 'wise' and 'virtuous' are now used almost as synonyms, and the argument runs as follows: The happy life is the life with no evil; pain and death are not evils (cf. sect.29); the only evil is vice; the wise/good man is free from vice; therefore his life has no evil and so is happy.

IX. 30 *Other theories*

121 a difference of opinion: Three groups of philosophers, each subdivided into three, are mentioned anonymously in sects. 30 and 31, only to be summarily dismissed. They are given in ascending order of approval by the Stoics – 'group A' who are completely wrong in excluding virtue from the good are the worst, 'group B' who are preferable in at least including virtue, and, in 31, 'group C', who are correct in linking the chief good to reason, but ridiculous in the conclusions they draw. 'uitiosē' here refers to defective argument rather than immoral implications, and so the translaton in the next section: 'have come to wrong conclusions'.

122 in placing ... preferable: This phrase has been transposed from the end of this complex sentence, where the summary is clear in Latin but clumsy in English – 'to all these (i.e. the three subdivisions of both A and B) I prefer those whoever they are (more exactly 'no matter of what kind', cf. *OLD* s.v. 'modus' 12b) who have placed the supreme good in mind (i.e. reason) and in virtue'. 'cuicuimodi' is Lambinus' suggestion for the genitive which the scribes obviously found problematic – MSS versions are 'cuimodi' (BER), 'cuiusmodi' (N), 'cuius modici' (V) and 'ante potui modo' (A).

123 identifying the chief good with (i) pleasure: the first subdivision of group A; in each of these three sub-divisions the virtue-excluding end was also thought to relate to the primary natural impulse. The earliest exponent of pleasure as both first instinct and highest good was the Cyrenaic Aristippus (cf. *Fin* 5.20), but the major figure of attack was of course Epicurus (cf. 2.35). That Epicurus advocated virtue as in the long run providing the most pleasant life tended to be ignored by his critics, or purposely misunderstood, cf. 'Letter to Menoecus' (DL 10.131-2) with *Tusc* 3.46-8.

124 (ii) freedom from pain: This would also include Epicurus (cf. 'the end of all our actions is to be free from pain and fear' DL ibid. 128) but Hieronymus is the main target, cf. *Fin* 2.35, 5.14 and 20. Hieronymus was from Rhodes but lived in Athens c. 290-230, first as a Peripatetic, and then as founder of his own school. Despite the lack of force in his main tenet, he became embroiled in personal abuse with other philosophers.

125 (iii) the primary natural state: The advocate is given as Carneades 'who was not the author of this view, but defended it for the sake of argument' (*Fin* 5.20). Antiochus, in his criticism of these different stands in book 5, points out that the *aim* of attaining the natural state, if not its achievement, belonged to Stoic doctrine, but, as has been shown, in the sense of self-preservation this was superseded by the life of virtue controlled by reason.

126 a second set of three groups: The sub-divisions of group B comprise those who add virtue to A (i), (ii) and (iii). So, B (i) there are those who combine virtue and pleasure as the chief good, named as Callipho and Dinomachus at *Fin* 5.21, *Tusc* 5.85, (ii) virtue and freedom from pain, as Diodorus *Fin* 2.34 and 5.21, and (iii) virtue and the natural state, the standard Aristotelian position. This will be given separate treatment in sect.41, because of the importance of rebutting the charge that Stoic ethics were basically Peripatetic, but with a new terminology. Polemo was head of the Academy from 314 to 276 b.c. (when Zeno himself studied there), and was famous more for his strength of character than the force of his teaching (cf. DL 4.17-19). Diodorus, who also taught Zeno, was the great Megarian dialectician; Callipho and Dinomachus are otherwise unknown.

IX. 31 *Difficulties even with the preferable alternatives*

127   a life of learning: Given books 5 to 7 of the *Republic* Plato might be thought to be the prime candidate here, but the present context is concerned with the disagreements among the Hellenistic schools, and at *Fin* 2.43 and 4.40 Erillus, the third century Stoic from Carthage, is the example given (the name has an initial aspirate in Greek), cf. *Fin* 5.73: 'knowledge (for him) was the chief good, and nothing else desirable *per se*, cf. DL 7.165-6 and Arnold 81-2. But why should those who devote their lives to knowledge be 'perabsurdi'? In *Tusc* 5.64-67 Archimedes is held up as a paradeigm example (along with Democritus and Anaxagoras) of one who lived a happy life precisely because he nourished his mind with scientific problems. Cato perhaps is more traditionally Roman, suspicious of science for its own sake (as in sect.37) and, while acknowledging the need for a grounding in theory, eager to emphasise the part played by practical wisdom, cf. n.131.

128   no distinctions to be made: for Pyrrho and Aristo who are implied here, cf. n.34, and also *Fin* 2.43, 3.12, 5.20-23.

129   he does not have a preference: Pyrrho lived his life according to the principle of *ou mallon* – 'no more this than that' – so that it did not matter to him, for example, if he ate or not, or whether he walked along a safe path or over a precipice, with the result that his friends were continually steering him from danger. Aristo emphasised more the complete indifference of everything except virtue. The theories of Erillus, Pyrrho and Aristo are given short shrift at *Off* 1.6.

130   to withold his assent from appearances: '<et qui>' was added by Heine after 'anteponentem' to provide a third subdivision of this group (the following 'ut' is given as 'aut' by B and E) and Lambinus inserted '<fore ut>' towards the end of the sentence to maintain the correct construction. After Plato's immediate successors in the Academy the scepticism of Pyrrho and Timon exerted an influence on its teaching, in the 'middle' period under Arcesilaus and in the 'New Academy' under Carneades and Philo of Larissa, and it is these and their followers who are referred to here as 'some Academics'. They denied the possibility of certainty, especially in epistemology and ethics, and urged rather that one should aim at 'suspension of judgment', *epochē*. Antiochus seceded from Philo to re-establish the 'old' Academy, cf. the diagram, *Intr.* page 11.

131 practical wisdom will be useless: The function of 'prudentia' is to guide our choice on day-to-day non-moral issues according to what is with or against nature, so that appropriate action ('officium') results. Without any employment for 'prudentia' the wise man would not be less good, but his virtue would have less scope or extension, cf. n.200.

132 eliminate: 'circumscribo' is like an ancient equivalent of 'bracket', and so 'take out of the reading', 'exclude', or (as here for rejected alternatives) 'eliminate'.

133 applying to the conduct of life ... conformity with nature: This sentence gives the important summary of the conclusions reached so far, before the next theoretical section on definitions. The supreme good embraces a theoretical knowledge ('scientia') of the way nature operates and a practical application of it ('prudentia'). 'Prudentia' chooses what is according to nature and rejects the opposite, and in so doing brings about the habit of conformity of human nature with nature as a whole, and thereby the happy life, cf. (outside of *Fin*) *Off* 1.110, *Ac* 2.131 (where the formula is 'honestē uiuere') and the exposition and evidence in de Vogel, iii 133-4. The theory as a whole takes to its logical conclusion the intellectualisation of ethics begun by Socrates, for whom 'being good' tended to imply theoretical knowledge and its practical application, and delinquency its deficiency, to be countered not by punishment but by education. For the role of 'prudentia' in choice cf. notes 131, 210, and for the necessity of understanding human, divine and cosmic nature cf. n.321. The Epicureans also urged that a knowledge of nature (in their case of atoms and void) was a necessary foundation for freedom from anxiety and so happiness.

X. 33 - 34 *The definition of 'good'*
(Section 32, which is concerned with the *technē* analogy, has been transposed to the more appropriate context of ch.VII. sect.25, cf. n.100.)

134 is capable of definition: It was (and is) notoriously difficult to define good, or the good. The Socratic search for a definition of *aretē* in the *Meno* characteristically foundered, in Plato's *Republic* (506d) an explanation is postponed indefinitely, and Aristotle, in his discussion at *EN* 1.7, suggests first that it is what is choosable for its own sake, and then connects it with 'well-functioning' (cf. of the innumerable commentaries on this, most recently Santas *Apeiron* 22, 75-100). Generally definitions tend to peter out into a list of 'goods' or of effects of virtue, or they replace one ambiguous term by another. The Stoics here first take the concept in abstraction, and then in its realisation in the individual.

135 what is naturally perfect: 'natura absolutum', but in the major MSS 'e' or 'a' natura, due to the similar phrase two lines below – 'e natura absoluto' (where 'absoluta' is an obvious manuscript error). The definition is that of Diogenes of Babylon, head of the Stoic school c. 170-150 b.c., teacher of Panaetius, and, with Carneades, a member of the famous and influential delegation from Greece to Rome in 155 b.c. (The subjunctive in 'qui definierit' is causal, i.e. I agree with him 'because he / in that he ...') The Greek version, attributed to the Stoics generally in the *Life of Zeno* (DL 7.94) is 'the natural perfection (τὸ τέλειον κατὰ φύσιν) of the rational as rational'.

136 that which is beneficial: The particular realisation of the general good as a process ('motus') or condition ('status') in the individual is a benefit (ōphelēma) to that individual, cf. DL 7.104 – 'to benefit is to set in motion or sustain according to virtue', and again 7.94, where the good connects with benefit as its source, in the virtuous act and by the agency of the good man.

137 (i) experience, (ii) combination, (iii) resemblance: The ways of coming to an understanding of a concept are given in more detail in Sextus (*Math* 3.40, 9.393). Through direct experience we are aware of different qualities, such as black, sweet and hard, and of such objects as man and horse. We can then have a 'notio' of the unknown through mental 'combination' of such direct sense-data, as of a centaur, for example, taken as a conjunction of man and horse, or through resemblance. Resemblance in turn may be by 'increase', as a Cyclops can be realised as a large man, or by 'decrease', like the unknown pygmy as a man on a small scale, or by 'likeness', when someone may be imagined from a familiar relative or from a portrait. (The philosophical problems of 'resemblance' were dealt with exhaustively by Plato in the second immortality argument in the *Phaedo*, 73c-74a). There is a slightly different list at DL 7.52-3, with general notions said to be gained by direct contact, by resemblance, by analogy, by transposition, by combination and by opposition (as death from life).

138 (iv) logical inference: 'collatio rationis', corresponding to *analogia*, and the way in which we come to an understanding or 'notio' of the good. Analogy involves relationships – a simple example is that 'as a shepherd to his sheep so a king to his people', and another one will be used in the next paragraph ('as honey is to sweet so virtue is to good'). The general awareness by analogy that will lead to a 'notio' of the good begins by studying the relationship of any object that is functioning well to the *telos* that belongs to it according to its nature, and continues in this way over a broad range of simple and then more sophisticated forms of life until in its highest form the relationship between function of a rational being and natural perfection is grasped.

139 its own inherent force: The good is in a class of its own; everything else is not only inferior to it, but operates on a different level, and nothing from this level (that of what is basically 'indifferent') taken in conjunction with the good, can increase it or affect it in any way.

140 just as honey: the first of a series of illustrations (the majority are in sects. 45 to 48) which show the gulf that exists between the good and 'indifferents', and which help us to an understanding of the concepts involved by the method of 'logical inference'. Honey (in the absence of sugar) was the basic sweetener in ancient cooking. The point of the analogy is that just as honey is counted not as one of many sweet things but as the essence of sweetness, so virtue is not one of many good things but the very essence of goodness. The judgment is not of *quantity* (as if one could achieve the sweetness of honey by piling up a number of foods that seem to be sweet but are not essentially so), but of *kind* ('genus'). Honey is the one and only essentially sweet substance as virtue is the one and only essential good.

141 value belonging to virtue alone: The classification of 'indifferents' into value-plus, value-minus and value-neutral, outlined in sect. 20 and explained more fully in 51, 52 and 58, is according to a scale of 'aestimatio' (*axia*) that admits of increase and decrease on a non-moral level. This is to be distinguished from the absolute worth of virtue, which alone belongs to the *genus* of 'good', on account of its own inherent force ('propria uis sua', n.139). This restriction of the use of 'good' to morality alone was the cornerstone of Stoic ethics, but, in its apparent contradiction to general human experience, appeared absurd. It gave rise both to Cicero's public ridicule of Cato's position in *Pro Murena*, and to his defence of some of the consequences in the *Paradoxes*.

X. 35 *The emotions are mental disturbances*

142 mental disturbances: Passion or emotion was defined by Zeno (e.g. at DL 7.115) as 'irrational and unnatural movement in the soul' or again as 'excessive impulse' (ὁρμὴ πλεονάζουσα, i.e.

impulse that is unnatural and out of the control of reason, cf.
Stobaeus, 2.7.10); this definition was translated by Cicero at *Tusc*
4.47, with the second alternative as 'appetitus uehementior'. In the
earlier discussion in ch.X of *Fin* 3 there had been a brief
explanation of vice both as an end result, when the wrong is in a
particular wrong action such as treason or violence, and as a
continuing disturbance of the soul. This is now developed further,
to clarify the theory in its own right, and, by taking the opposite
condition, to help in understanding the 'good' mental state. The
general position is that the soul, as *logos* and *pneuma*, must be
maintained physically in the correct tension, in harmony within
itself, then the resulting actions will be moral, and the agent's life
good and therefore happy. If however it is in the wrong condition,
in discord and disturbance, then the resulting actions will be
immoral, the life vicious and so unhappy. The Stoics continually
looked inwards to the mental state for the explanation of the
virtuous or vicious life rather than outwards, to what is done. And
it is excessive emotion that wrecks inner harmony and warps
judgment. For detailing of the evidence and general discussion of
this topic cf. especially Zeller 228-38, Arnold ch.14 'Sin and
weakness', Bréhier 58-60, I. G. Kidd 'Posidonius on the emotions'
Long *Problems* 200-15, de Vogel iii.92-95, Long and Sedley sect.65
'The Passions', and M. Frede 'The affections of the soul' in
Schofield *Norms*, 93-110.

143   I could call them diseases: 'morbi' in the plural for
specific serious illnesses is rejected as taking the medical metaphor
to extremes in the Latin for what, in the Greek, are more like
malfunctions of a disturbed soul, cf. *Tusc* 3.7, 4.10. The theory of
psychic illness and its therapy is probably Pythagorean in origin,
and appears in its most sustained form in Plato's *Gorgias*,
culminating in the unpleasantly vivid description of the 'mass of
weals and scars' on the unjust man's soul (*Gorg* 524e-525b), but
most philosophers saw themselves as offering a 'cure for souls'. (To
balance the modal with infinitive 'poteram appellare' editors
generally change the following 'conueniet' to the imperfect
subjunctive 'conueniret'. The MSS also have after 'uidetur' the
clause 'nec eae perturbationes ui aliqua naturali mouentur' which
was deleted by Madvig: it is an obvious and at this point
inappropriate duplication of the similar phrase at the beginning of
the next sentence.)

144   four main classes: After the long parenthesis on
translation, the subject 'perturbationes animorum' is picked up
again with 'omnes eae'. The four classes relate to mistaken
judgment about present and future good and evil, and in the

exhaustive detail of their numerous sub-divisions aim to classify the range of human emotion, cf. DL 7.111, taken from Zeno's work *Peri pathōn*, and Vergil *Aen* 6.733 where the four arise from the imprisonment of immortal mind in mortal body. The first category is grief (*lupē*), which is not the *feeling* of pain (which of course is beyond one's control) but an erroneous assent to the physical feeling or the mental imagining as a real evil, whereas the only evil is vice; the sub-divisions include pity (i.e. grief at another's supposed misfortune), jealousy and mental agony or anxiety. Fear, secondly, is an expectation of supposed evil and includes shame (the expectation of losing one's reputation), terror at having to act positively, and the agony of suspense. Thirdly improper desire is irrational longing for what one believes, incorrectly, to be good, and subsumes hatred (desire for future ill for another), anger (the desire to avenge a supposed evil) and lust.

145 the pleasant excitement of a mind aroused: The fourth class, *hēdone*, which Cicero translates here by 'laetitia' rather than 'uoluptas' (cf. n.1, but 'elatio uoluptaria' in the gloss here), to be understood as the release of restraint in the mistaken assumption that good is present, cf. the definition at *Fin* 2.14 of 'uoluptas animi', synonymous with 'laetitia' as 'elation of the mind under an irrational conviction that it is enjoying some great good'. This is to be distinguished from *chara*, 'rational elation', which is appropriate for the wise man, cf. below, n.147.

146 fancies and sentiments of an unstable character: 'omniaque ea' unusually takes the gender of the second predicate 'iudicia' rather than of 'opiniones' or of the subject 'perturbationes'. The main classes of emotion and their sub-divisions are all to be explained on Stoic theory as mistaken beliefs and judgments about present and future good and evil. Cicero himself makes use of this in the essay on grief that is book 3 of the *Tusculans*, especially at 3.67 when he agrees that grief is due to 'iudicium' and can be adopted and set aside at will, and his conclusion at 3.71, after citing numerous exempla of misfortune bravely borne, that 'grief is not natural but a question of belief'. Courage, which involves knowledge of what is truly evil, is the virtue to counter grief and fear, and self-control, the application of knowledge of what is truly good, corrects improper desire and delight. These basic connections of applied knowledge to virtue, and false belief to unrestrained emotion, had already been examined in the Socratic arguments of Plato's *Laches* and *Charmides*. In physical terms in Stoic psychology grief and fear were connected with contracting and shrinking of the *pneuma* of the soul, and desire and delight as its stretching and swelling, and these continual movements were also the soul's 'fluttering', indicating the instability of the emotionally immature (cf. Stobaeus 2.7.1). Plutarch gives an appropriate commentary on this instability: 'Desire and anger and fear and the rest are corrupt opinions and judgments, which do not arise about just one part of the soul, but are the whole commanding faculty's inclinations, yieldings, assents and impulses, and, quite generally, those activities which change rapidly, like children's quarrels; their fury and intensity are volatile and transient owing to their weakness.' (cf. *virt. mor.* 447a, translation based on Long and Sedley, i.412)

147 always free of them: Since the Stoic understood true good and evil, he would be immune to false judgments about them in the present and future, and so free from these destabilising and corrupting emotions. In this 'apathy' lay the austerity of Stoicism, so attractive to Roman idealism, exemplified in both the elder and younger Cato, and still considered its identifying feature. Yet the wise man would not be completely apathetic, but, with reason always in control, he could be in a condition of 'proper feeling' (*eupatheia* cf. DL 7.116). There were three such states, again with various sub-divisions (i) *chara* or 'joy', the rational elation that was the counterpart of delight, and included the state praised by Democritus as *euthumia* – 'calm cheerfulness', (ii) *eulabeia* or 'caution', which, as rational avoidance, was set against fear, and (iii) *boulēsis* or 'wishing', a reasonable 'looking forward to' rather than irrational craving, and covering the conditions essential to social relations of benevolence and friendship, cf. further on sects. 69 and 70.

XI. 36 *Support from general consensus*

148 apart from the three schools: (i) those of Aristippus (the Cyrenaics) and Epicurus, considering pleasure to be the supreme good, (ii) of Hieronymus, with freedom from pain, and (iii) of the Peripatetics and Carneades, cf. on sect. 30. Carneades, who was mainly instrumental in founding the New Academy with its sceptical leanings, adopted the Peripatetic stand here as a debating point against the Stoics, cf. n.171.

149 especially of the Stoics: An unnecessary 'Stoicis' after 'his' was deleted by Lambinus and subsequent editors. 'haec defensio' in the next sentence is idiomatic for 'huius rei defensio' – defence of this position. Some MSS have 'perexpedita' following 'perfacilis' rather than 'expedita', and then 'quamquam' for 'quam' in the last sentence. Other philosophers, the Peripatetics in particular, included virtue or what is right as *a* good, the Stoics claimed it as the one and only good.

150 gain his object blamelessly: The Stoics followed Socrates in claiming that no one desires evil *per se* (cf. *Gorg* 467a-8e, *Meno* 77d-78b), but we are naturally inclined towards the good, cf. n.83. Subsequent history has unfortunately disproved this optimistic generalisation that rational man would not deliberately and under no compulsion choose criminal means to achieve his end.

XI. 37 *Wisdom and courage are esteemed for their own sake*

151 the secrets of natural science: a slightly expanded translation of 'illa quae occulta nobis sunt'; the example given refers to astronomy. An understanding of natural science was necessary for the Stoics as the foundation of their physics (cf. sect.73), and the pursuit of the higher mathematics involved in Hellenistic astronomy was an example of the love of rational activity for its own sake, developed from its first appearance in children (cf. n.63), and characteristic of the greatest of human achievements. It was however regarded with some suspicion by the Romans generally, cf. n.127 on the rejection of 'scientia' as an end in itself. Vergil notoriously rejected astronomy in favour of government as a Roman vocation (*Aen* 6.849-51), yet Cicero himself had translated Aratus' *Phaenomena*, a poem on astronomy, and this was soon to be followed by the *Astronomica* of Manilius.

152 unless they bring some pleasure or profit: The flourish of rhetorical questions conceals the obvious objection that anyone familiar with golden age mythology, Plato's *Republic* or Lucretius book 5 would answer that primitive rural societies are less concerned with 'uoluptas' and 'utilitas' than are advanced civilisations.

153 pleasure at heart: lit. 'mental pleasure', and presumably equivalent to the *chara* or 'proper joy' (cf. n.147) of rational emotion, produced here by the contemplation of *exempla* of wisdom and courage.

154 of the Africani: the two Scipios, called by Vergil 'two thunderbolts of war, Libya's destruction' (*Aen* 6.842-3). Scipio Africanus Major (236-184 b.c.) defeated Hasdrubal at Barca in the second Punic war and won Spain for Rome; he then invaded Africa and finally conquered Hannibal at Zama in 202 b.c. Political hostility, supported by the elder Cato, led to his eventual disgrace and exile. The younger Scipio (185-129 b.c.), his grandson through adoption, was responsible for the settlement of Numidia and the final destruction of Carthage at the end of the third Punic war (146 b.c.). His opposition to the Gracchan reforms was probably the cause of his death in suspicious circumstances during the subsequent general disorder. In his admiration for Greek literature and philosophy he established the 'Scipionic Circle', which included the Greek historian Polybius, the Stoic philosopher Panaetius, and aristocratic Romans with similar cultural intersts. The Circle provided a focus for the emergence of Hellenic studies at Rome.

155   of my great-grandfather: Cato the Censor (234-149), most famous for his stern traditional morality, his opposition to the infiltration of Greek influence into Rome, and his insistence on the destruction of Carthage. He was a skilled orator (Cicero knew of 150 speeches), and his great works on agriculture and on Roman origins were the foundation of Latin prose. The Scipios and the elder Cato soon joined the 'exempla' of an idealised Roman past, and they were favourites of Cicero, cf. *Somnium Scipionis* at the end of *De Republica* (which involves both Scipios), *De Senectute* with the elder Cato as main speaker, and *De Amicitia*, which gives Laelius' friendship with the younger Scipio as the paradeigm.

XI. 38 *What is wrong is intrinsically repulsive*

156   proper education: 'ingenue' more exactly as 'befitting the free-born'. The (highly subjective) argument from general consensus continues with the converse of sect.36. As even the most depraved would prefer to gain their objectives innocently rather than unjustly, so the best people instinctively shrink from the vice which they see exemplified in criminals and those who waste the resources of their rationality.

157   unless the wrongness, by its very ugliness, acts as a deterrent: cf. Glaucon's challenge to Socrates on Gyges' ring (Plato *Rep* book 2) that he must show why a man must act rightly even if he had the ring of invisibility and could do wrong with impunity, and (adds Adeimantus) even if he could buy off divine punishment after death. The Stoic answer was that right action was the consequence of the working of nature within humanity as well as the external aim of rational desire. The recognition of this by the individual involves the awareness of the claims of divine law, of which human laws are the instantiation in political societies. Cicero uses comparable language elsewhere, in his theory of the origins of justice in *De legibus*: 'Reason ('ratio') established and fully developed in the human mind is law, and so the most learned men think of law as practical reason ('prudentia') with the power to command right action and forbid wrongdoing ... the commands and prohibitions of nations summon us towards what is right and away from what is wrong, but such power is older than nations and states, being co-eval with god who guards and rules heaven and earth; there can be no divine mind without 'ratio', and divine 'ratio' establishes right and wrong ... so reason, derived from the nature of the universe, urges men to right conduct and diverts them from wrongdoing.' (*Leg* 1.19, 2.9-11).

158 nothing is less to be questioned: The sentence summarises in uncompromising form the conclusion of this long section on the nature of the good that started at the beginning of ch. VIII, covering sects. 27 to 38.

XI. 39 *The consequences of wrong conduct*

159 those neutral effects which result from it: more exactly 'such neutral effects as are procured ('comparentur' is generic subjunctive) by it'. This is in the sense that 'prudentia' exercises continual selection on a non-moral level of what is according to nature.

160 cowardice: Guyet's 'timiditatem' for the MSS 'temeritatem', needed as the counterpart to 'fortitudo' (sometimes also given as 'ignauia') to complete the quartet of basic vices corresponding to the four cardinal virtues of wisdom, courage, justice and self-control. As wisdom is the key virtue, and the other three are variations of it, so 'stultitia' is the fundamental vice, and the others represent aspects of this false knowledge or folly. Such folly is more positively wrong than the median position held by ignorance in the scale: false knowledge – ignorance – true knowledge. *Paradoxes* IV and V deal with the two devastating consequences of 'stultitia', namely madness and loss of freedom.

161 to be avoided: The gender of the gerundive attached to feminine nouns varies; the MSS here have 'fugienda', -am' and '-as'.

162 do not apply to bodily harm: The malfunctioning of reason shown in the four cardinal vices is not reprehensible because of any physical flaw (the criminal may enjoy the best of health), but because the psychic defect may cause the individual to explode into particular violent actions, cf. on the examples given at n.101.

163 "vices" rather than "evils": on Cicero's translation here cf. *Tusc* 4.34, where, for the opposite of 'uirtus', the more general term 'uitiositas' is preferred to 'malitia', which is used more of a particular vice.

XII. 40 *The Latinising of philosophy*

164 how clear: for 'ne' or 'nae' emphasising a personal pronoun cf. n.40; 'uteris' is to be understood with the ablative 'uerbis'.

165 giving her Roman citizenship: Cato's monologue is interrupted by this section in which Cicero compliments Cato once more on his skill in establishing a Latin philosophical vocabulary, and so making the subject at home in Rome, rather than being so obviously a Greek import, cf. sects. 5 and 16, and n.50.

166 Stoic philosophy especially: on the particular difficulties of the 'spiky' style of the Stoics cf. sects. 3, 5 and 19, and the Preface of the *Paradoxes*.

167 I know there are some: an ironic reference to the Epicureans on the grounds that they used the evidence of sense-perception as their sole criterion (called 'the assent of silent nature' or 'the unspoken approval of nature' because awareness of sense-perception is immediate and requires no verbal interpretation, cf. notes 10 and 11); Cato ignores the fact that they also maintained that the senses could provide *indirect* evidence where perception was inadequate (as for atoms and void) by confirming or refuting the hypotheses of the theory.

168 classifications and definitions: cf. further the criticism at *Fin* 1.22: '(Epicurus) does away with definitions, has no theory of division and partition (i.e. classification into genus and species), leaves no guidelines on inference and deduction, or for dealing with sophistries or distinguishing ambiguities'. For the re-instatement of the Epicureans here and an examination of their logical methods cf. Long '*Aisthesis, prolepsis* and linguistic theory' *BICS* 1971, Sedley 'On Signs' and Dumont 'Confirmation et disconfirmation' in Barnes ed *Science and Speculation*, 239-303.

169 I shall soon have to use: 'iam' here for 'soon'. During the following months Cicero was to write the *Tusculans*, *De Natura Deorum*, *De Fato* and *De Officiis*, all of which required the Latinisation of Greek philosophical terms.

XII. 41 *Crucial disagreement with the Peripatetics*

170 their ignorance of logic: a startling claim to make about the followers of the man who laid the foundations of European logical theory, but after Theophrastus, his immediate successor, the main body of Aristotle's technical philosophy was little discussed (apart from Strato's interest in physical theory), the texts themselves had been sent to Alexandria and the school was in decline. But at the time of Cicero's writing, Andronicus of Rhodes was engaged in the mammoth task of arranging and editing the Aristotelian *corpus*, and so smoothing the way for the great commentaries that were to follow.

171 your Carneades: Carneades of Cyrene (214-129 b.c.), head of the Academy in the early second century; under his leadership the sceptical tendencies begun by Arcesilaus were further strengthened until what was virtually a different school, the New

Academy, emerged. Carneades was a member of the famous embassy of the philosophers in Rome in 155 b.c. (cf. on Diogenes, n.135), when he gave the exciting and unsettling pair of lectures for and against justice. Although he wrote nothing, this style of disputation, arguing for and against different philosophical positions, carried out with incisive wit, careful detail and brilliant exposition, made him the scourge of the schools. His scepticism on the possibility of attaining knowledge and his consequent 'witholding of assent' were tempered by his theory of probability and of 'presentations' of greater or less conviction. Cicero, who tended towards eclecticism himself partly as a result of his legal training in arguing for both sides, was inclined to sympathise with Carneades (and so called by Cato 'yours').

172 made it a key issue: Madvig and the purists complain that the sentence is anacoluthic, and would delete 'rem' after 'quam tractatam', but this picking up of a noun after a digression is in Cicero's style, and an obvious help to the reader, cf. n.144. They would also change 'appelletur' to 'appellatur' on the grounds that either the present indicative is required if the clause is parenthetical, or an imperfect subjunctive if it is dependent on the indirect speech.

173 not about facts but terminology: That there was no substantial difference between Zeno and his predecessors, especially the Peripatetics, on the theory of the final good, is at the heart of Cicero's own attack on the Stoic position in book 4, especially sections 19-41, cf. Summary; other relevant passages are *Fin* 5.15-20, *ND* 1.16, *Tusc* 5.24 (on Theophrastus) and 32. At *Off* 1.2 Cicero says that his own ethical position is not very different from the Peripatetics, and in fact goes back to Socrates, and at 3.11 he maintains that there is only a minimal disagreement between the Stoics' claim that virtue is the only good and the Peripatetics' that it is so great that other additions do not count.

174 much more substantial than verbal: Carneades' objection was that the Stoic *proëgmena*, defined as what was according to nature, were simply an alternative description of the Aristotelian 'natural goods', and that the function of wisdom in selecting them shows that they are to be included in the 'end for man'. The Stoics had a three-pronged reply; (i) they identified 'right' and 'expediency', so that there was only a single aim, whereas the Peripatetics separated them, (ii) the Stoics saw right action as reason in action rather than a consequence of it, and (iii) what was 'natural' was not static, but became gradually more sophisticated as it shifted from what was life-preserving to what was rational as the individual human matured from infancy through adolescence into adulthood. Cf. the discussions by Rist 'Aristotle and the Stoic good' *Stoic Philosophy* ch.1, Kidd 'Stoic intermediates and the end for man', in Long, *Problems*, 150-72, Irwin 'Stoic and Aristotelian conceptions of happiness', in Schofield, *Norms*, 205-44, and Long and Sedley sect.64.

XIII. 42 - 43 *Differences on the length and degree of happiness*

175   the philosophy of those: 'illorum ratione', so Lambinus and the editors for the MSS 'illo / illa ratione' or 'illa ratio est' to give a masculine plural antecedent to 'qui'.

176   who count pain an evil: This gives the converse of the earlier disagreemnt with the Peripatetics; for the Stoics virtue is the only good and vice therefore the only evil. They maintain that those who count pain (which is out of our control) as evil deprive us of mastery of our own lives and means of happiness. The extreme consequence of this, that the wise man is happy even on the rack, left them open to a ridicule which they were ready to accept, cf. n.114 and *Paradox* II, and the 'plain question' again of *Tusc* 5.14 – 'Can anyone really be happy while being tortured?'

177   on the rack: The 'eculeus' (or 'equuleus') was used to extract court evidence from slaves (on the assumption that they would not tell the truth voluntarily). The name means 'little horse', and the torture seems to have been a kind of impalement, involving sitting on some unpleasant and probably pointed wooden device, with the weight of the body increased by attaching weights to the arms and legs. Rich's *Dictionary of Classical Antiquities* s.v. has an engraving from Mirandola in north Italy. The common Greek verb for 'torture' is *strebloō*, meaning literally 'wrench' or 'twist', and may refer to a similar impalement, or to stretching on a cross or breaking on a wheel.

178   the wise man's happiness is secure: cf. n.113 on the happy life as the righteous life, and the main discussion at sects. 27-29; also *Tusc* 5.19: 'Philosophy will ensure that the man who has obeyed its laws shall never fail to be armed against all the hazards of fortune; that he shall possess and control, within his own self, every possible guarantee for a satisfactory and happy life.' (trans. Grant).

179   the mental attitude: cf. *Tusc* 5.76 (trans. Grant again): 'The most formidable obstacle to adopting a moral standard seems to be pain. When its fiery torches intimidate us they threaten the complete destruction of all the courage, character and endurance that we can muster. So does this mean that moral goodness is forced to succumb to pain? When pain comes, does the wise and steadfast man's happiness have to bow down before it? Heaven forbid!' The passage is followed by interesting examples of those who endure pain without flinching, like Spartan boys and Indian gurus; here the support is from the well-known phenomenon that pain from wounds is barely noticed in the heat of battle.

180   three classes of goods: These are (i) of the soul, comprising virtue, and much the most important, (ii) external goods which act as the instruments of virtuous action (such as wealth) 'for it is impossible to do good deeds without resources', and (iii) physical advantages of family, children and personal beauty 'for a man is scarcely happy if he is ugly, or of low birth, or solitary or childless' (cf. *EN* 1099a29-b8, also Plato *Euthyd* 279a-b, *Phil* 48e, *Laws* 743e).

181   a man will be happier: The sentence has a complex structure, and the general sense is: 'it does not follow, if having three classes of Peripatetic goods [(i), (ii) and (iii) in the previous note] supposedly means that more of (iii) and (ii) implies greater happpiness, that then ['ut' picked up again after the long explanatory conditional clause] we the Stoics should agree that more of (iii) implies greater happiness; cf. next note.

182   what *we* truly call goods: i.e. right actions, *katorthōmata*, cf. notes 79 and 189, and sect.55. The wise man's happiness could not be increased by the introduction of more material and physical goods (for these are indifferent) or even by multiplying his good deeds. Every *katorthoma* is a complete manifestation of each and every form of virtue in rational activity and, as such, an instantiation of perfect happiness. A series of *katorthōmata* cannot therefore add to that happiness or increase its value, cf. on sects. 46-47.

XIII. 44 - XIV. 45 *There is no good but virtue*

183   if both wisdom and health are desirable: Wisdom counts as a Peripatetic good of the soul, and health a good of the body; both, for them, could be classified as 'expetenda', whereas for the Stoics only virtue is 'expetendum'. The two together are not worth more than wisdom alone because they are different in *kind* and so cannot be added. The whole is a re-wording, in the Peripatetic context, of the point made more generally in sect.34, and illustrated with the 'honey' analogy.

184   We put a certain value on health: Wisdom as virtue is the only good and alone is 'expetendum' ('to be desired'), health, on the non-moral level but in the 'value-plus' category as inherently according to nature, is 'sumendum' or 'seligendum' ('to be adopted', *proēgmenon*, cf. notes 69 and 88). The primary instinct is for self-preservation, involving a well-formed and sound body, and the first 'officium' is to keep in one's natural condition; with advancing years however reason takes over from instinct, and desire for the good supplants that for the physical natural state, cf. notes 54, 60, 72, 80 and below n.234. At the end of the *Tusculans* (5.112-7) Cicero gives some interesting examples of those who did not find a physical handicap a hindrance to the moral life. He includes some famous blind people – Appius Claudius, C. Drusus, Cn. Aufudius and, in Cicero's own house, the Stoic Diodotus, who continued philosophising, playing the lyre and teaching geometry after losing his sight.

185 right action without pain: the converse point to that discussed at n.183. The addition of health to wisdom makes no difference for the Stoic, nor would its subtraction; the Peripatetics are making a categorical mistake in adding and subtracting health and pain to wisdom and virtue in this way.

186 as the light of a lamp: These illustrations, to show the immeasurable difference between virtue and the so-called goods of the body (like health) are vivid, and their source, if not Cicero's own invention, unknown. As is a lamp (in brightness) to the light of the sun, a drop (in size) to the Aegean sea, a penny (in amount) to Croesus' millions, a step (in length) to the journey to India, so is health or any other external advantage inferior (in every way) to the final end of virtue. (At *Tusc* 2.30 Cicero says that there is little to choose between Plato, Aristotle and the Stoics here in that they all give such pre-eminence to virtue that goods of body and fortune are insignificant and paltry in comparison. But for the Stoics the difference is more one of kind than of quantity, so uncountable and immeasurable as to be virtually infinite – no number of lamps is equal to the sun's light, nor will adding one drop to another ever produce the vastness of the ocean.)

187 what belongs to the body: 'corporearum' is generally accepted for the MSS 'in corporearum' or 'in corpore harum'.

XIV. 45 contd. - 47 *Appropriateness is in the limit*

188 suitability: *eukairia* from *kairos* which is 'due proportion' (hence the proverbial '*kairos* is best in all things' Hesiod *WD* 694), but especially 'the due time', and particularly in medical contexts for the right time for treatment. *Kairos* in this sense must be 'seized' or 'grasped' or it will be lost, but as a moment, rather than a time of any duration; cf. Plato *Phaedrus* 272a on *eukairia* and *akairia* as suitable moments for the orator, and Stobaeus 2.7.11e (SVF iii.136) where *katorthōmata* include *eukairēmata* ('opportune acts') along with *eutaktēmata* ('acts of orderly behaviour') and *euschēmata* ('acts of decorum').

189 right conduct: *katorthōsis* introduces another technical term. The Greek third declension feminine nouns in *-sis* tend to be for a state or condition resulting from the related verb, and the neuter in *-ma* for a particular instance; in Latin feminine nouns in *-io* connect with the supine of the verb, as 'cognitio' from 'cognosco' and 'effectio' (the example here) from 'efficio'. *katorthōsis* ('recta effectio'), which includes a series of *katorthōmata*, now defines the supreme good, being equivalent to 'living harmoniously' and to 'that very good which rests in agreement with nature', cf. n.133.

190 not improved by length of time: Once a man attains the qualities of right conduct, harmonious life and agreement with nature he has reached the summit of human achievement. As with mountaineering, once the peak is reached the length of time one stays there is irrelevant. The theory of *eukairia* is fundamental to the controversial equality of right acts, cf. the converse implications for vice *Paradox* III.20: 'Acting wrongly is like crossing a boundary, and once you have done it an offence has been committed. How much further you go when once you have crossed over makes no difference to the gravity of the offence'.

191 a shoe: more exactly 'a boot', of which a number of Greek types seems to be included under the Latin 'cothurnus': (i) *endromis*, a high boot, laced in front and with toes uncovered to give flexibility, especially for running; (ii) *arbulē*, a primitive boot of raw hide used by country people, and (iii) *cothornos*, a high laced boot used in hunting, with a platform sole by tragic actors, and in art in an elaborate form by some gods, notably Dionysus and Artemis. The cothurnus in any guise could not have been an exact fit as the straight sole did not distinguish right from left (so it was used metaphorically of someone who changed sides frequently). It would have improved the simile if Cicero had used the Latin word 'calceus', which was for a shoe or low boot made on a last and distinguishing right from left.

192 would not be preferable: Bentley and Madvig change the passive 'anteponentur' or 'anteponerentur' in the MSS to the active 'anteponent' to give a personal subject, namely 'the Stoics'.

193 They fail to recognise: Many people do not understand that appropriateness varies with the context. Childbirth and death are 'good' if of short duration, health if of long duration, a shoe if the limit is reached. A 'good' shoe fits, and it is not a better shoe if bigger, and (since only one pair can be worn at a time) the number of pairs owned is irrelevant. Virtue and wisdom for the Stoics resemble the shoe in this respect, that appropriateness is in the limit, and for virtue any increase cannot be in degree but only in scope, cf. n.200. The Epicureans had a similar theory with regard to pleasure – once the limit was reached pleasure could not be increased but only 'varied'.

XIV. 48 *There are no degrees of virtue*

194   according to their theory: The sentence is mildly anacoluthic, as 'iisdem placere' is, strictly speaking, redundant after 'ratione illorum', but such resumption after a parenthesis is not uncommon, cf. n.172. Those referred to are given as the Peripatetics, DL 7.127, but it would appear generally obvious that one man may have more wisdom and goodness than another, whether taken together or separately.

195 act rightly or wrongly to a greater degree: so Chrysippus (DL 7.101) on there being no *anesis* ('lowering') or *epitasis* ('heightening') in the intensity of what is good, cf. Seneca *Ep* 66.8 – 'nihil inuenies rectius recto ... quid accedere perfecto potest?' ('you will find nothing righter than right ... what can enhance that which is perfect?'), DL 7.127 – according to the Stoics, 'just as a stick must be either straight or crooked, so a man must be either just or unjust', and Cicero *Paradox* III.26 – 'I cannot listen to someone who is only slightly out of tune'. One is either virtuous or not, and once there, there is no 'better' or 'worse'. The physical aspect of being in a state of virtue is to have the *psyche* in the correct tension ('habitus', *hexis*), and this again can have no degrees. Wisdom and goodness are interchangeable here, since wisdom organises the soul harmoniously; it brings it into accord with nature as a whole, and the condition of being in such accord is the state of virtue.

196 Just as drowning men: the first of two striking similes to show that there can be no intermediate state, cf. Plutarch *adv Stoic* 1063a, and also the different version at DL 7.120 quoting Chrysippus (*Ethical Questions* book 4): 'A man a hundred stades from Canopus and a man one stade away are equally not in Canopus, so too he who commits the greater sin and he who commits the less are equally not on the path of right conduct.' Cf. the extract from *Pro Murena* given in the Appendix, and Plutarch's essay *Against the Stoics on common conceptions* passim, and in support cf. *Paradox* III.

197   just as a puppy: The similes are slightly different in Plutarch (1063a): 'Just as a man in the sea being an arm's length from the surface is drowning no less than one who has sunk five hundred fathoms ... just as the blind are blind even if they are going to see again a little later, so those who are making progress, right up to when they seize on virtue, stay foolish and immoral'.

The substitution of the puppy (who is blind for a short time after birth) makes the simile more exact as well as more engaging.

198 about to open his eyes: 'appropinquat' is the editors' emendation of the MSS 'ut propinquat', and in the next line 'ad uirtutis habitum' is an old correction for 'ad uirtutis aditum (additum R)'.

199 some progress towards the state of virtue: A consequence of these 'paradoxes' that all right actions are equal and similarly all wrong ones, and that there can be no degrees of virtue or vice, was that progress was impossible. In practice. however, and especially in the Romanisation of the strict tenets of the early Greek Stoics by Panaetius, more emphasis came to be placed on progress (*prokopē*) through the indifferents towards what is more in accordance with nature than on the gulf separating the indifferents from virtue, cf. the simile of the king's court, sect. 52.

XV. 48. contd. *The 'extension' of virtue and vice*

200 both can be expanded and extended: It has been shown that virtue does not admit of degrees, one is either in the state of virtue or out of it, either in tune or out of tune. However the concession is made that although one cannot be more or less good, one's goodness can have more or less scope, as Seneca speaks of 'broad' and 'narrow' virtue ('uirtus lata' and 'uirtus arta' *Ep* 74.28). A king may not be 'better' (i.e. more virtuous) than a beggar but his good actions have a broader range – his wealth gives him opportunities for generosity, and his power the means to dispense justice, cf. *Off* 2.52-3. Conversely a scoundrel in high office has wider scope for doing harm – his malevolence and injustices may be on a grand scale.

XV. 49 - 50 *Digression on wealth and virtue*

201 Diogenes: Diogenes of Babylon (c. 240 – 152 b.c.), pupil of Chrysippus, and head of the Stoic school after Zeno of Tarsus. He was influential in bringing Stoicism to Rome, both by being one of the 'embassy of the philosophers' in 155, and particularly through his pupil Panaetius, cf. n.135.

202 wealth: This discussion on wealth interrupts the theoretical argument on the final good (hence the parenthesis), and belongs perhaps as a note to sect. 51 or with the separate discussion of reputation in 57, since wealth and reputation were the two most important and problematical of the external so-called 'goods', cf. n.213. It was especially difficult for the Romans to accept either wealth or 'bona fama' as indifferent, which is probably why Cato gives each separate treatment.

203 even granting: The MSS 'ut in ea' is emended to 'uti ea' ('uti' as the old form of 'ut') by Baiter, and editors generally, cf. Martha (Budé) app. crit. p. 34 and the translation – 'mais encore de les tenir dans leur dépendance'. (Martha also offers a justification for keeping the paragraph in its place here, as dealing with external 'goods' after the physical ones.)

204 act as a guide: Wealth may be a means for physical and external advantages (including pleasure), but has no essential connection with the good, being at best a 'guide' towards it ('dux'); cf. on wealth as a sub-division of plus-value indifferents, n.233. (Some Stoics thought that courting the rich was an acceptable occupation, cf. DL 7.189, and Aristotle *Rhet* 1391a10.)

205 but if wisdom is a good: 'at' generally for the MSS 'aut'. In the next sentence MS P has 'cogitationes' for 'cognitiones', and in sect.50 the majority have 'commendationis' for 'commentationis'.

206 cognitions and comprehensions ... awaken desire: for the technical terms (which are alternative translations of *katalēpseis*) cf. n.61. 'Appetitio', here 'proper desire', is stimulated by what is in accordance with nature and leads to the emergence of reason (cf. *Fin* 4.48, *Ac* 2.24), and so is the basis for both virtue and the skills.

207 even if we grant: The whole rather involved argument is in two sections with subdivisions: (A) (i) if wealth is necessary for health and pleasure, if they are goods then wealth is, but they are not, so wealth is not a (physical or external) good; (ii) virtue is the only good, wealth is not essential for virtue, therefore wealth is not a (moral) good. (B) If virtue is a skill, skills need money, therefore virtue needs money, but (i) skills connect not with money but with cognitions of the sensible world which arouse (proper) desire in the rational mind, and (ii) virtue, although comparable to a skill, differs in that (a) it is wholly rational ('requires deep meditation') and (b) continues unremittingly ('involves steadfastness, strength and perserverance'), cf. the general argument, notes 94-103.

XV. 50 contd. *The theory of difference*

208 Aristo: often connected with Pyrrho for his denial of any distinction at all among the non-moral indifferents, cf. the quotation at Sextus *Math* 11.64: 'without exception things indifferent between virtue and vice have no difference at all', and the comparison to alphabet letters, none of which has priority by nature, but only according to the context. On the resulting carefully chaotic life, especially of Pyrrho, cf. n.34.

209 no function ... for wisdom to perform: cf. Erillus at *Fin* 5.23, who 'in saying that there was no good but knowledge ('scientia') destroyed every motive for rational thought and every context for appropriate action'. But for the Stoics it was knowledge of the comparative relativity of the indifferents as aspects of the working of nature that produced the correct mental attitude towards them. It may well have been the disagreement on this very topic that caused Zeno to leave the Cynics.

210 make any choice: Theoretical wisdom's reflection on nature results in practical wisdom selecting correctly what is according to nature and rejecting the opposite, and, from the converse position, progress can be made towards wisdom by acquiring the habit of appropriate choice along nature's guidelines, otherwise 'practical wisdom will be useless', cf. n.133.

211 a distinction does exist: for the preliminary report on the sub-division of indifferents cf. on sect. 20; a more detailed theory now emerges. Virtue is the only good and secures happiness, vice is the only evil and ensures misery; what about everything else? If everything else is absolutely indifferent (as for Pyrrho and Aristo) then life becomes chaotic, wisdom is useless, and there is no guide for day to day living. To combat this, i.e. to bring order into the conduct of life, to expand wisdom's scope and to help with daily, non-moral decisions, all that was not virtue or vice, the *adiaphora* or 'media', were sub-divided. As long as it was borne in mind that the indifferents were not in any true sense 'profitable', that they could not contribute to happiness or misery, and that their value was only relative and on a non-moral level, then they could be divided into (a) those according to nature, with plus value, to be preferred, (b) those contrary to nature with minus value to be rejected, and (c) those that were completely indifferent. For examples in each category cf. notes 213-5, and for the connection with appropriate action notes 242-6.

212 to some neither: Cicero does not give any examples in this category, and the two known are whether the hairs on the head are odd or even, and whether a finger points in this direction or not, cf. DL 7.104, Sextus *Math* 11.59.

XV. 51 *Examples of difference*

213 given a plus value: For Zeno 'good things are wisdom, self-control, justice, courage and everything which either is virtue or partakes of it; evil things are foolishness, lack of self-control, injustice, cowardice and everything which either is vice or partakes of it; indifferents are as follows: life and death, reputation and lack of it, pain and pleasure, wealth and poverty, disease and health and the like' (Stobaeus 2.7.5a). Indifferents are then divided into those with plus value that are 'inherently according to nature' (physical advantages), or 'productive of what is according to nature' (external advantages), and their opposites, cf. n.68. Life itself is what is primarily according to nature, and then follow the accompanying physical advantages (cf. n.55). These are listed more comprehensively in *Ac* 1.19 as those physical goods of the Academics which have their starting-point in nature, and are said to differ in name only from Stoic *proēgmena* – health, strength and beauty of the whole, sound senses, and also particular excellence in the different parts, as speed in feet, strength in hands and clarity in voice. External advantages, 'productive of what is according to nature', include the problematic wealth and fame (cf. notes 202 and 235); the list at DL 7.106 adds 'noble birth' (*eugeneia*), although it is difficult to see how this could be a matter for selection, except for one's descendants. In a Roman context Cicero discusses military commands and consulships (*Rep* 1.27), and concludes that, provided that they are not taken up for profit or glory, they are not only preferable but necessary. The earlier list (DL 7.106) puts qualities of mind ahead of the physical and external categories within *proēgmena*, listing *euphuia* ('natural ability'), *technē* ('skill') and *prokopē* ('progress'), for which cf. sect.52..

   214   others not of this kind: There are no further details extant of this sub-division and its contrary. The *proēgmena* mentioned in the previous note have 'much value' and are worth preferring, these have 'sufficient' value, hardly enough to motivate their adoption, and similarly there are those with too little minus value to support their rejection. The five part scale of value in full would be: (i) of plus value, (ii) of sufficient value, (iii) completely indifferent, (iv) of less value, (v) of minus value.

   215   of minus value: the converse of 'plus value', and also divided into (i) physical disadvantages – death primarily, then pain, loss of sensation and (added at DL 7.106) disease, weakness, mutilation, ugliness and the like, (ii) external disadvantages – poverty, disgrace (the opposite of 'reputation') and low birth (balancing *eugeneia* above, exile would also be included), (iii) disadvantages of mind – lack of ability, lack of skill and similar. These are all contrary to nature and to be rejected, provided that there is no conflict with the overriding claims of virtue. Cf. further *Fin* 1.41 on the life of pain to be avoided in Epicureanism, and *Tusc* 3.81-3 on various kinds of 'distress' and the appropriate consolations.

   216   Zeno's distinction: Zeno's break with the Cynics was probably mainly due to his rejection of their extreme position in taking everything that was not virtue as worthless (cf. n.209). Zeno's reinstatement of some value among the indifferents, to enhance the physical condition and give material for practical wisdom and 'scope' for virtue, in turn caused the defection of Aristo. Zeno's position was reaffirmed by Hecato, Apollodorus and Chrysippus (DL 7.102), who further distinguished the Stoic stand on indifferents from Academic 'goods' by arguing that the *proēgmena* could be put to better or worse use and so could not count as 'good' (an argument that goes back to Plato's *Meno* 78c-e, that wealth is neutral, and gains its moral connotations from the ways in which it is acquired and used).

217 he still coined new words: for Zeno's vocabulary cf. *Fin* 5.90 on the subtleties of terminology but basic general agreement between Stoics and Academics on the scale of values and the predominance of virtue, also notes 13, 18 and 47.

XVI. 52 - 53 *The king and courtiers*

218 In a royal court: This famous simile illustrates the gulf between indifferents and the good, the sub-divisions of indifferents, and the theme of progress (*prokopē*). The setting would be particularly appropriate to the court of the Great King, i.e. the King of Persia, where the monarchy was hereditary, and so was not only the highest ranking office but of a different kind; promotion and demotion however would be possible among the courtiers according to a strict protocol, cf. Stobaeus 2.7.7g: 'In a court the *proēgmenoi* do not include the king, but they are ranked in line (*tetagmenoi*) after him.

219 those who have some state office: They have duties, responsibilities and powers which give them status, but this is still negligible beside that of the king (for example. they would all have to prostrate themselves before him).

220 what takes first place: 'primorie loco' codd., 'primo ordine' Madvig, 'primo loco' Heine.

221 "promoted": Latin translations for *proēgmena* are 'producta', 'promota', 'praeposita' and 'praecipua', and of *apoproēgmena* 'remota' and 'reiecta'.

222 "indifferent, but with some value": In the simile the king is supreme and corresponds to the good (virtue); the courtiers, who are all second but have different ranks, correspond to what has plus value. These are morally neutral in themselves and neither harm nor benefit, but have more or less value relative to their use, and as means to the end. When morality is not involved, 'preferential reason' (*proēgmenos logos* cf. Stobaeus 2.7.7g) grades them, and suggests their adoption in so far as they are according to nature. Progress is then possible (like promotion through the ranks) towards the highest state of (the non-moral) life – that of habitual selection of what is most according to nature. Roman Stoics in particular tended to emphasis the theme of progress rather than that of the great divide between the virtuous and non-virtuous.

223 this residue: The 'praeposita' are reached by a process of division: (i) everything into good, evil and indifferent, (ii) indifferents into what is according to nature and what contrary, (iii) what is according to nature into what has sufficient and what has much value (cf.n.214), (iv) what has much value belongs in the category of 'praeposita' (comparable to those closest to the king) and then further ranking of these by 'preferential reason' is possible (cf. previous note).

XVI. 54 *The illustration of the dice*

224 throw a dice: A 'talus' ('dice') made of stone or bronze (and so called from the small foot bone that was originally used) had four flat sides, one opposite pair broader and the other narrower, with rounded ends. Numbers 3 and 4 were marked on the former, and 1 and 6 on the latter. Four 'tali' were usually thrown together – the best score ('Venus') was to have four different numbers facing up, the worst ('canis' 'dog') has to have four the same. There was also a cube dice ('tessera') marked out with dots for numbers on each of the six faces (as the modern one), three 'tesserae' were thrown together with similar scoring. Cf. *Div* 2.85 where casting lots is compared to playing with 'tali' or 'tesserae'. and 1.23 where, if four 'tali' are thrown and a 'Venus' results, that is due to chance, but obviously not if this happens a hundred times in a hundred throws.

225 so that it falls upright: If the 'talus' were to fall 'rectus' initially this would be a preliminary advantage, but to stay 'rectus' (i.e. on a narrower side) would be more difficult. Cicero's point can be taken more easily from the more familiar 'tessera': if the aim is to cast a '6', any other number is irrelevant, but a '5' is closer than a '1'.

226 similarly: The good would then be comparable to the '6', and the *proēgmena* ranking '1' to '5'. As in the royal court simile, some are closer to the top grade than others, but how close is essentially irrelevant.

XVI. 55 *Ends and means*

227 the division of goods: Further details of the kinds of 'praeposita' follow in sect.56, but first Cato gives a brief summary of the division of true (i.e. moral) goods into final, instrumental and both; for the Greek sources cf. DL 7.96, Stobaeus 2.7.5k and also b-h.

228 (i) *telika*: what is essentially related to the end or goal, namely 'right actions' – 'honestae actiones' (along with 'recte / recta facta' and 'officia perfecta' as translations of *katorthōmata*), cf. notes 79 and 189.

229 (ii) *poiētika* instrumental, or means to the end. The only example Cato gives is of a friend (the DL passage adds 'and the advantages derived from him', and Stobaeus 'and also a prudent man' (as n.227); cf. the discussion of friendship at sect.70, with the problems arising from using a friend too obviously as a means.

230 (iii) **those which are both**: wisdom above all, for harmonious living is the goal, and this is having the wisdom (*logos*) of the soul in harmony with itself and with the cosmos as a whole, cf. notes 77 and 133. It is the means in that the wisdom of the moral agent necessarily ensures that his actions are right, and, as practical wisdom (*phronēsis*, 'prudentia') is productive of them. The passages from Stobaeus and Diogenes Laertius include all the virtues as ends and means (and obviously so as they are aspects of wisdom, cf. n.99) but also suggest more complex divisions. There are goods of 'process' that are not virtues, such as joy, cheerfulness and confidence, of 'state' like well-ordered leisure, stability and concentration, and of 'character' which include the cardinal virtues as skills and other non-skill virtues like greatness of soul. From another point of view the virtues are *hexeis* ('conditions', or as Long and Sedley translate 'tenors'), as are love of music, literature and geometry. And there are corresponding lists of genera and species of evil (cf. Zeller's exhaustive footnote, p.21, and Long and Sedley sect. 60). Such lists show indulgence in detail for its own sake; Cato confines himself to the main guidelines, here and in the following section.

231 **essentially related**: <in> is added before 'illo genere' by Davison, and 'id' deleted before 'efficiens' by Bayter, cf. Martha (Budé) app. crit.

XVII. 56 *The sub-divisions of the class of things preferred*

232 **preferred** (i) **on their own account**: The example – 'a certain style of feature and expression, stance and deportment' is covered by the quality of 'grauitas', so important to the Romans. Expression and deportment indicating 'grauitas' are to be chosen in preference to those which do not, but in the wise man they would be the consistent outward expression of inner harmony. The 'praeposita' which are to be chosen *per se* are intrinsic to him as *epigennēmatika* of his virtuous status and activity, cf. n.103. The type of deportment desirable for itself as according to nature is elaborated at *Fin* 5.35: 'There is a certain form of bodily activity

which keeps movement and posture in harmony with nature, and any error in these, due to distortion or deformity or abnormality – for example if a man were to walk on his hands, or backwards instead of forwards – would make him appear alienated from himself, as if he had stripped off his proper humanity and hated his own nature. Some kinds of sitting and slouching suggest a physical perversion of human nature, whereas controlled and well-regulated deportment shows that one is in harmony with nature' (trans. from Rackham).

233 (ii) for their effects: The one example is, somewhat surprisingly, money, but the ground has already been cleared for its inclusion, cf. sect.49; the just and wise use of wealth extends the scope of virtue and benefits one's fellow men, cf. sect.65.

234 (iii) for themselves and their effects: Sound senses and good health are included in this category, cf. n.60. They are to be selected as being according to nature, as having advantageous effects, and as being appropriate ends in themselves, all on this non-moral level.

XVII. 57 *The classification of reputation*

235 a good reputation: Where does 'bona fama' belong in the division of indifferents? The early Stoics, including Chrysippus and Diogenes (of Babylon, cf. n.201) counted it as completely different, following the Cynics and the other Diogenes in his blatant disregard for what people thought of him, cf. DL 7.115: '(The Stoics) said that as there were certain infirmities of the body, like gout and arthritis, so there is in the soul love of fame (*philodoxia*)'.

236 apart from its utility: For 'detracta' MSS B and E have 'detractata quidem'; presumably the 'utility' lies in the great 'scope' for virtue a man of reputation has to influence others (cf. n.200).

237 stretching out a finger for: The phrase occurs twice in Plutarch allegedly quoting Stoic theory – 'We ought not to extend a finger for the sake of *phronēsis*' (*Stoic rep* 1046d), and 'the non-wise man does not even extend a finger for the sake of (the good)' (*adv Stoic* 1061f).

238 the Stoics who came after them: There appear to be no details extant of a confrontation between Carneades and the Stoics on this topic. Presumably the shift of reputation from the category of completely indifferent to 'praeposita' that are 'preferred for their own sake' (n.232) was made or approved by Panaetius to counter contradictions pointed out by Carneades, and in the general modification of extreme Stoic doctrine to the Roman context.

239 adopted for its own sake: Although Cato as Cicero portrays him is not concerned with reputation, Cicero's own position was ambiguous. On a personal basis he was, or had been earlier, very concerned about it (even writing an epic poem on his own consulship), and it features significantly in his defence of Archias. In *Tusculans* 1 the interest of political leaders, poets and artists in their enduring fame is taken as evidence of awareness after death (cf. 1.32-34, 91 and Douglas' notes ad loc), later it is seen as a consolation: 'Death is faced with most serenity when the failing life can console itself with the reputation it has won ... the dead, although without sensation, are not without their own 'goods' of praise and glory ... glory may have nothing in itself to justify desiring it, but it follows virtue like a shadow' (*Tusc* 1.109; cf. the glory won by his son that consoled Achilles, Homer *Od* 11.540). In *Tusculans* 3 (3.3-4) Cicero distinguishes a 'phantom' glory dependent on fickle public opinion from the true one – 'the agreed approval of good men, the impartial verdict of judges deciding honestly on outstanding merit; it returns to virtue the echo of her voice, and, because it usually accompanies right actions ('recte facta', Cicero's translation of *katorthōmata*) good men should not disdain it'.

    240 the interests of our children: MSS BE read 'non dicuntque propter usumque ut' which transfers 'propter usum' from the individual's fame to his children. On the duties towards one's heirs, cf. on sect.65.

    241 we shall still have: 'tamen' emphasises the preceding phrase with concessive implication: 'still – although we will not be alive to enjoy it'. In contrast the 'Dream of Scipio' preaches the insignificance of fame, both spatially, in the limited area of the inhabited world it can reach, and temporally, cf. Cicero *Rep* 6.21-4.

XVII. 58 *Appropriate actions*

    242 to perform appropriate action: The concept of 'officium' (*kathēkon*) was introduced in sect.20, where the first appropriate action was said to be to keep in one's natural condition, and the second to hold to what is according to nature and reject the opposite. When appropriate actions become habitual, guided by maturing reason and in harmony with nature, circumstances are ripe for the emergence of the good. 'Officia' are morally neutral, involving neither good nor evil, but result from appropriate choice derived from reason and following nature. Such choices are common to wise and non-wise alike in day to day living, where courses of action continually have to be adopted or rejected; the guiding principle for the rational agent is consistent selection of what is according to nature, rejection of what is contrary.

243 **on this neutral level**: 'in his rebus'. Although not concerned with right or wrong, 'officia' involve reason to a greater or less extent and can be ranked by being given more or less approval in a way comparable to the ranking according to value of the corresponding 'praeposita'. Approval for 'officia', like the value of 'praeposita', derives from the principle of their accord with nature, cf. *Fin* 4.48: 'What is according to nature provides the motive for conduct and appropriate action'.

244 **a rational explanation of the performance**: the standard criterion for 'officium' (*kathēkon*), cf. DL 7.107, Stobaeus 2.7.7g and the requirement of *eulogos apologia*, *Off* 1.8 'ratio probabile' and *Ac* 1.37. More explicitly this is of *kathēkon meson* ('officium medium'), which is contrasted with *katorthōma* ('recte factum' or 'officium perfectum', cf. n.79).

245 **Since ... neither good nor evil**: This section looks suspiciously like an alternative, perhaps earlier and less precise version of the previous paragraph. It reduplicates the main points (and in the last clause the precise wording), namely that there are morally neutral actions between virtues and vices called 'officia' which have some advantage and so are to be approved and adopted; this advantage stems from their being motivated and performed according to the dictates of reason.

XVIII. 59 *Appropriate action is common to all*

246 **sometimes acts on this neutral level**: cf. *Off* 3.15 for 'officia' as 'sort of second level right actions' ('secunda quaedam honesta'), not belonging exclusively to the wise but common to all who are innately inclined towards virtue ('uirtutis indoles', cf. on n.63). Standard Roman heroes are listed not as being wise in the strict Stoic sense, but, because of their consistent observance of 'media officia', they have the semblance ('species') of wise men; cf. n.72 on habitual appropriate choice which becomes unwavering and in harmony with nature. The 'officium' of the wise man is 'medium' in that it is concerned with indifferents, but also 'perfectum' (and so *katorthōma*) because (i) he brings infallible judgment to bear on the situation, and (ii) he has inner psychic harmony, and it is the psychic state and the related will or intention rather than the act itself that provides the moral criterion. The theory is something like that of the Christian 'state of grace', where the soul's being in the right relation with God gives a special lustre to ordinary activities; cf. Bevan *Stoics*, 73-4: 'The *kathēkonta* set before the common man are not a different set of duties, a different scheme of action, from those set before the sage ... but neutral, becoming good only when filled with the spirit put into them by the wise man'.

247 **action imperfectly performed:** A second 'autem' between 'erit' and 'etiam' was deleted by Lambinus, who also changed 'facit' in the next line but one to 'fit'. For the example and conditions which can make returning a deposit a wrong action cf. Plato *Rep* 332a. The point is that returning a deposit is basically neutral although 'praepositum', the sort of action performed by someone progressing towards virtue. It is only a moral act when the agent is virtuous and knows what is rightly due (i.e. exercises justice as an aspect of wisdom). That the morality of giving lies in the intention rather than the act itself can be illustrated by comparing the widow's mite to the Pharisee's largesse; cf. also the discussion in Long and Sedley ii. 359).

248 **From this:** The argument runs: (i) some things (those according to nature) are 'praeposita' and to be adopted, and this adoption is appropriate action; (ii) the primary impulse for self-preservation (starting from self-love, cf. n.54) is common to all; (iii) the primary impulse motivates the adoption of what is according to nature, therefore (iv) all (the wise and the unwise) perform appropriate action.

249 **what we call the neutral level:** When virtue and vice are not involved, all are open to adopt what is according to nature, so appropriate action for wise and unwise covers primarily selecting the physical benefits first of staying alive, and then keeping in health and avoiding what is harmful (in contrast to the chaotic lives of Pyrrho and Aristo), then, in maturity, also taking up the advantages and performing the duties connected with more complex *proēgmena*; these will be detailed in the remaining sections of the book.

XVIII. 60 - 61 *Suicide*

250 **the question of leaving life:** If life, like everything else on the non-moral level, is basically indifferent, then the most primarily practical question is whether to stay in life or not – is suicide ever justified as an 'officium', an appropriate act? Socrates in the *Phaedo* (62a) is quite definite: god has positioned us like soldiers on guard duty, and we are not to leave until he gives the sign and imposes *anankē* ('necessity'). (Socrates himself was a suicide in that, according to Athenian law, he had to administer his own death in the form of drinking the hemlock, but Plato's *Apology*, and Xenophon's much more so, hint at Socrates deliberately courting death by delivering a provocative defence.) Cicero himself adopts the *Phaedo* line in the 'Dream of Scipio', cf. *Rep* 6.15: 'you must not abandon human life except at the behest

of him by whom it was given you'. Cato, the Stoic spokesman here, two years previously had committed a dramatic suicide (stabbing himself after reading the *Phaedo*) rather than submit to Caesar at Utica. Cicero attributes his suicide to strength of character, suitable for Cato, but perhaps not for his companions: 'Cato had been endowed by nature with "grauitas" beyond belief, which he had himself strengthened with unwavering consistency, always staying true to his purpose with fixed resolve, and so it was fitting for him to die rather than look on the face of the tyrant' (*Off* 1.112, cf. Plutarch *Cato* 67-70). Brutus, to whom *De Finibus* was dedicated, would kill himself two years hence, after his defeat at Philippi in 42 b.c., and ten years later Cicero's friend Atticus ended his life to avoid further illness.

251 the appropriate action is to stay alive: Life and death are indifferent, neither good nor evil on Stoic theory (cf. *Tusc* 1.85-95 on the consolation that death is not an evil), and the Cynics and early Stoics were ready to show this by their actions. According to the tradition Zeno, after breaking his toe in a fall, which he saw as a 'sign' that it was time for him to go, held his breath until he died. Cleanthes turned a medically recommended fast into terminal starvation – as death was indifferent he 'might as well' continue (cf. DL 7.28, 176). Sometimes the argument went the other way – if death was indifferent a wise man had no motive to kill himself. There was for example an interchange with Pyrrho which the Cynics and early Stoics may well have approved – when asked why he did not die if death did not matter, Pyrrho replied 'because it does not matter'. But when life was seen as having 'plus value', being in the class of 'praeposita', then living or dying became a question of calculation on the non-moral level – if one's life 'for the most part' was according to nature, then one should stay, if for the most part contrary to nature then 'withdraw from a house that is no longer weather-proof'. (The Epicureans talked of departing at the end of a banquet, or being ready to go when one's 'lease' on life was finished, cf. Lucr 3.938-9, 971; for the Stoics one could leave the 'banquet of life' in mid-course, cf. the references at *SVF* 3.768, and also n.252 below.)

252 or seems likely to be so: 'Rational departure' (*eulogos exagogē*) from life was justified in the service of one's country or to save a friend (and for this cf. the Roman tradition of 'deuotio' – the commander sacrificing himself for his country's victory); as far as oneself was concerned pain, mutilation or disease were reasonable causes (because the life according to nature was no longer possible without health and sound senses), to avoid being compelled to a wrong action (cf. 'death before dishonour') or for incipient insanity (the last two would mean the life of virtue was no longer possible, cf. DL 7.130, Stobaeus 2.7.11, Clement *Strom* 2.6; also Diogenes the Cynic – 'reason or the rope' DL 6.24). Refusal to submit to tyranny was also a justification, and particularly appropriate in Rome, starting with Cato's opposition to Caesar, and then with the Stoics in the empire. Whatever the motive, death was not seen as a form of cowardice, or escapism from life's ills (as with Aristotle, cf. *EN* 1138a9), but to show indifference to life or (especially with the later Stoics) as an expression of moral freedom – the occasion *par excellence* for a display of fortitude and philosophic calm. The motives for suicide and voluntary self-sacrifice in Attic tragedy are also relevant: Jocasta, Deianeira and Ajax died from shame, Phaedra from shame, and to protect her honour and the status of her children, Evadne from love of Capaneus, Antigone for her brother, Alcestis her husband, Macaria to save her country, and Iphigeneia for the freedom of Greece. Cato's famous 'last words' were in the tradition of heroic death-speeches in tragedy as well as those of philosophers.

253 to stay alive although wretched: If life for the most part was according to nature, i.e. if one were healthy and with sound senses, with a modicum of wealth, well-spoken of and the like, and since length of time was irrelevant (cf. n.190) the non-wise might as well stay alive. Plutarch found this position absurd, cf. *Stoic rep* 1042c-d, *adv Stoic* 1063 c-d, 1064c-f.)

254 wisdom's subject matter: cf. n.209 – the indifferents give a role to practical wisdom by providing the subject-matter for selection and rejection in relation to what is according to nature and what contrary.

255 that a man stays alive: A lacuna is generally assumed in the clause which would provide a subject for 'retinetur' (hence <ille> Schiche), although the verb could be taken as impersonal passive – 'it is not because of virtue that there is a staying / being held in life'; Madvig suggests an expansion: 'neque is qui uirtute utitur retinetur', but with un–Ciceronian lack of elegance.

256 i.e. in accordance with nature: It is preferable to leave life once the 'suitable exit' (*eulogos exagogē*) has been determined by the calculus of what is according to nature *versus* what is not. (Madvig, followed by Martha, transposed this parenthesis to the end of the sentence as a gloss on 'beate uiuere' rather than 'opportune facere'.)

257 ought to stay alive: cf. n.251 above, and in general Rist's chapter on Stoic suicide (*Stoic Philosophy*, 233-55), and Miriam Griffin's comprehensive articles on 'Philosophy, Cato and Roman suicide' (*G & R* 1986, 64-77, 192-202). The injury that the unjust

man has done to his soul is not only out of all proportion to any
physical or external disadvantages, but belongs on a different level.
Once a man's psychic state is wrong true misery follows, despite
apparent prosperity, and so whether he lives or dies is irrelevant.
The reasoning here is the logical extension of the Socratic *dictum*
that there is no compensation for harm to the soul (i.e. injustice in
the general sense of vice) in any wordly 'goods', cf. *Gorgias* 527b,
Apol 28d, *Crito* 49b-d.

XIX. 62 - 63   *Parental love as the natural basis for social
relations*
   258   **love of parents for their children:** According to the
oikeiōsis theory (cf. notes 53-56) the infant primarily feels
attachment for himself, and his first natural instinct is for
self-preservation. But almost immediately the mother too is seen as
belonging to himself, so the instincts of self-love and
self-preservation extend to her. Then, as the child grows through
adolescence to maturity, there is further expansion - to the family,
then to the extended family and local community, to the state and
finally the world-state, the 'cosmopolis' (cf. n.273; for the ever
widening circles cf. Hierocles in Stobaeus 4.27.23, and also
Aurelius 3.1.9 on *oikeiōsis pros anthropous*). From the mother's
point of view her child is naturally and instinctively 'her own', and
this symbiotic bonding is similarly a microcosm of community, state
and world-state affiliations.
   259   **men living together:** as for Aristotle man is a *politikon
zōon*, i.e. an animate creature designed by nature to live in a
political community; for the Stoic *politeia* cf. Plutarch *fort Alex*
329c. Cicero, with his own political interests, is especially
concerned with this topic, cf. *Off* 1.12: (As a consequence of
parental love) 'nature prompts men to form communities and
political associations, and to take part in them himself'. His work
on *Laws* has a similar foundation, starting from book 1: 'We are
born for justice, and law ('ius') is based not on opinion but on
nature, which can be clearly understood from the fellowship and
community of men, for nothing is more like than we to one
another' (*Leg* 1.28); cf. also *Fin* 5.65: 'Nothing is more glorious or
wider-ranging than the fellowship of men, the alliance and sharing
of interests and love itself ('caritas ipsa') of man for man. This
starts immediately on birth, since children are loved by their
parents and the household is bound by the ties of marriage and
parenthood; it then spreads gradually beyond the home to relatives,
in-laws, friends, neighbours, fellow-citizens and political allies, and
ends by embracing the whole human race'.

260 the structure of our bodies: for the teleology of nature cf. notes 55, and 265 below.

261 then make no provision: cf. *Off* 1.11 for nature endowing every living creature with the instinct for self-preservation, and, extending from that, the instincts for reproduction and care for the young. The argument that 'nature does nothing in vain' was first used for primary *oikeiōsis* (nature would not bring living creatures into existence and not give them the means to survive through the instinct of self-preservation), and is repeated in this second context: our bodies are designed by nature for the procreation of children, and it would be absurd for nature to have this design without providing for the children to be cared for, therefore nature impels parents to love and care for their offspring.

262 even in animals: As with primary *oikeiōsis* the principle in its first stages includes animals as well as human families. Animals suffer distress in giving birth to and rearing their young (the screams of labour are the very cry of nature), and this impulse, the desire for a child and its well-being, overcomes the pain of childbirth and the anxieties and risks involved in caring for the young. Interesting examples of animals caring for their young (including turtles and crocodiles) as a result of nature's providence are given in *De Natura Deorum* 2.129.

263 no man should be seen as a stranger to another: cf. Terence *The Self-Tormentor* 77: 'homo sum, nihil humani a me alienum puto' ('I am a man, and nothing to do with men is foreign to me'), spoken by the old Chremes as an excuse for interfering in his neighbour's private life. Cicero also quotes the line at *Leg* 1.33, and cf. *Off* 1.50 on the basic principle of the 'societas' of the whole human race, developed further in 3.26-27. The Stoic theory of social relations, which Cicero approves in his own right as well as in the *persona* of Cato, was that men are equal by nature, there are no class distinctions or slaves by nature, but all aim at the same end, are subject to the same law, and are endowed with reason, therefore we are all parts of one connected whole. Consequently (i) in benefiting others we benefit ourselves, and (ii) the love and care we show to our neighbour (even our enemy) is of the same kind, and has the same source, as the love and care that parents show towards their children.

XIX. 18 *Comparative usefulness of bodily parts*

264 some of the limbs: Section 18 has been moved from its position after 17, where it is obviously out of place in the theoretical discussion of rational activity. This seems to be its most appropriate context, since the need men have for each other is illustrated (i) from interdependent parts of the body ('membra' here as in the next note) and (ii) mutual help in the animal world.

265 hands, legs and feet: Such parts of the body are to help each other and the whole, cf. *ND* 2.134-5 for the *telos* of parts of the body, and also *Fin* 5.35; the theory is first given in detail in Plato's *Timaeus* 69-81 and developed by Aristotle, e.g. *Phys* 2.8; for social cooperation as the functioning of a living organsim cf. *Off* 3.22, and for the amputation of diseased parts from the body politic (such as tyrants) cf. 3.32.

266 a kind of decoration: for the peacock cf. Plutarch *Stoic rep* 1044c-d on Chrysippus, where the beauty of the peacock's tail is nature's sole aim here, and where it is even suggested that the peacock is for the sake of the tail. (Cherniss's note to the Loeb text, *Plutarch's Moralia* xiii, 503 is instructive, with a list of ancient criticisms of this kind of teleology).

267 a man's breasts and beard: The examples are Peripatetic, cf. Aristotle *PA* 688a19, Theophrastus *Met* 10b7-8 and 10.

XIX. 63 contd. *Examples from the animal world*

268 Some limbs have been produced for themselves: A refinement on the previous point: some limbs help the body as a whole, as legs to walk on, hands to work with; others, like eyes and ears, have a similar use - to guide the body, give warning of danger and the like, but they are also ends in themselves when eyes are used for looking at beautiful sights and ears for hearing beautiful sounds.

269 the mussel called the "pina": Large animals can manage on their own, cooperation among smaller creatures illustrates the need members of the human race have for each other, and the dependence of their societies on mutual help. A pina is a mussel that clings to rocks with beard-like filaments, and the pinatores a kind of small shrimp that lives in its beard (rather than in the shell itself); the mussel gives the shrimp protection and the shrimp in return acts as a warning 'look-out' for its host, cf. Aristotle *HA* 547b28 (and *pinophulax* 547b16), Plutarch *soll an* 980b, Aristophanes *Wasps* 1510, Pliny *NH* 9.142; at Cicero *ND* 2.123 the cooperation is for food collecting - the shrimp looks out for food, the mussel traps it, and the two feed together.

270 ants, bees and storks: Ants and bees are standard examples of job allocation and mutual cooperation in animal communities, the ants on their hill and bees in their hive. Storks are less obviously so, but because they nest and migrate together they have a community life.

271 Much closer is the bond: Natural affiliations in groups of animals bring them to live and work together in communities for mutual advantage and the good of the whole; much closer (surely) are the natural ties which bind men to each other in the organisation and administration of social groupings and political states, with all contributing to the general welfare. Such idealism is poignant in the mouth of Cato, who fought and died in civil war.

XIX. 64 *The cosmopolis and related duties*

272 The universe is governed by divine will: This is a central Stoic thesis from Cleanthes' *Hymn to Zeus* to Seneca's *De Prouidentia*, and was set out most forcefully in Cicero by the Stoic spokesman Balbus: 'I believe that the world and all parts of the world were structured at the beginning and are governed at all time by the providence of the gods ('prouidentia deorum' – i.e. the collective will of the gods, also encapsulated in Zeus/Jupiter, *ND* 2.75, 133 and cf. *Paradox* II). The main arguments were from the existence of gods, whose wisdom and power ensured all for the best, from animate nature pursuing ordered generation and growth, and from the wonder of the world's design. Apparent evils could be accounted for as 'blessings in disguise' or in the long run for the general good. The counter-position was summed up succinctly by Lucretius: there can be no divine providence because the nature of the world is so very imperfect – 'tanta stat praedita culpa (2.181).

273 city or state belonging jointly to gods and men: Such citizenship was based on the common possession of reason and of respect for law, cf. *ND* 2.154 – 'the world is as a home that men and gods share, or as a city for both', and also *Leg* 1.23. Historically the concept of the world-city or *cosmopolis* began with the Cynics, and may well have been influenced by Macedonian policies of breaking down state boundaries and bringing together Greek and barbarian, cf. Plutarch *Alex* 45, Arrian *Alex* 7.11. When the *imperium Romanum* was practically co-extensive with world empire, the Roman citizenship could be seen as world citizenship, cf. Aurelius 'the *cosmos* is as a *polis*' 4.3.2. The Stoics could include slaves as slavery was due to fortune not character, cf. *Paradox* V. On the whole question cf. Baldry *Unity of Mankind*, esp. 151-66 and G.R. Stanton 'The cosmopolitan ideas of Epictetus and Marcus Aurelius' *Phronesis* 13 (1968), 183-95.

274 looks to the general interest: The citizens of a *polis* obeys its laws and respects the rights of his fellow-citizens. In the *cosmopolis* to which all belong it would follow that the rights of all men have to be respected. This may well be the origin of the concept of the rights of man or 'human rights', at least in the sense of civic and social rights transcending state boundaries, cf. Aurelius again 3.1.4 – 'it is in man's nature to care for all men', and Seneca *Clem* 2.5 – 'no school is more kindly or gentle <than the Stoics>, none more full of love for men or more concerned for the common good'.

275 he who betrays his country: The forceful phrasing here, that one who abandons the advantage and welfare of others in his own interest is more criminal than the 'proditor patriae' suggests a general understanding of the concept of 'human rights', cf. the discussion *Off* 3.21-26 where nature is aligned with the law of nations ('ius gentium'), and an unjust action is more contrary to nature than death, poverty or pain, and below, notes 314-5 on Law. 'utilitas' and 'salus' cover such basic requirements as Locke's 'life, liberty and property' (cf. n.298), or at least food, shelter and a minimum standard of living, cf. the details of the Universal Declaration on Human Rights, 1948.

276 fittingly more precious: The saying *cosmpolitēs eimi* ('I am a world-citizen') is attributed to Diogenes the Cynic (DL 6.63) and was probably read back from him to Socrates. Cicero uses the context in the *Tusculans* (5.108), not however with reference to the duties of world-citizenship but as a consolation in exile. But here he is more conscious of his definition of a *polis* at *Rep* 1.39 as an association 'with respect to justice and a partnership of the common good'. Personal *oikeiōsis* extends from self to family and eventually to *polis* and *cosmopolis* (cf. notes 53-55, 271 and below 300).

277   who suffers death for his community: The underlying sentiment is altruistic in the extreme. The *polis* or *patria* requires the lives of its citizens when threatened (cf. Plato *Crito* 51b), the cosmopolis that one holds any other human life dearer than one's own, cf. *Off* 3.27: 'If nature prescribes that one man looks to the interest of another man *whoever he might be* (quicumque sit), just because he is a man, the interests of all men, in accordance with that nature, are common; ... we are all subject to one and the same law of nature and, since this is so, wronging anyone else is forbidden by it.

278   a familiar line of Greek verse: ἐμοῦ θανόντος γαῖα μιχθήτω πυρί 'once I am dead let earth be mixed with fire' followed by – 'I don't care, I'm alright', cf. Nauck fr. 513, perhaps from Euripides' *Bellerophon*. The line is called 'an old saying' by Dio Cassius (58.23), uttered frequently by Tiberius, and also by Nero (cf. Suetonius *Nero* 38). Not to care if the world collapses after one's death is against humanity, cf. next note. According to Seneca the line is 'one of the many striking but odious sayings that have made their entry into human life and become famous' (*Clem* 2.2); cf. similarly 'après moi le déluge'.

279   take thought for those who will come after us: Humanitarian action should extend in space, beyond city boundaries, even when contrary to individual interest, and also in time, to future generations, even if irrelevant to individual profit. The issue, sometimes known as 'inter-generational justice', takes on new urgency in the present ecological crisis; cf. letters to *The Times* July 18 1989 and the drafting of a 'Universal Declaration of the Rights of Posterity'.

XX. 65 - 66   *The duty of material and intellectual bequests*

280   making wills: Basic instincts are at work here: biologically our genes struggle to reproduce themselves and ensure the survival of the species, morally there is an urge to care for our descendants, who are 'dear' to us. The attachment that children have instinctively for their parents (cf. the *oikeiôsis* references in note 276) is complemented by that of parents for their children, even post-humously. For the latter Cicero cites here the evidence of death-bed wills, at *Tusc* 1.31 adoptions and wills, but he also sees the wise law-giver as analogous to the farmer who plants trees of which he will never see the fruit.

281   life in complete isolation: Only animals (below men) and gods (above) were thought to be able to live alone, a concept which was fostered by the supposed related etymology between *therion* and *theos*.

282   a community according to nature: The observation that pleasures pall in isolation could be used by the Stoics to counter Epicurean hedonism and support the primacy of the instinct for men to gather into a community. This had been most famously expressed by Aristotle at *Pol* 1253a3, that man is 'naturally a political animal', i.e. a living creature born to live in political association with his like, cf. note 259.

283   principles of practical wisdom: Typically it is the principles of *prudentia* above all that the Roman Stoics wish to be handed on, so *Off.* 1.158: 'Every *officium* that safeguards the bonding and association of men is to be preferred to that arising from scientific theorising ('cognitio et scientia').

284   not only to learn, but also to teach: If living according to reason is the human *telos* (cf. notes 75, 77-8, 83, 91) then the fostering of reason is a natural instinct – in ourselves in learning, and in others in teaching. Teaching is a natural *officium*, and in fact the best service that we can render to others. (Again the idea is still current, as the duties of transferring 'practical wisdom' to the Third World are debated.)

XX. 66 contd. *The duty to protect the weak*

285 the natural condition of bulls to fight: As a consequence of putting the interests of others before one's own there comes the particular duty (seen here in terms of natural impulse) to protect the weak. There are *exempla* for this among both animals (below men) and gods above. Although lions are mentioned in the Homeric poems in similes and metaphors, and were perhaps at one time native to Greece and Italy, it is doubtful whether there could have been verification of the imposing confrontation cited here. Bulls tend rather to fight other bulls – for a heifer or for leadership of the herd.

286 Hercules: (the Greek Herakles), who travelled the world in his labours, clearing it of monsters and preparing for the emergence of civilisation, was a favourite hero first of the Cynics (Antisthenes allegorised the monsters slain as vices overcome) and then of the Stoics, cf. *Off* 3.25, and also *Tusc* 2.22, where Cicero translates the account of his final sufferings from Sophocles *Trachiniae*, and sets him with Philoctetes and Prometheus for his noble endurance of pain. cf. also Seneca's description: 'malorum hostis, bonorum uindex, terrarum marisque pacator', *Ben* 1.13.3.

287 Liber: an old Roman god who was assimilated to the Greek Dionysus/Bacchus, and, like Herakles, was born of Zeus' liaison with a mortal woman. He came from the East, and with the vine brought civilisation (later to include the theatre) to Europe; it was appropriate to connect his name with his activity as 'liberator'; cf. Cicero's explanation *ND* 2.62.

288 "Optimus" and "Maximus": "best" and "greatest", the main titles of Jupiter on the Capitoline, but he also took over the titles of the Greek Zeus, particularly appropriate for the Stoics as *sōtēr* ('salutaris' – 'saviour') and *xenios* ('hospitalis', patron of stranger-guests, who were especially vulnerable, and so under the care of the highest god.)

289 steadfastness in battle: A temple to 'Iuppiter Stator' ('holding firm') was erected to commemmorate Romulus' victory over the Sabines, cf. Livy 1.12.

290 his guardian care: Not only the security of Rome but the welfare of the whole human race depends on Jupiter. Zeus/Jupiter could for the Stoics be just another term for or aspect of *pronoia*/'prouidentia', cf. note 272 above.

291 no concern for one another: If we want the gods to love and care for us then it follows that we must ourselves love and care for others, a striking parallel to the precept 'do as you would be done by'. (There is a textual crux with 'uiles', Gruter's reading for 'cules' A, 'eules' R and 'ciuiles' BE.)

292 by nature we come together: a development of the metaphor of the 'body-politic'. As we use parts of our body to work for the whole without thinking about it, so we become functioning parts of a political association naturally, before understanding how or why, cf. n.265.

293 no scope for justice or benevolence: The society of one's fellow-men provides scope for the public virtue of 'iustitia' as citizens and for the personal 'beneuolentia' as individuals, cf. note 200.

XX. 67 *Man has no duty towards animals*

294 they do not think that law unites men and animals: According to Stoic doctrine (quoted DL 7.129) there are no rights (*mēden dikaion* 'nothing owed by law') that men need show to other living creatures because of their 'unlikeness', i.e. their lack of reason. At 7.107 however the Stoics maintain that even in plants and animals there can be seen appropriate actions (*kathēkonta*). In addition the arguments for *oikeiōsis* is based on the impulses common to animals and men, especially in self-preservation, family attachments, care for the young, and, in some cases, community life (cf. sect.63).

295 Chrysippus put this clearly: Diogenes gives his sources at 7.129 (see previous note) as Chrysippus, *On Justice* book 1, and Posidonius *On Appropriate Action* book 1; cf. also *ND* 2.61, 140-2, 154, *Off* 1.105 'how far superior man is by nature ...', *Leg* 1.23, 25, 36 (on no reason or virtue in animals, and man alone being erect), but also *Fin* 5.25-6 and 37-9 on the shared nature of men and animals, and *Off* 1.50 on animal courage, despite deficiency in reason and speech.

296 make use of animals for their own advantage: The Stoics argued that since animals have no reason (*logos*) they are outside the law; therefore they have no rights and men have no duties towards them. On the contrary plants and animals are for the use of man, sheep for example to provide warm clothing, dogs to keep watch, oxen to pull the plough, mules to carry, birds to give signs and many (along with plants) to provide medicines (Cf. for the details *ND* 2.158; much of this connects with the 'technical' discoveries that further man's progress, cf. Prometheus great speech *PV* 442-71.) The Stoics went further, and allowed animals, birds and fish to be used for food. But what about the use of animals for pleasure? Cicero (in the *ND* passage cited) allows hunting both for food and the healthy exercise it affords the hunters; hunting bears and lions also gives practice in courage, cf. Porphyry *abst* 3.20.1 quoting Chrysippus. Logically the Roman Stoics would here have an argument for the large-scale slaughter of animals practised, from Pompey onwards, to amuse the people at the games. The contrast with the Pythagorean concern for other life and the simple pleasures of the Epicureans is striking.

XX. 67 contd. *Private property is justified*

297 he who deviates from it unjust: As a citizen is bound by civil law so is a world citizen by natural law; 'ius ciuile' extends to 'ius gentium' which is also 'ius naturale', cf. n.275 on the unjust man as traitor to the *cosmopolis*. (For 'migraret' MS A has 'negaret').

298 as the theatre: As the theatre is a public building but seats are allocated to individuals, so, although the city and the world are open to all, individual ownership of property can be justified. Only a few seats were allocated in the Greek theatre, and these mainly to visiting dignitaries, but every citizen could have a place, and in fact might be paid for attending. So this striking analogy, of property rights to a limited number of theatre seats, is more likely to be a Roman modification of strict Stoic theory.

299 individual possession of private property: The legitimate possession of wealth was a continuing problem for Roman Stoics, and was not solved by the consensus that everything belongs to the wise, which gives them wholesale licence (*panteles exousia* DL 7.125, misleadingly translated by Hicks in the Loeb as 'a perfect right'). If wealth was honestly acquired (i.e. inherited or earned) and honestly used without harming others, then it could be classed as of plus value, cf. notes 201-7. The logical consequence of cosmopolitanism was to give away everything, but individual property rights could be secured by civil law (founded on divine law, cf. n.273), and property tax in fact was only levied in an economic crisis. In further special pleading it was suggested that since individual resources are limited and the needy limitless, generosity must be 'regulated', but we are encouraged to share what costs us nothing – water, fire and honest counsel for example, cf. Cicero's struggles with his principles at *Off* 1.51-2, 2.73, 85.

XX.68 *Political and personal duties*

300 to take part in politics and government: As reason develops and we become aware of the instinct to extend self-attachment to the family and society, and to understand that we belong by nature to a political association governed by justice and law, we then recognise a natural duty to serve society. The wise man therefore will help to promote laws which further the well-being and security of the citizens, and so advance virtue and happiness. In this appeal to a life of service to the community Stoicism, in sharp contrast to the apathy of the Epicureans, was in sympathy with traditional Roman ideals. On the political life as giving scope for 'greatness of spirit' cf. *Off* 1.72, and as leading to its astral home for the soul after death *Rep* 6.16, 26; there is also the affirmation *Rep* 1.1: 'the human race has been given by nature such a need for virtue and such a love of defending the common welfare that its force defeats the charms of leisure and the pleasant life'.

301 by taking a wife: Love of children for parents and parents for children is a natural instinct (cf. notes 54-6, 258, 279), and so the wise man acts in accordance with nature in marrying and raising a family – wife and children complete his domestic life as taking part in politics does his civic life. The 'duties' that are listed here belong not to the extremely rare Wise Man, but to all who aim to fulfil their human potential. The Cynics (cf. note 303) rejected family and state ties, the Epicureans advised caution in starting on a family because of the likely threat to one's *ataraxia* ('tranquillity of spirit'). In general the Hellenistic schools valued women more highly than Aristotle had done; they were admitted into the Epicurean Garden, and respected by the Stoics, especially at Rome, with the tradition of the idealised 'matrona'. Portia, daughter of Cato and wife of Brutus, came near to qualifying as a 'wise woman'. (Cato himself however divorced and remarried his wife Marcia, 'lending' her to a childless friend.) On the position of women in Roman Stoicism generally cf. Arnold 276-7, 287, 318, 348, 367.

302 even homosexual love if pure: an expanded translation of 'sancti amores' to clarify the point at issue. The standard line, in the tradition of Plato's *Symposium* and *Phaedrus*, was that 'the wise will feel affection for the young man who shows by his outward appearance (*eidos*) a character inclined to virtue', – the aim of philosophic *eros* is not sexual intercourse but *philia*, so DL 7.129, and cf. also *ND* 1.79 'philosophers have always enjoyed the company of young men', *Tusc* 4.72 and *Off* 1.46 on the wise man's love without lust.

303 Cynic principles and way of life: The early Cynics, the 'dog' philosophers, lived open lives in the streets, naked and shameless, and in their self-sufficiency and extreme cosmopolitanism rejected family and state ties. The early Stoics adopted their shamelessness in theory, advocating women in common and 'free' mating as in the animal world, and even incest and cannibalism, cf. DL 7.131 and 188 on the reported views of Zeno and Chrysippus.

304 others completely deny this: The attempt to break down all taboos was not a practical or acceptable option for later Stoics and especially at Rome; Panaetius modified Stoic extremism in this as in other areas. (Martha in the Budé reports some MSS variations in the two sentences: arbitrantur – arbitramur E, Cynicorum – cunctorum BE, si qui – si quis BEP.)

XXI. 69 *Benefits and injuries*

Section 69 on moral terminology is irrelevant to the general discussion of the wise man's duties, and is out of place; perhaps it should be transposed to the theory and theoretical terminology of sections 48-51.

305 "benefits" and "injuries": The wise man is by nature made for society and action (*koinonikos* and *praktikos* DL 7.123); 'benefits' are the practical effects of his right action, and as such affect everyone. On the *cosmopolis* theory, he who benefits one benefits all, and if one suffers, all, as parts of the organism, suffer with him.

306 of equal value: from the agent's point of view, since right actions are all equal the benefits that result from them are equal, cf. section 48, and also *Paradox* III.

307 "disadvantages" and "advantages": Cicero is having some difficulty with translating the Greek terms in this section as Latin does not have nouns from 'prodesse' and 'nocere' in the way that the Greek nouns correspond to the verbs, and 'commoda' does not have the sense of 'good use' that is in *euchrēstēmata*.

308 of unequal value: 'commoda' and 'incommoda' are sub-categories of 'praeposita' and 'reiecta'. They are universal in that they can be applied to all (like the 'benefits and 'injuries' in note 305) but not equal in that grading is applicable in a non-moral context; a person may become richer or poorer but not more or less good, cf. on sections 52 and 56. In what may be a parody, Plutarch reports that if the wise man wags a finger all benefit, cf. *Stoic rep* 1041c-d.

309 right and wrong actions are not considered universal: Right and wrong actions are equal but not universal, for right actions are restricted to the few wise, wrong actions to the many non-wise. And for the wise man right action ('honestum') converges rather than conflicts with advantage ('commodum' or, as in the discussion in *Off* 3, 'utile'; cf. n.317 on 'utilitas'.

XXI. 70   *Friendship*

310   Friendship should be cultivated: Friendship was a topic of great interest to ancient philosophers, the most famous texts on the subject being Plato's *Lysis*, *Symposium* and *Phaedrus*, Aristotle *EN* books 8 and 9, various Epicurean *dicta* and Cicero's own essay *De Amicitia* (where Laelius, like Cato here, is a paradeigm, in his friendship with the younger Scipio, of the ethical theory he is propounding). The Stoics elevated friendship to the category of *ōphelēma* ('emolumentum') as a virtuous activity of the good rather than as only, or merely, a life-enhancing 'praepositum', cf. n.307 above, and the definition n.136. Whereas 'societas' and 'caritas' belong to men in general, 'amicitia' is directed to an individual within that generality. But there were two main difficulties with the Stoic theory, if friendship is to be cultivated: i) if the wise man is self-sufficient he has no need of a friend, and ii) only the wise are capable of friendship, which puts it beyond the reach of the majority of mankind, cf. DL 7.124.

311   as dear to the wise man as his own: 'ratio' here, as commonly in Cicero, for 'business' or 'affairs' rather than 'reason' or 'intelligence'. On the general principle cf. the definition at DL 7.124: 'By friendship the Stoics mean a sharing of all that has to do with life, wherein we deal with our friends as with ourselves'. Cicero's own definition is: 'a consensus in all things divine and human, along with good will ('beneuolentia') and affection ('caritas'), *Amic* 20; cf. Sallust's famous 'idem uelle atque idem nolle' *Cat* 20, and the 'second self' vocabulary, e.g. Aristotle *EN* 9.4, and Cicero's 'alter ego' *Fam* 2.15.4, 'alter idem' and 'exemplar sui' ('a mirror-image of oneself') *Amic* 80 and 23.

312   a view to personal advantage: The traditional dilemma between acting altruistically (in the friend's interest) and selfishly (for one's own) coincide in the cosmopolis. To benefit another, like acting justly by one's neighbour, is to benefit oneself, cf. notes 274 and 277. The guidelines for apparent conflict between *duty* and friendship are summarised by Cicero at *Off* 3.43-6.

313   pursued for their own sakes: Despite the high value the Epicureans placed on friendship, it was pursued for basically selfish ends according to their opponents, cf. the exposition and criticism at *Fin* 1.65-70 and 2.82-5, and also *Off* 3.118. But the Stoics too could also see the friend as a means, even if in the higher Platonic sense of a guide to wisdom, cf. n.229. Cicero's own conclusion is that friendship derives from nature *because* it is free of calculation of profit – the association itself is profit enough, cf. *Amic* 27, 31.

XXI. 71 *Law*

314 Law exists by nature: Cicero's own legal training guaranteed his particular interest in this subject, resulting in his compositions *De Republica* and *De Legibus*. He was himself particularly sympathetic to the fundamentals of Stoic legal theory here, cf. his definitions: 'Law is right reason ('recta ratio') in agreement with nature, universal, unwavering and everlasting' *Rep* 3.33, and: 'Law is the distinction between just and unjust in accordance with nature, the most ancient and primary principle' *Leg* 2.13, and cf. 1.23 and 35. These definitions derive directly from the Stoic tenet: 'Justice is by nature, not convention' (cf. DL 7.128), which in turn has its roots in the *nomos/physis* controversy of fifth century Athens, but also echoes many of the sayings of the Stoics' favourite Presocratic, Heraclitus.

315 even to hurt anyone: 'iniuria' is etymologically the negation or deprivation of 'ius', and so contrary to nature, cf. *Leg* 1.33: 'we are so made by nature as to share the sense of law with one another', and *Off* 3.23: 'the aim of law is to keep inviolate the association of citizens, and the breaking of the bond is (therefore) punishable by death, exile, imprisonment or fine'.

316 to associate or conspire: The cabals of oligarchs were a constant threat to the stability of the Greek democracies. At Rome the Catilinarian conspiracy had been the most notorious (cf. *Paradox* IV), and that against Caesar was imminent.

317 equity can never be divorced from advantage: cf. *Leg* 1.42: 'Justice is one, binding all human society, based on one law, and this law is right reason applied to command and prohibition'. The subsequent discussion concludes that justice has to be founded on nature rather than 'popular decrees, rulers' edicts or judges' decisions'. The inter-connection of justice, law, reason and nature was thought to ensure absolute standards, and conformity with them is to the advantage of the rational man in his civic life, comparable to the claims of friendship in his private life, cf. n.312 on the coincidence of altruism and advantage in true justice and friendship.

XXI. 72 *Logic*

318 dialectic: 'dialectica', like 'physica' is feminine, with 'ars' (the Greek *technē*) understood. (In the same sentence, for the generic perfect subjunctive 'didicerimus' 'whatever we have learned', MSS P and R have 'diceremus' 'whatever we say' and A the impossible 'didiceremus'.) Chrysippus' original thought and extensive writings on logic made considerable advance on Aristotle's work, especially in propositional logic, and ensured the central importance of the subject in Stoic philosophy. Dialectic could be taken either as co-extensive with logic, or, from its Socratic/Platonic inheritance, as the sub-division concerned with spoken argument in question and answer. Skill in the subject was needed (i) to avoid being tricked by eristic sophistry or clever persuasion into assenting to what is false, (ii) to defend one's position in positive argument and the refutation of fallacies, (iii) as a method of instruction which the Stoic was duty-bound to undertake, cf. n.284, and (iv) to test hypotheses in the search for truth; cf. DL 7.47: 'without dialectic the wise man would be liable to stumble in argument, for by means of it true and false are distinguished, the plausible and the ambiguous articulated, and question and answer proceed methodically.

319 the skill is correctly called virtue: cf. DL 7.46: 'dialectic is a virtue embracing other virtues', as for Plato it was the summit of philosophical achievement, and for Aristotle the tool (*organon*) of the whole of its range.

XXII. 73 *Natural Science*

320 natural science: To live in harmony with nature requires knowledge of nature, and both Epicureans and Stoics emphasised the necessity of understanding the physical world as a sound basis for ethical theory and practice. The Epicureans started from the atomic theory of Democritus to produce a coherent theory of innumerable worlds in a random cosmos that had no place for divine guidance or human immortality. In contrast Stoic physics started from the ideas of the Presocratic Heraclitus, and resulted in an enclosed cosmos, controlled by providence and divine intelligence, vitalised by fire and *logos* in individuals and the whole.

321 the principles of both nature and divine life: cf. *Fin* 5.44 'knowing ourselves requires the intense study of nature', and 5.58 on the classification of studies as (i) of cosmology and the secrets of nature, (ii) the theory and practise of politics, and (iii) the virtues taken separately and as a whole. The report is from Antiochus, but the principle also Stoic. In general however the Roman Stoics did not practise what they preached here, there was a characteristic disinclination to engage in such 'scientia' (apart from astronomy), and no Latin work to counter the exposition of Epicurean physics by Lucretius in his *De Rerum Natura*. On the Stoics and 'divine life', cf. n.324.

322 the maxims propounded of old: The first two maxims cited 'know thyself' (γνῶθι σεαυτόν) and 'nothing in excess' (μηδὲν ἄγαν) were inscribed on the front of the temple at Delphi, the former particularly was taken to heart by Socrates, cf. Plato *Phaedr* 230a, also *Prot* 343a, and is quoted again at *Fin* 5.44. 'Follow god' (ἑποῦ θεῷ) perhaps originated in this form with the Pythagoreans, but it was a common Greek sentiment, given a particular context by the Stoics; there does not seem to be a Greek equivalent extant for 'tempori parere'. A number of such maxims were attributed indiscriminately to the original 'Seven Wise Men' of the seventh and sixth centuries. The most common list is: Solon, Thales, Pittacus, Cleobulus, Chilon, Bias and Periander – whether by chance or intention, each is from a different Greek city.

323 **the power nature wields:** Knowledge of natural science brings with it an understanding of oneself and one's own relationship both to the external cosmos and to one's fellow men. This in turn provides in political life the theoretical grounds for justice and in private life for friendship, cf. notes 312 and 317 on the interconnection of nature, justice and friendship.

324 **reverence to the gods:** Religion is the recognition by man of his relation to deity, and so theology too for the Stoics involved the understanding of their physical and cosmological theories. In these the Stoics tended to treat the deity as singular – this is the case in the main arguments for divine providence, and for god as both active priciple (vital, intelligent and fiery) and as the all-pervasive *pneuma* in the passive material of the cosmos. The plural tended to be used in arguments for the existence of gods (e.g. from 'universal consensus') and in allegorising individual gods as aspects of the world-god, already a re-interpretation of the traditional Olympian Zeus. The Stoics showed reverence to deity in prayer and praise (the most famous example being Cleanthes' 'Hymn to Zeus'), and also in 'following god' (cf. the maxim, n.322) by consistent living and willing cooperation with the workings of nature. The allegorising of traditional gods, and the re-interpretation of their myths as parables of the truths of natural science, meant that the Stoics could, with good conscience, take part in traditional ceremonies, cf. Balbus' explanation, *ND* 2.60-71.

XXII. 74 *The beauty of Stoic philosophy*

325 **amazing sequence of subject-matter:** The Stoics presented their philosophy as a system of three parts – logic, physics and ethics, with numerous sub-divisions and definitions. The whole was compared to an orchard with wall, trees and fruit, or to a city, or to an egg, or, because the parts were inseparably entwined and mutually dependent, to a living organism, with logic like the bones and sinew, physics the flesh and blood, and ethics the soul, cf. DL 7.40 and the references at Long and Sedley sect. 26 on 'the

philosophical curriculum' and sect. 32 on 'definition and division'.

326 welded: 'coagmento' is a common Ciceronian verb for joining, glueing or cementing together; 'coagmentatum' therefore is the editors' usual suggestion for a metaphor which obviously gave the scribes trouble, as 'cocimentatum' A, 'cociomtatum' R, 'coaugmentatum' BEN and 'coagumentatum' V.

327 the whole would topple: for 'ullam' Martha suggests 'unam' ('if you move *one* letter'), comparing *Fin* 4.53. A philosophical curriculum requirews a sequence of subjects for purposes of exposition (cf. n.325), but, as the comparison to a living organism showed, the whole is a unity with all the parts indissolubly linked, so that understanding of one part involves the understanding of all (and hence the strict dichotomy between those with wisdom and those without). Intelligent nature, logical language and rational behaviour are inter-connecting aspects of the one *logos*; the smallest change would alter, and so destroy, the whole. The Stoics were so convinced of the rightness of their philosophy in its totality that this was seen as a strength rather than a danger.

XXII. 75-76 *Panegyric of the Wise Man*

328 how dignified, how splendid: To finish, Cato gives up his 'spiky' style to launch into the panegyric of the wise man, and the clarion call to philosophy and virtue. For the panegyric cf. DL 7.117, 122, but Cato sprinkles Roman illustrations among the Greek. The difficulty was in naming anyone who had actually reached the status of 'wise man' ('rare as the phoenix' was one comment). Possible candidates were Hercules and Ulysses among heroes, Socrates, Diogenes, Zeno and Chrysippus among philosophers, and in Rome Cato himself; cf. examples offered from Roman history *Fin* 5.64, and a list of names rejected at *Off* 3.16.

329 must always be happy: cf. sections 28 and 29 (notes 112-120).

330 Tarquin: named in legend as 'the Proud' ('Superbus') and driven from Rome with his son Sextus for a series of atrocities, culminating in the famous 'rape of Lucretia'. Brutus, his nephew, and Lucretia's husband became the first consuls of the Republic, established after the expulsion. Stories connected with the kings at Rome and the foundation of the Republic as recorded in Livy were well-known fabrications dating from about 300 b.c. when the Romans gave themselves an invented history which exaggerated their conquests, enhanced their character, explained their customs, and, with Tarquin, provided a Roman version of a Greek tyrant.

331   **Sulla:** Sulla was appointed dictator in 81 b.c. after returning from the East and restoring order in Italy, but at a price; the final episode was the cold-blooded massacre of 80,000 Samnite prisoners-of-war. The office was given to Sulla for life, rather than the usual 6-month period, although he abdicated before his death in 78 b.c. Greed and self-indulgence were proverbially added to his cruelty (although a recent biography by Arthur Keaveney attempts to exonerate him). The office of dictator was literally 'magister populi' ('master of the people') with the same ambiguous senses of teacher/controller/tyrant that are in 'master', and so allows Cato his pun.

332   **Crassus:** Marcus Licinius Crassus, nicknamed 'Dives' ('the Rich'), consul in 70, and (as a result of the first triumvirate of Caesar/Crassus/Pompey) with Pompey in 55. The years between his consulships were spent in increasing his already magnificent fortune, and using it without scruples in political dealings. His wealth however could not match the military power and reputation of Caesar or Pompey, and in an effort to equal them he undertook a disastrous (and unnecessary) mission against the Parthians, which ended in his defeat and death at Carrhae in 53 b.c.

333   **truly handsome:** The superiority of moral over physical beauty had been one of Socrates' main themes, and was instantiated in himself. Tallness was admired among the Greeks, but Socrates was short, on the stoutish side, and notoriously snub-nosed, one of the reasons why Aristophanes caricatured him in his comedy, the *Clouds*; for the inner beauty however, cf. Alcibiades' character sketch at the end of Plato's *Symposium* from 215b.

334   **a free man:** on moral freedom contrasted with true slavery, cf. *Paradox* V headed: 'Only the wise man is free and every fool is a slave'.

335   **Croesus:** the last king of Lydia (560-546 b.c.), and, like Crassus in Roman times, proverbial for his wealth. Solon, the wise man alluded to here, had refused to include him among the three happiest men, and warned that, because of the uncertainties of life, no one could be called happy until he had died well. Croesus later led an expedition against the Persian king Cyrus, misled by the Delphic oracle that foretold the fall of a great empire if he did so. He was defeated, and when he called 'Solon' on his death-pyre, Cyrus, on learning the reason, set him free in sympathy. The famous story (chronologically impossible and a complete fabrication) is given by Herodotus, 1.29ff and 86-87.

336   **more to be encouraged than philosophy:** Heuristic writing, especially the encouragement to philosophy, was a literary genre in the ancient world; Cicero's own essay on this, the

Hortensius (which so moved Augustine, cf. *Conf* 3.4.7) is no longer extant. For Cicero's part in continuing the tradition, and 'taking the glory of philosophy from the weakening hand of Greece and bringing it to Rome' cf. *Tusc* 2.5, 5.5-6, *Off* 2.5-6, *Fin* 1.3, and Intr.V.

337 more godlike than virtue: *Fin* 3 began with the defeat of 'uoluptas' and ends with the triumphant victory of 'uirtus' – righteous living achieved by individual reason consistently in harmony with nature and divine providence, the sole means to happiness and the fulfilment of human potential.

SUMMARY

De Finibus Bonorum et Malorum IV

In the first book of *De Finibus*, the Epicurean case had been put by Lucius Manilius Torquatus, and was answered by Cicero in his own *persona*. He attacked in particular the Epicurean assumption that pleasure is the one good, and, in pointing out the many inconsistencies in the Epicurean position, claimed that Epicurus' own way of life was at variance with his teaching. In book four Cicero again is the dissenting voice, countering the main points of the Stoic theories, arguments and assumptions that Marcus Cato had expounded in book III, but with more sympathy for the heart of Stoic ethics - that virtue is the *summum bonum* - than he had shown for the Epicurean claims for pleasure. In the initial banter between Cato and Cicero the two are to act as in a court of law, with Cicero now allowed a three-hour limit in which to answer Cato's case for the Stoics. (1-2)

The first topic to clarify is the originality of the Stoic system. Cicero claims that the older Platonists, including Zeno's own teacher Polemo, already held the three basic propositions later put forward by the Stoics, that men have (i) a natural aptitude for virtue, (ii) an innate desire for knowledge, and (iii) a disposition towards association with their fellows, and a communal life that embraces all humanity. (3-5)

The Platonists' elegant style compares favourably with that of the Stoics, their clarity and fluency being superior to the Stoics' hair-splitting fussiness, pin-pricking syllogisms and unnecessary neologisms, all of which aim to win over the mind and not the heart, and consequently extinguish rather than kindle the student's enthusiasm. In Logic there was no need to add to or alter what the Peripatetics had already achieved, and in any case the Stoics neglected Topics, and, despite Chrysippus' compendious elaborations, made no improvements to the study of the subject. [This fourth chapter of book IV is a breath-taking dismissal of the vast quantity of original work by the Stoics on propositional logic.] Similarly in Natural Science Cicero says that the Stoics generally copied the Peripatetics, believing like them in four elements, one world, and a divine cosmic mind, but disagreeing on the substance of the soul, rejecting Aristotle's fifth element in favour of fire. So on most of these points Zeno merely echoes the master (Aristotle), but without his energy, originality, comprehensiveness and attention to detail. (5-13)

But the central topic is Ethics, and the understanding of the content of the good for man. Where is the Stoic originality in this area? Polemo had said that the good was 'to live according to nature', which involves knowledge of causation, the performance of 'officia' and the enjoyment of what is natural. The foundations of Stoic ethics - the doctrine of self-preservation as the primary natural instinct, the art of living ('ars uiuendi') and the primacy of wisdom - were already laid. And the case was similar with many of the details. The union of man and woman in marriage and the love of parents for children were according to nature, and wisdom emerged from nature as the excellence of the soul and the source of justice, temperance and other particular virtues in the full flowering of the moral life. What the Stoics did was to make virtue the only good, and to change the terminology of non-moral goods (such as health and sound senses), and call them the equivalent of 'praeposita' ('preferred') and 'sumenda' ('to be taken up') rather than 'expetenda' ('to be desired'), while what are commonly considered evils, such as exile and confiscation of property, are 'reicienda' ('to be rejected') but not 'fugienda' ('to be shunned'). How could a legal or political system possibly be run on such principles? Do you deal with Hannibal at the gates by saying that loss of country, captivity and death are indifferent? (14-23)

Cato argues that all these are merely 'popular ' objections, and the analysis should go deeper. There is agreement that the earliest impulse given by nature is for self-preservation stemming from self-love, and that the aim and chief good is the life according to nature, that is the moral life. One basic problem for the Stoics however is to reconcile the beginning, the natural instinct to stay alive, which is physical, with the end, to live the virtuous life, which is intellectual. Where along the line is the body to be so completely discarded? and how can it be discarded if we are to live a life according to nature, and nature has given us both body and soul? The good as virtue alone could only be appropriate for a disembodied mind. (24-29)

Cicero tries to maintain a sense of proportion. The tiniest additions - a penny to the wealth of Croesus, another day to a happy life (cf.

3.44-5) may be eclipsed, but physical good and evil are not of this kind. Facing a session with a torturer would require the summoning of all one's resources of courage and endurance, and just is not comparable to the loss of a bottle of oil; all is not equally indifferent. And in any case the whole does comprise the sum total of its smallest parts, Croesus' wealth is made up of its pennies, the happy life of a series of happy days. (29-33)

It is generally agreed that the good is analogous for all species of living creatures, deriving from self-love and the impulse to preserve their constitution, so why should man alone neglect the body? Is the consensus for preservation only of the *best* part, but it could not then be a universal principle and cover the different species. Furthermore, if it is the function of wisdom to take over from nature and perfect the individual, it cannot be exclusively concerned with either body or mind alone, but of the two together. Indeed, wisdom does not abandon the lesser parts, but safeguards and controls them in its pilotage of the individual's whole life. And not even mind can be satisfied with virtue alone, but, being located in a body (and not freely suspended in some unimaginable state), desires also to be free from pain. To deprive wisdom of the care of the body is to make it sterile, subverting nature rather than acting in accord with it. (34-42)

All those who restrict the good life to the virtuous life are wrong, but not all to the same degree. Pyrrho was worst, because he tried to dispense with desire altogether, and Aristo next, since he relied on chance motivation. The Stoics resemble them, but at least give wisdom a sphere in which to operate when it adopts what it according to nature and rejects the opposite; yet the Stoics still say that these primary objects, although 'preferred', are irrelevant to happiness, and this again is an abandonment of nature. Cicero was prepared to stop here, but was encouraged to continue by Cato, so he adds that it would have been better for Zeno to start from the standpoint of his Platonist teacher Polemo than that of Pyrrho and Aristo - he would not then have found himself divorcing nature from happiness. (43-48)

The next move is to attack the syllogism of 3.26 and the sorites of 28. The major premise of the syllogism: 'bonum' = 'laudabile', 'laudabile' = honestum', therefore 'bonum' = 'honestum' is unacceptable to most philosophers, and to ordinary people, who would say that health, riches, fame and the like were good but not necessarily praiseworthy. A similar step in the sorites ('quod expetendum' = 'laudabile') would halt that argument too, for what is desirable is also not necessarily praiseworthy. In addition, moral syllogisms should correct our lives and not just our terminology; just to say that pain, although odious and contrary to nature, is not an evil does not help us to endure it. (48-52)

Zeno was consistent in his logic, and did not flinch from pressing an argument to its conclusion, however absurd it might be. But if a conclusion was unacceptable (and the argument valid) then the premise too should not stand. And this is the case with such consequences as 'the wise alone are happy', 'the unwise are all miserable', and 'all sins are equal', for common sense and the way things are and truth itself cry out against them. (52-55)

Zeno then proceeded to make his position more credible by juggling with the terminology. What others called 'goods' were sneaked in as 'valuable' and 'according to nature'. But if the terminology already fitted the principles, and the Stoics agreed with the principles, why change the names? In effect there is very little difference between the emphasis placed by the traditional philosophers (i.e. the followers of Plato and Aristotle) on virtue compared with goods, and by the Stoics on it compared with their 'things preferred'. (56-63)

Cicero continues by taking up the similes of the drowning men and the puppies (3.48). He maintains that there must be a difference between those nearer the surface of the water and those in its depths, and between the puppies just about to open their eyes and those newly-born, for otherwise Plato would be no more mentally and morally aware then the monstrous Phaleris. People do advance and make real progress, and more appropriate similes would be those of applying ointment to weak eyes or giving medicine to the sick - day by day these improve, and similarly those who pursue virtue gradually overcome their vices. And if the absurd conclusion that 'all sins are equal' derives from the assumption that the 'summum bonum' does not admit of increase, then that too should be re-thought. (64-68)

How can we possibly manage our lives if it makes no difference whether we are well or ill, free from pain or in agony, cold and hungry or warm and fed? And when Zeno tried to avoid the worst absurdities of his position with his classification of indifferents into those to be preferred and according to nature, and those to be rejected and contrary to nature, the result is that he agrees with

Aristotle in substance but not in terms, and with Aristo in terms but not substance; such a position well deserved Marius Piso's ridicule. (69-73)

Finally the panegyric on the wise man is criticised. That he alone is handsome, free and a citizen, whereas the rest are ugly, slaves, exiles and mad, is patently absurd, and generated the Paradoxes (which Cicero had already adopted, elaborated and popularised in his essays on them). There is also an unflattering reference to the jury of the *Pro Murena* speech (cf. Appendix) in which these same paradoxes, as held and practised by Cato, had been mocked. The example of the captain with a cargo of gold or straw (cf. Paradox III) is again introduced, as well as that of the so-called equality of attack on a slave or one's father. The Stoics, while clinging to their own terminology, are constantly veering between the positions of Aristo and of Aristotle. Panaetius was the great mediator, softening the harsh doctrines of the early Stoics, and adopting a style of great clarity. (74-79)

Cato and Cicero then part company, and Cato promises a counter-refutation. Cicero may be ready to accept the substance if not the terminology of Cato's Stoicism, but Cato is uncompromising to the end. (79-80).

COMMENTARY
Paradoxa Stoicorum

The *Paradoxes* were sent to Brutus at the beginning of the spring of 46 b.c., between January, the date of the major work mentioned in 5, and April, when Cato died at Utica. Some of the essays however may have been sketched out over ten years earlier, especially IV, which is in the form of a 'diatribe' (the genre of moral invective) directed at Clodius, who was killed in 52 b.c. VI similarly almost certainly involves Crassus (whose disastrous Parthian campaign ended in 53 b.c.), and V, the attack on luxurious living, would inevitably bring Lucullus to mind.

The six essays are given a unity as developments of individual Stoic 'admirabilia' (Cicero's translation of *paradoxa*), and, according to the description in the Preface, as popularisations of some of the most difficult and provocative doctrines of the Stoa. Cicero had mocked them in 63 b.c., in his defence of Murena, in a legal move to discredit Cato's prosecution in the case, but in this work he faces the challenge of making them acceptable to the general public. The brusque arguments that will be used in *Fin* 3 are here tempered with professional skills, as Cicero puts into practice a main thesis of his oratorical works - that the orator himself is a moral teacher. (For a list of some of the rhetorical devices used, including repetition, amplification, asyndeton, hendiadys, metaphor and clausulae patterns, cf. Molager's introduction to the Budé edition, sect. VII: 'Style et valeur littéraire'.)

The *Paradoxes* are of particular interest in this deliberate linkage of rhetoric and philosophy, and in the application of Greek maxims to a Roman setting. The sermonising of the Cynics and early Stoics was easily assimilated to the native Roman satirical genre; and this tradition, which started with Lucilius and continued in Lucretius, would lead eventually to the satires of Juvenal. Its particular Roman flavour is here enhanced by the use of *exempla* taken from early Republican history, a store-house that Vergil would draw from (especially in the Pageant of Heroes in *Aeneid* 6 and the Shield in book 8) and also Livy, in the opening books of his history.

PREFACE

The Preface combines the dedication to Brutus, the connection with Cato (the paradeigmatic Stoic, and expositor of Stoic doctrine in *Fin* 3), and Cicero's own aim of making difficult doctrines, which had originally been presented in an uncompromising style, more generally acceptable. The light touch of Cicero's own approach to his task had its own tragic irony, when the appearance of these essays was followed almost immediately by the news from Utica of the suicide of Cato, who died as he had lived, in the spirit of these maxims. The appropriateness of allowing Cato later to speak in his own persona in *Fin* 3 becomes apparent.

1   topics: 'locus' (Greek *topos*) is a semi-technical term for the specific context of an argument, here a philosophical one contrasted with 'communes loci' in 3; cf. the opening of Cicero's own *Topica*, and on 'commonplaces, *De Orat* 3.106.

the forum and the assembly: the two stages for public oratory. 'Forum' can be specifically for the courts of justice there, or generally, as in 4, 'in the street'. Cicero has in mind the 'average man', but cf. on 33.2

little tiny syllogisms: on Stoic style cf. *Fin* 3, notes 66-67, 107, 164-6 (including praise for Cato's clarity); also *Brutus* 120: 'Stoic oratory is too tight and concise for a popular audience'.

3   that persuasive speech cannot make acceptable: for the range of topics that the orator masters, cf. *De Orat* 2.65-70. Once the fundamentals of his craft have been learned, the orator, like the painter, can tackle a variety of subjects. For Gorgias' claim that the orator, as a general persuader, is superior to experts in individual fields, cf. Plato *Gorg* 452e.

adding rhetorical flourishes: for an example, cf. the panegyric of the wise man that concludes *Fin* 3. (In some manuscripts the contrast is destroyed with 'nullis' inserted before 'oratoriis ornamentis'.)

I have amused myself: Cicero, 'ludens', deprecates his achievements, suspecting perhaps that Brutus might not be enthusiastic about such popularisation, but at least they are authentic 'minora'; cf. the concluding simile.

4   'paradoxes': 'admirabilia' is Cicero's translation here of the Greek *paradoxa*; at *Fin* 4.74 he uses 'uerborum praestigiae', i.e. 'verbal trickery'. They are the basis for Cicero's raillery of Cato in *Pro Murena* (cf. Appendix), and for his criticism of Cato's Stoicism at *Fin* 4.74-78. The particular *Socratic* paradoxes were generally reduced to two: (i) virtue is (some kind) of knowledge, and (ii) no one does wrong willingly.

5   has already appeared: i.e. the work *De claris oratoribus,* a history of oratory in dialogue form between the *personae* of Atticus and Brutus, written during the previous winter, and more generally known as *Brutus*; cf. Douglas' introduction to the work, xi-xiv.

'propositions': *thetika,* Cicero likes to use philosophical 'theses', i.e. propositions assumed but requiring proof, as subjects for rhetorical rather than logical treatment.

Phidias's Minerva: This great statue of Athena, over 30 feet high, made of gold and ivory, and set in the Parthenon in 438 b.c., is described by Pausanias (1.24.5) and survives in smaller copies; cf. the account with reconstruction in John Boardman *Greek Sculpture of the Classical Period* (London 1985) 110-12: 'It is impossible to assess the effect of such a colossal figure, the strong verticals of dress and support, the crisp detail of cast and chased metal, and the shining flesh ...'. In comparing his *Paradoxes* to small pieces from Phidias' workshop, did Cicero suppose that there was a literary equivalent to the statue itself? The wording is ambiguous.

PARADOX I

'Only what is right is just' - μόνον τὸ χαλὸν ἀγαθόν. This paradox is at the heart of Stoic ethics, cf. *Fin* 3.21 (notes 77-80), 27 (notes 109-111) with the converse: 'nothing is evil except vice' at 29 (notes 114-117). The generalisations of *Fin* 3 are illustrated here by *exempla* taken mainly from early Roman history, before Stoicism reached Rome. The 'old Roman' - austere, thrifty, courageous and incorruptible - could easily be idealised as a 'natural' Stoic.

6   I have never supposed: 'numquam me hercule ego'; Cicero perhaps protests too much that he personally never considered wealth or high office desirable, cf. Paradox VI on his comparatively modest possessions. His great denunciation of worldly goods comes in the 'Dream of Scipio', cf. especially *Rep* 6.25 on contempt for human rewards for one's efforts - 'let virtue by her own charms lead you to true glory'.

lust's thirst is never quenched: cf. similarly Plato *Gorg* 493 on the myth of the Danaids, and Lucretius book 3: 'we are never filled with the joys of life, (1.1010) and 'we long for what we do not have, and when we have that, we long for something else, and open-mouthed we thirst unceasingly' (1082-4), and also 4.1100 (the lover) 'thirsts in the torrent'.

8   true reason ... public opinion: The contrast first appears in Xenophanes, fr. 34, then in Parmenides' division into *Aletheia* and *Doxa*; it was fundamental to Socrates' stand in the *Apology* and *Crito*, and then to Plato's epistemology and metaphysics, especially as set out in *Rep.* books 5-7.

Bias: one of the Seven Sages, who were adopted by the Stoics as their predecessors. The seven are listed in Plato *Protagoras* 343a (with some irony as being pro-Spartan), but there were some variations in the list. It is notable that the seven came from differents cities in the Greek world.

9   only what is moral, right and virtuous is, I think, good: the main theme of *Fin* 3, cf. esp. 27-29, and 39. Cicero in his own person then criticised this position in book 4 (cf. Summary), preferring to take virtue as the highest rather than the sole good. Throughout these *Paradoxes* Cicero writes more from the Stoic position presented by Cato in *Fin* 3 than from his own in *Fin* 4.

10   rather far-fetched: 'odiosora' ABV(1), 'oscuriora' in marg. F, 'obscuriora' M, 'obscuria' V(2), cf. Molager's *app.crit.* 'obscuriora' (lit. 'rather dark') is preferable, given the metaphor of illumination that follows.

the life and actions of great men: In accord with the respect for 'mos maiorum' and the reverent attitude to family ancestors Roman writers   constantly used *exempla* from their past (rather than arguments) to substantiate ethical positions. To this end the grey area of early Roman history became peopled with colourful figures of dubious historical veracity, and set in contexts suitable for moral comment, admiration and imitation, cf. for Cicero's advice in the practice in oratory: 'Citation of *exempla* from antiquity gives the speech authority, credibility and delight' *Orator* 120.

11   Romulus: Rome's own mythical founding hero, born, in the Greek tradition, of a god and a mortal woman (Mars and Rhea Silvia), and heroised as the god Quirinus. The 'steps which led him to heaven' included, in the myth, the murder of his brother and the rape of the Sabine women. On this topic cf. most recently Bremner and Horsfall 'Roman Myth and Mythography', BICC suppl. 52 (1987).

12   Numa Pompilius: traditionally the second of the seven kings of Rome, to whom was attributed a series of religious institutions, and an anachronistic meeting with Pythagoras in south Italy.

the rest of the kings: Tullus Hostilius, Ancus Marcius, Tarquinius Priscus and Servius Tullius. The seventh, Tarquinius Superbus, was expelled after his son's rape of Lucretia. It is likely that there was a 'regal period' in early Roman history, but the names, except perhaps that of Tarquin, are probably fictitious. Lucius Junius Brutus, ancestor of the present addressee, and founder of the Republic, is generally accepted as a historical figure, but not such embellishments as the cruelty to his sons; for the details and authenticity, cf. Ogilvie's commentary on Livy 1-5, especially pp 210, 218-34.

Gaius Mucius: given the cognomen 'Scaevola' (i.e. 'Lefty').

According to the legend he defiantly held his right hand in a burning brazier in front of the Etruscan king Porsenna, whom he had failed to kill; for the details, cf. Ogilvie, loc. cit. 262-6. He was immediately used as an *exemplum* for the endurance of pain.

Cocles: Horatius Cocles, who, in the legend, held back the army of Porsenna single-handed from the Sulpician bridge while it was being demolished, and then swam to safety.

Decii: father and son, one or both of whom, in the time of the Latin wars, was said to have brought victory to the Romans by 'devotio', a formal vow dedicating oneself and the enemy to Tellus and Di Manes (the gods of earth and the dead), followed by a suicidal charge into the enemy ranks.

Gaius Fabricius: consul in 282 b.c., and an *exemplum* of incorruptibility when he refused the bribes of Pyrrhus. He is often linked with Curius (cf. next note, 38, 48 and *Rep* 3.40).

Manius Curius: cognomen 'Dentatus' (because he was born with teeth), four times consul between 290 and 274 b.c., victor over the Samnites, and at Beneventum he forced Pyrrhus to withdraw. He was said to have been cooking his dinner when an embassy of Samnites arrived; he refused their gold, saying that he preferred to rule the rich rather than be rich himself.

Gnaeus and Publius Scipio: cf. Lucretius 3.1034 and the 'two thunderbolts of war' (*Aen* 6.842). 'Propugnacula' might be either offensive (as 'battering rams') since they took the initiative at the beginning of the second Punic war against Hasdrubal in Spain in 215 b.c. (they were both killed soon after), or defensive, with a pun on the name 'scipio' - 'staff' or 'support'.

the older Africanus: Scipio Africanus Maior, 236-184 b.c. As consul in 205 he took the second Punic war into Africa, and eventually defeated Hannibal at the battle of Zama.

the younger: Scipio Aemilianus Africanus Minor, 185-129 b.c., son of Aemilius Paullus and adopted by the son of Africanus Maior. He is the subject of the *Somnium Scipionis* ('Dream of Scipio', Cicero's Platonic type myth at the end of *De republica*), in which both his father and adoptive grandfather appear and exhort him to achieve immortality through a life of service to the state. Elected consul (under age) in 147 b.c. Scipio brought the third Punic war to an end, and on his return to Rome he took a stand against the Gracchi and their legislation, and this was the probable cause of his sudden death. He was a cultured Hellenist and founder of the famous Scipionic circle, an enlightened group of similar minds, who ensured the introduction of Greek literature and (through Panaetius) Stoic philosophy to Rome.

Cato: Marcus Porcius Cato the Censor, 234-149 b.c., great-grandfather of the Stoic Cato, renowned for his moral, social and economic severity, and for his hostility to Carthage. He was also against the Scipios and the infiltration of Greek culture into Rome, although he is said to have relented, and learnt Greek in his eighties. His own book *De agricultura* is the first continuous work in Latin prose.

14   pleasure is the ultimate good: for those who advocate pleasure as the 'summum bonum' cf. *Fin* 3, notes 1, 57-8, 123.

   nature has given you a mind: reason and right action characterise human life and set it above that of animals, cf. *Fin* 3, especially notes 83, 273, 294.

15   merits most praise ... justifiably be proud: for the syllogisms and sorites cf. *Fin* 3, 27-28 with notes.

   the more intense it is: cf. the references given in 6 above, and also Lucretius 4.1068: 'the cancer thrives and festers on its nourishment, and day by day the madness grows'. The Epicureans eschewed intense and unsettling pleasure as vehemently as the Stoics, cf. Introduction III.

PARADOX II

The life of virtue is the completely happy life' - αὐτάρκης ἡ ἀρετὴ πρὸς εὐδαιμονίαν.   The axiom, in this wording, is attributed to Zeno, Chrysippus and (linked with 'greatness of soul') to Hecato, cf. DL 7.128. The coincidence of virtue and advantage in the happy life of the truly good man was constantly reiterated, cf. *Fin* 3. 10, 26, 27 (with notes 31, 106 and 113), *Off* 1.6, 3.11-13. It is the main topic of book 5 of the *Tusculans*, and Brutus himself wrote a treatise *De virtute* on the theme of this Paradox. The essay gives two *exempla*, Regulus and Marius, then introduces Cicero's own case, before widening into a more general 'diatribe'.

16   Marcus Regulus: later to figure in Horace's famous ode, 3.5. As consul in 256 b.c. Regulus, towards the end of the first Punic war, led the first Roman force to enter Africa. He seemed to have had little understanding of the African situation, and was outmanoevred, defeated and captured by the Carthaginians. He was sent to Rome to negotiate peace terms, or at least an exchange of prisoners, and, after dissuading the senate, kept his oath to Carthage and returned to captivity. Whether he was subsequently tortured (by having his eyelids removed and then being exposed in the desert, cf. Dio 11) or eventually died 'from neglect' is disputed. The story is muddied by the tradition of 'Punic perfidy' fostered by the Romans, and by the horrors Regulus' own family inflicted on

Punic hostages at Rome. As with many of Cicero's *exempla*, Regulus as heroic oath-abiding patriot is of dubious historicity. Cf. also Cicero's use of Regulus at *Off* 3.99 and *Fin* 2.65: 'Virtue shouts that Regulus was happier tortured by sleeplessness and hunger than Thorius banqueting on his bed of roses'.

Gaius Marius: 157-86 b.c., the great army reformer, from Cicero's own Arpinum, and, like him, a 'nouus homo', reaching the consulship although not a 'nobilis'. In his 'fortunate days' Marius enjoyed unparalleled 'auctoritas', being consul six times, victor over Jugurtha in Africa and the invading German tribes - the Cimbri and Teutones. In adversity, betrayed by the upper class, the 'Optimates', whom he had supported at Rome, he fled to Etruria, conscripted his veteran army there, and returned to capture Rome. His return, and his seventh consulship (with Cinna), were notorious for the harassment and slaughter of his political opponents. Cicero wrote an epic poem on Marius, of which the only substantial extant quotation, on the omens foretelling Marius' greatness, is given at *Div* 1.106.

17 You have no idea at all, you fool: Whom is Cicero addressing? Certainly not Brutus, but, from the threats of death and exile, it might be Clodius (cf. Paradox IV) or, given the 'nights of worry and deliberation' mentioned below, possibly Catiline, whose conspiracy was defeated and its leaders executed in Cicero's famous consulship of 63 b.c. In Paradox III the addressee is an anonymous objector to the extreme Stoic position on the equality of all wrong acts, in VI he may possibly be the notoriously wealthy Crassus. But the tradition of the diatribe did not require a specific name as the recipient of moral exhortation or invective.

what is the result of my efforts?: In *Tusc* 5 Cicero later set up an idealised Wise Man as the *exemplum* of the happy life attained solely through self-sufficient virtue. Here Cicero uses his own service to the state, and the ingratitude it met with, as a model for the struggle to be independent of the caprices of fortune. From numerous references to Cicero's efforts, cf. *Mur* 3: 'res publica magnis meis laboribus et periculis sustenta'.

18 who think of the whole world as one city: for this cosmopolitanism cf. *Fin* 3.64 and notes 272-7. The contrast between true and apparent exile is developed at length in 29-32.

a guilty conscience stings you: cf. again the remarkable resemblance to Lucretius 3, here to lines 1010-23 on the allegory of the Furies as stings of conscience: 'mens sibi conscia factis / praemetuens adhibet stimulos terretque flagellis'.

19 a life to be praised ... to be desired: cf. 15 above, and the references to *Fin* 3.27-28.

PARADOX III

'Wrong acts are all equal as are moral ones' - ἴσα τὰ ἁμαρτήματα καὶ τὰ κατορθώματα. The Latin version 'aequalia esse peccata et recte facta' was missing in the MSS and supplied by Orelli; the version at *Fin* 4.55 is 'recte facta omnia aequalia, omnia peccata paria'. (On *katorthōmata*, translated as 'recte facta' , cf. *Fin* 3.24 and n.97.) Of all the paradoxes this was the hardest to accept, cf. *Fin* 4.55 where 'common sense, the way things are and truth herself' violently object, and it was the one most mocked (cf. the passage from *Pro Murena* in the Appendix). For the Stoics the slightest difference makes all the difference, and there are no gradations, or increase or decrease, in virtue and vice; the harshest arguments and the most impressive illustrations were produced to hammer the point home, cf. from *Fin* 3 on the puppy and the drowning man (48), the shoe that fits (46), the king and courtiers (52), and the list starting with the light of a lamp (45).

20   Wrong acts are gauged ... by the vices of the human agents: cf. *Fin* 3. 24, 35 and especially 39 with notes. The Stoics judged right and wrong not by the external action but the inner psychological state; right actions resulted from the healthy soul in the correct state of tension (*tonos*) and in harmony with nature, wrong ones from the diseased soul. Progress could only be made by a change in the agent's *psychē*, from ignorance to knowledge and from mental sickness to mental health.

   A pilot wrecks a ship: the motivation arising from the psychological state determines the morality of an action, not the apparent seriousness of the act itself. In the metaphor used in this paragraph, once the boundary between virtue and vice is crossed it makes no difference how far one goes in the territory. The pilot is incompetent if he loses his cargo, whatever it is, the adulterer is a victim of lust whether with a prostitute or high-born virgin.

21   virtues are alike: the converse position - returning a debt is just, whatever the amount, the self-controlled man masters all desires. Justice and self-control are aspects of virtue as a whole, the perpetual harmony of reason inevitably resulting in moral acts, cf. 22 'una uirtus est consentiens cum ratione et perpetua constantia'.

23   Socrates ... was clever and wise: cf. the reply of the Delphic oracle that no one was wiser than Socrates, and interpreted by him to mean that ignorance like his own was a wiser state of mind than to think that one knows when one does not (cf. Plato *Ap* 21a-23b);

for Socrates' discussion on the unity of the virtues cf. *Protag* 329c, and for the linkage of virtue with knowledge, cf. Introduction II. One of Socrates' convictions was that we should heed not the opinion of the many ('of porters and labourers' as Cicero puts it here), but of those few whose understanding we respect.

what power is there: The underlying principle goes back to Draco in seventh century Athens who 'wrote his laws in blood', decreeing the same death penalty for trivial thefts as for sacrilege and murder. When asked why, he replied that small offences deserved it, and there was no greater penalty for more serious offences, cf. Plutarch *Solon* 17.1-2.

24 killing one's father and killing a slave: cf. *Fin* 4.76; the question was discussed most famously in Plato's *Euthyphro*.

the citizens of Saguntum: the counter-example to show that the motive, not the action, should be judged. Saguntum was a city in south-east Spain, allied to Rome and finally taken by Hannibal in 219 b.c. The siege was fiercely resisted, and after eight months the citizens finally set fire to their homes, and in some cases to themselves and their families as well, cf. Livy 21.14. The incident precipitated the second Punic war.

26 only slightly out of tune: Cf. *Fin* 4.75 where Cicero, in objecting to the Stoic position, distinguishes 'all the lyres equally are out of tune' from 'all the lyres are equally out of tune'; but the Stoic position he defends here makes more sense, for there are actually no degrees of being 'in tune'. ('peccantem' obviously has to be understood with 'in nugis' from the previous 'peccare', and Rackham in fact prints the participle in the Loeb text.)

the length of his fingers: an illustration of only a slight difference in measurement; Molager however in the Budé text (110 n.5) suggests a reference to poets using their fingers to count off the metrical feet or to stress the beat.

PARADOX IV

'Every fool is mad' - πᾶς ἄφρων μαίνεται, also given in the plural in the Latin as 'omnes stultos insanire'. Because of the way in which this essay develops, and the unsatisfactory text of its opening, it has sometimes been assumed that a second paradox is involved here - that only the wise man is a citizen, the fool is an exile. Molager however, in the Budé introduction (pp 31-37), argues for the unity of the Paradox in the *exemplum* of Clodius, whose character and hostility to the state provide convincing evidence of madness, cf. from the *Pro Murena* extract the combin-

ation 'fugitiui, exules, hostes, insanos', and also *De Orat* 3.65
'serui, latrones, hostes, insani' as Stoic terms for the foolish. Cicero
presents himself in this essay as the wise and caring states- man,
the true citizen wherever he is, in contrast to Clodius as madman,
law-breaker and so exile even when living at Rome. It is generally
assumed that this essay was written during Clodius' life- time (cf.
the introductory note to the *Paradoxes*), but Cicero may have
found it appropriate to take his earlier clash with Clodius, and its
assumed contrast of sanity with madness, as a lesson relevant to 46
b.c., the year of the publication of the Paradoxes. In that year
Caesar held sway in Rome, was appointed dictator for ten years,
and started on a sweeping programme of domestic legislation.

27   you (Clodius):   the addressees of individual *Paradoxes* are
kept anonymous (cf. above on 17) although here there is no doubt
of this identity.   Publius Clodius, named Pulcher ('Handsome'),
92-52 b.c., was, after some difficulty, formally transferred to the
plebs in 59 b.c., and so was able to stand as tribune and initiate a
series of popular measures. Audacious and unscrupulous, he was
used to foster the ambitions of both Crassus and Caesar, but was an
implacable enemy of Cicero from 61, when Cicero gave evidence
against him for violating the Bona Dea rites (cf. below on 32). In
retaliation Clodius re-enacted a general edict of exile for anyone
who had executed a Roman citizen without trial, which would cover
Cicero's treatment of the Catilinarian conspirators. Cicero won
widespread support at Rome and in Italy, and the senate put on
mourning in sympathy with him, but there was no backing from
Caesar or Pompey. The consul Gabinius, in league with Clodius,
forbade the mourning, Clodius mobilised his public army, and
Cicero was forced to leave Rome. A second (unconstitutional) act
banned him 500 miles from the city, and he spent an unhappy year
in northern Greece. (Cato was also removed from Rome with a
mission to Cyprus.) Pompey eventually rallied, reinforced the
Italian delegations and strengthened his position in Rome through
the services of the tribune Milo, who set his own gang against that
of Clodius. The consuls and senate recalled Cicero, and in
September 57 b.c. he enjoyed a triumphant return through Italy
and acclamation in Rome itself. Clodius was killed in a brawl with
Milo at the beginning of 52 b.c., and his supporters burned down
the senate-house as a pyre for his corpse.

   you are actually mad: After 'dementem' here the text
becomes corrupt, with 'insanire' or in some MSS a lacuna before
'rebus', and then 'ad uictum necessarius esse inuictus potest' ('is
possible to be unconquered by what is essential for nourishment'

with a pun on 'uictum'/'inuictum'). It is doubtful whether lacunae covering the whole of the paradox 'every fool is mad' and the introduction of a second 'only the wise are citizens' can be assumed here, cf. the introductory note to this Paradox.

What is a city?: Cicero had examined at length the origins and definitions of law, justice and political communities in his *De republica* and *De legibus*, completed at about the same time as the *Paradoxes*. As with Lucretius' famous account of the origins of society (5.1135-60), political life, contrasted with anarchy, is said to be characterised by the election of magistrates, obedience to law and respect for sanctions.

the remnants of Catiline's conspiracy: Catiline himself, who had attempted to overthrow the established government during Cicero's consulship, had been defeated in battle, and the ring-leaders executed; the illegality of this execution was the cause of Cicero's own subsequent banishment. Catiline's following included an assortment of violent discontents - from the poor, the degenerate aristocracy, Sulla's veterans, and the dispossessed, cf. Sallust's description, *Cat* 21.

28 a city that did not exist: Cicero claims that in the year 58 b.c., when Rome was virtually run by Clodius, the constitution was in abeyance. Clodius' legislation as tribune secured the distribution of free corn, the relaxation of the censorship, the strengthening of the tribunician power and the restoration of political clubs (*collegia*) - a programme described as the 'systematisation of hooliganism', *CAH* ix.524.

pulling down my walls: Cicero's town house on the Palatine and his villas at Tusculum and Formiae were destroyed; when Clodius tried to auction the contents no one would bid for them. The houses were subsequently restored at public expense, cf. *Harusp* 16.

29 my godlike steadfastness of mind: 'diuina animi mei constantia' - Cicero appropriates to himself thecharacter of the Stoic sage. He claims that the energetic vigilance which saved the state from Catiline's anarchy continued in his stand against Clodius; but his exclusion from the coalition of Caesar, Pompey and Crassus in 60 b.c. removed him from centre stage in Roman politics.

my glorious return: Cicero's return from exile in Greece was publicly acclaimed. His own account of the journey through Italy and the welcome in Rome is preserved in a series of speeches he gave on his arrival before the senate, the people and the college of pontiffs (*Post reditum in senatu, Post reditum in Quirites* and *De domo sua*; the authorship of these speeches was formerly in doubt, but is now accepted as Cicero's), cf. also Att 4.1: 'When I reached the Capenan gate the temple steps were crowded; the people showed their joy with great applause, a similar crowd cheered me all the way to the Capitol, and on the Capitol and in the forum there was an extraordinary gathering'.

foreign nations: Although many cities, especially in Greece, offered Cicero hospitality in his exile he was extremely dejected 'gazing in the direction of Italy like a disconsolate lover, and without the serenity one would have expected from his philosophical leanings', cf. Plutarch *Cic* 32.2-5, and Cicero's letters to Atticus from Thessalonica, *Att* 3.8-21.

family and domicile: 'natura ac loco' is perhaps more simply 'place of birth'. The noun 'natura' (but not the related adjective 'naturalis') is rarely associated with its root meaning 'born' (cf. 'nascor' 'natus sum').

30   a massacre in the forum: Of many similar riots, the reference is perhaps to that of 1 June 57 b.c. when Clodius made use of a band of gladiators from his brother's funeral rites.

Spartacus: The famous Thracian gladiator who led the slave revolt of 73 b.c., defeated three Roman armies, and was finally cornered by Crassus in south Italy three years later. The survivors were rounded up and crucified along the Appian Way by Pompey.

31   all criminals ... are exiles: Clodius was guilty of the main crimes which, if the laws of the Republic were respected, would have resulted in the change of status from 'ciuis' ('citizen') to 'hostis' ('public enemy') and the penalty of exile. These were possession of a weapon with criminal intent, murder, arson and sacrilege, cf. *Pro Milone* 18-19, 72-78, *Pro Sestio* 69.

temple of the Nymphs: a target because of the public record stored there, which could provide 'evidence of Clodius' criminal activities.

32 the inner shrine of the Good Goddess: The annual ceremony of the sacred Roman goddess of fertility (who was connected both with the Roman Fauna and the Greek Hygeia) was held at night in the house of the Pontifex Maximus; his wife presided, and it was exclusively female. In May 61 b.c. Clodius had gate-crashed the ceremony disguised as a flute-girl, and was later discovered. In the subsequent trial for sacrilege Cicero gave evidence against Clodius, and so incurred his lasting enmity. Caesar, who was then the Pontifex Maximus, refused to testify, but divorced his wife Pompeia on the grounds that 'Caesar's wife must be above suspicion', cf. Plutarch *Caes* 10.6.

PARADOX V

'Only the wise man is free, and every fool is a slave' - μόνος ὁ σοφὸς ἐλεύθερος καὶ πᾶς ἄφρων δοῦλος. The lack of wisdom, which brings with it the failure to understand what is truly good and evil, beneficial and harmful, and so the inability to act as one would truly wish, is the most damaging bondage. The wise man, on the other hand, from his state of psychic harmony, exercises his wisdom in the right calculation of what is according to nature and rejection of the opposite; in this lies his freedom and guarantee of happiness, *Fin* 3, notes 105-6, 133, 209-210, 254. The slavery of the tyrant, who least of all achieves what he really wants, was first analysed by Socrates in Plato's *Gorgias*, and the enslavement of reason to desire in the tripartite soul was further elaborated in the Platonic psychology of the *Republic* and *Phaedrus*. (The problem of *akrasia*, of knowing what is right but not doing it because overcome by passion, pleasure, lust, fear and the like, appears first in the *Protagoras*, 352b - 357e, before its fuller development by Plato, and then by Aristotle in his *Ethics*.) Cicero himself gave a vivid portrayal of the theme in his narrative of the sword of Damocles hanging over Dionysius, tyrant of Syracuse (*Tusc* 5.61-2), and reiterated the point in the panegyric of the wise man at the end of *Fin* 3 - 'he will be called king more truly than Tarquin, more truly master of the people than Sulla'. From the other side, this Paradox, like IV and VI, is also ridiculed at *Pro Murena* 61 - 'only the wise, even if they serve in slavery, are kings, we, who are not wise, are "fugitiui" (a contemptuous term for runaway slaves who, in deserting, forfeited all rights). Despite the indirect reference to Lucullus and his fish-ponds in 38, the essay is a general diatribe on the reversal of values, Roman in the main pun on 'imperator' and its cognates, and in the lively sketches of contemporary *mores*. The specific attack on the destructive influence of sex, avarice, ambition and fear is again very much in the tone of Lucretius, cf. especially the opening lines of *RN* books 2 and 3.

33 commanding-officer: 'imperator' was used in the Republic particularly of the highest military commanders; they were always senators, originally consuls, defending Rome and Italy, and then the provinces as proconsuls. In the last century b.c. the position was used (and abused) to win over the loyalty of the legions to individuals rather than the state. It was also a title of honour conferred on a general after an important victory, and given most often to Pompey. It eventually was adopted permanently by the

Roman emperors, whose power rested above all on the support of the armies. 'imperium' was the word for the authority conferred, and the related verb is 'impero'. But 'impero' was also widely used outside any formal or military context for 'command', 'dominate' of one person over another, and with various object-clauses for 'give orders that'.

a very intelligent audience: Cicero writes as if addressing a wider readership than Brutus (in the Preface) or Clodius (in the previous Paradox) or an indefinite 'tu', and on the assumption that it accepts certain general philosophical if not specifically Stoic premises, cf. on 17 above.

34   **as the wise poet says:** the author is unknown, but the *dictum* goes back to Heraclitus fr. 119 - 'Character for man is destiny', i.e. each man has within himself control of his own present and future state in the role assigned to reason.

35   **the submission of a spirit:** To maintain the paradox, the Stoics need to define slavery not in terms of external circumstances (where it could not be maintained) but of the inner disposition.

36   **whom a woman commands:** The lover as slave or captive of his mistress was a standard *topos,* and elaborated by Cicero's poetic contemporaries - Catullus and his circle, and Lucretius in book 4, 1060-1190. But such a situation is seen here as less deplorable than enslavement to *objets d'art* as status symbols.

Aetion .. Polyclitus: the former was a fourth century artist, most famous for his 'Marriage of Alexander and Roxane', painted about 325 b.c. Polyclitus of Argos was the leading sculptor of the second half of the fifth century, who specialised in figures of athletes, but was also renowned for his statue of Hera, which rivalled Phidias's Athena, cf. Pausanias 2.17.4, and the end of the Preface above.

38   **Lucius Mummius:** consul 146 b.c., who sacked Corinth in that year and broke up the Achaean confederacy. He sent the treasures of Corinth back to Rome, and so started the interest in Greek and especially Corinthian works of art, cf. Horace *Ep* 2.1.193, Vergil *Aen* 6.836, Pliny *NH* 35.24, 37.14, Pausanias 7.16.7-9. Mummius was so uncultured that he told the contractors responsible for transporting the priceless pictures and statues to replace any lost (cf. Velleius 1.13.4), and his soldiers were said to have played draughts on the paintings (Polybius 39.2).

Manius Curius: cf. above on 12.

his supply of lamprey: Despite Cicero's great friendship with Lucullus, the extravagance of his table, house, gardens and fish-ponds would be instantly recalled in this criticism, cf. *Fin* 3, n.26, Plutarch *Luc* 39-41. For the type of red mullet, with a beard-like fin, cf. Cicero *Att* 2.1.7, Juvenal 5.92, Pliny *NH* 9.30.1.

40 Cethegus: Publius Cornelius Cethegus, who first allied himself to Marius, fleeing with him in 88 b.c. and returning the following year, but he then sided with Sulla. He was of undistinguished patrician family and held no recorded office, but he was a key figure in the complicated intrigues of the 70s, especially in the allocation of military commands. The older Antonius and Lucullus both had to negotiate with him for their commands.

his moll Praecia: for the restoration of the name in a corrupt text cf. Molager (Budé) *app. crit.* Given the state of the text, 'moll' in the translation is perhaps admissible colouring, cf. Plutarch *Luc* 6: 'No public measure was passed unless Cethegus favoured it, and Cethegus did nothing without Praecia's approval'.

41 Lucius Crassus: Lucius Licinius Crassus 140-91 b.c., consul and censor, and father of the the more famous Marcus Crassus. He was the great orator of his generation, whom Cicero admired and took as his model, and made the chief speaker in his *De Oratore*. There are three candidates for the specific speech referred to: (i) Crassus' first major appearance, (119 b.c.) prosecuting Cabirius Carbo, (ii) his support of the Lex Servilia Caeponis (106) on mixed juries of equites and senators, and (iii) his 'swan-song' in 91, supporting the legislation of Marcus Drusus on enlarging the senate, distributing land to the people and enfranchising the Italians.

PARADOX VI

'Only the wise man is rich' - μόνος ὁ σοφὸς πλούσιος. The paradox that only the wise man is rich, however poor, is elaborated in a Roman context (except for the passing reference to Danaus), and Cicero again uses his own case as an illustration of the moral point he wishes to make. This theme is also treated at the end of *Fin* 3, in the panygeric of the wise man who is 'more truly rich than Crassus, who, if he had not been in want, would never have agreed to cross the Euphrates... truly the one who knows how to make use of all things will be said to own them'. The Stoic *exempla* from the early Republic are brought in again, although even Cicero begins to suspect that the reader may be getting bored with Manius Curius (cf. 12, 38, 48 and 50), but we also have an insight into the seamy side of acquiring a fortune in the last decades of the Republic. It was a common theme of the diatribe, and also very Epicurean, to say that the rich man is the one who needs little, There is a touch of hypocrisy in Cicero's demure remarks about his 'slender income' when he was said to own a house at Rome and seven others in the country, and, in another context (*Phil* 2.40), boasted of the large legacies he received as evidence of his popularity.

42   Are you the only rich man?: For the addressee as a general 'you' but with an implicit particular reference, cf. on 17, 27 and 33.

44   Danaus: His fifty daughters were the victims of an arranged marriage to their first cousins, the fifty sons of Aegyptus; they fled from their suitors and gained asylum in Argos. They were however eventually compelled to marry but, with the exception of Hypermestra, they all killed their husbands on their wedding night. As a punishment they were condemned to fetch water for ever in leaky jars in Hades, which Lucretius interpreted as an allegory for the attempt to satisfy insatiable desires. There was no question of a dowry however - the Egyptians enforced their rights by conquest.

45   maintain an army: the only reference to the size of an 'exercitus' as six legions with cavalry and infantry auxiliaries. Pompey was the first to raise a personal army on a large scale, boasting that a legion appeared if he stamped his foot. The cost of maintaining an army was estimated at about 4 million sesterces, which would be eight times Cicero's own (very comfortable) income, cf. *Off* 1.25, and below on 49. Crassus needed an army and military success to compete with Caesar and Pompey, but setting up as 'imperator' brought about his own defeat and death at Carrhae in Parthia in 53 b.c.

46   the terrible harvest: The revenge that Sulla wreaked on his enemies in the civil wars on his return to Italy and Rome in 82 b.c. was unforgettable. Samnite prisoners were slaughtered en masse after the battle of the Colline gate, and over five thousand citizens appeared on the dreaded 'proscription' lists which made lives and property forfeit. Prominent senators and wealthy business men were proscribed as much for their possessions as their principles.

48   Fabricius ... Curius: for these much-used *exempla* of incorruptibility cf. 12 and 38.

the generosity of Africanus: Scipio Africanus the younger (cf. on 12), son of Publius Scipio, who was adopted by the elder Africanus. The other son Quintus, the younger Scipio's brother, was adopted by Fabius Maximus, and so took his name.

49   600 sestertia: i.e. 600,000 sesterces.   The sum would be comparable to the annual income of the prosperous upper class (and of a popular actor like Roscius), and not much larger than Cicero's own 'slender' one. The hundred sestertia Cicero made from the property deal mentioned here would be the equivalent of the annual income from ten small farms, or, in a different context, would cover the pay of a 100 centurions for a year.

50 Manius Manilius: consul 149 b.c., who started the siege of Carthage in the third Punic war and was reinforced by the younger Africanus (cf. on 12 and 48). He was a founder of civil law, and appears with Scipio, Laelius, Scaevola and others as a speaker in Cicero's *De republica*. His house in the 'Keels' district would be between the Esquiline and Caelian hills, in one of the poorer areas; his farm at Labicanum was near to Tusculum.

GLOSSARY OF STOIC TERMS

Greek	Transliterated Greek	Latin	English
τὸ ἀγαθόν	to agathon	bonum	the good
ἄλγος	algos	dolor	pain
ἀδιάφορον	adiaphoron	indifferens	indifferent
αἴσχρος [opp. καλός]	aischros	inhonestus, turpis, prauus	wrong, immoral
ἁμάρτημα	hamartēma	peccatum	wrong action
ἀξία	axia	aestimabilia	of plus value
ἀπαξία	apaxia	inaestimabilia	of minus value
ἀποπροηγμένα	apoproēgmena	reiecta, remota	to be rejected
ἀρετή	aretē	uirtus	virtue
βλάμμα	blamma	detrimentum	harm
δυσχρηστήματα	dyschrestēmata	incommoda	disadvantages
ἔννοια	ennoia	notio	concept
ἐπιγεννηματικόν	epigennēmatikon	consequens	coming after
εὐδαιμονία	eudaimonia	beata uita	happiness
εὐκαιρία	eukairia	opportunitas	opportunity
εὐχρηστήματα	euchrestēmata	commoda	advantages
τὸ ἡγεμονικόν	to hēgemonikon	ratio	reason
ἡδονή	hēdonē	uoluptas	pleasure
καθῆκον	kathēkon	officium	appropriate action
κακία, τὸ κακὸν	kakia/to kakon	uitium, malum	vice, evil
καλός	kalos	honestus, rectus	right/righteous, moral
κατάληψις	katalēpsis	cognitio, comprehensio	understanding
κατορθῶμα	katorthōma	recte factum, officium perfectum	right action
λυπή	lupē	aegritudo	grief
οἰκειοῦσθαι	oikeiousthai	sibi conciliari	to have affection for oneself
ὁμολογία	homologia	conuenientia	harmony
ὁμολογουμένως ζῆν	homologoumenōs zen	conuenienter uiuere	to live in harmony
ὁρμή	hormē	appetitio animi	instinct

πάθος	*pathos*	perturbatio animi	mental disturbance
τὰ πρῶτα κατὰ φύσιν	*ta prōta kata physin*	prima/initia naturae principia naturae principia naturalia	what is primarily according to nature
ποιητικά	*poiētika*	efficientia	effective of
προηγμένα	*proēgmena*	praeposita, promota	to be preferred
προκοπή	*prokopē*	progressio	progress
τελικά	*telika*	ad summum bonum pertinentia	that which leads to the end / to the good
τέλος ἀγαθῶν	*telos agathōn*	summum/ultimum bonum, finis bonorum	the supreme/ highest, ultimate good
φύσις	*physis*	natura	nature
ὠφέλημα	*ōphelēma*	quod prodest	benefit

BIBLIOGRAPHY

J. Annas 'The Hellenistic Version of Aristotle's Ethics' *The Monist* 73 (1990), 80–96
– and J. Barnes *The Modes of Scepticism* Oxford 1987
E.V. Arnold *Roman Stoicism* Cambridge 1911
E.M. Atkins 'Justice and Societas in De Officiis' *Phronesis* 35(1990), 258–89
C. Bailey *The Greek Atomists and Epicurus* Oxford 1928
– *Epicurus: The Extant Remains* Oxford 1928
J. Barnes, J. Brunchswig, M. Burnyeat, M. Schofield eds *Science and Speculation* Cambri◊ 1982
E. Bevan *Stoics and Sceptics* Oxford 1913
E. Bréhier *The Hellenistic and Roman Age* Chicago 1965
J. Brunchswig 'The 'cradle' argument in Epicureanism and Stoicism' in Schofield *Norms*, 1▮ 44
M.L. Clarke *The Roman Mind* London 1965
– *The Noblest Roman: Marcus Brutus* London 1981
H. Cherniss *Plutarch: Moralia* xiii.2, Cambridge Mass. 1976
C.J. De Vogel *Greek Philosophy III: The Hellenistic-Roman Period* Leiden 1959
N.W. De Witt *Epicurus and his Philosophy* Minneapolis, 1954
A.E. Douglas *Cicero: Brutus* Oxford 1966
– *Greece and Rome: New Surveys in the Classics: Cicero* Oxford 1968, with addenda 1978
– *Cicero: Tusculan Disputations I* Warminster 1985
– *Cicero: Tusculan Disputations II and IV* Warminster 1991
J.-P. Dumont 'Confirmations et Disconfirmations' in Barnes *Science*, 273–303
L. Edelstein *The Meaning of Stoicism* Cambridge, Mass. 1966
– and I.G. Kidd *Posidonius* vol i 'The Fragments' Cambridge 1972
– 'The Philosophical System of Posidonius' *Journal of Roman Studies* 49(1959), 1–16
T. Engberg-Pederson 'Discovering the Good: *oikeiosis* and *kathekonta* in Stoic Ethics' ◊ Schofield *Norms*, 145–83
W.W. Fortenbaugh ed. *On Stoic and Peripatetic Ethics: The Work of Arius Didymus* Ne◊ Brunswick 1983
M. Frede 'The Stoic Doctrine of the Affections of the Soul' in Schofield *Norms*, 93–110
J. Glucker *Antiochus and the Late Academy* Gottingen 1978
H. Gorgemanns '*Oikeiosis* in Arius Didymus' in Fortenbaugh *Stoic Ethics*, 165–89
M. Griffin 'Philosophy, Cato and Roman Suicide' *Greece & Rome* (1986), 64–77, 192–202
– and J. Barnes (eds) *Philosophia Togata* Oxford 1989
R.D. Hicks *Stoic and Epicurean* London 1910
H.A.K. Hunt *The Humanism of Cicero* Melbourne 1954
B. Inwood *Ethics and Human Action in Early Stoicism* Oxford 1965
T. Irwin 'Virtue, Praise and Success: Stoic Responses to Aristotle' *The Monist* 73(1990), 59–7◊
J. Kaimio *The Romans and the Greek Language* Helsinki 1979
G.B. Kerferd 'The Search for Personal Identity in Stoic Thought' *John Rylands Bulleti◊* 55(1972), 177–96
– 'The Origin of Evil in Stoic Thought' *ibid* 60(1978), 482–94
– 'Cicero and Stoic Ethics' in J.M. Martyn ed. *Cicero and Virgil* Amsterdam 1972, 60–74
I.G. Kidd *Posidonius* vol ii 'Commentary' Cambridge 1987
– 'Poseidonius on the Emotions' in Long *Problems*, 200–15
– 'Stoic Intermediates and the End for Man' in Long *Problems*, 150–72
W.K. Lacey *Cicero and the End of the Roman Republic* London 1978

A.A. Long *Hellenistic Philosophy* 2nd ed. London 1986
  – ed. *Problems in Stoicism* London 1971
  – 'Aristotle's Legacy to Stoic Ethics *Bulletin of the Institute of Classical Studies* 15(1968) 72–85
  – 'Soul and Body in Stoicism' *Phronesis* 27(1982), 34–57
  – and D.N. Sedley *The Hellenistic Philosophers* Cambridge 1987 vols i and ii
P. Mitsis *Epicurean Ethical Theory* Cornell 1988
J. Moles *Plutarch: Life of Cicero* Warminster 1988
A.D. Nock 'Posidonius' *Journal of Roman Studies* 49(1959), 1–16
S.G. Pembroke 'Oikeiosis' in Long *Problems*, 114–49
E. Rawson *Cicero: a Portrait* London 1975
  – *Intellectual Life in the Late Roman Republic* London 1985
M.E. Reesor *The Political Theory of the Old and Middle Stoa* New York 1951
J.M. Rist *Stoic Philosophy* Cambridge 1969
  – *Epicurus: an Introduction* Cambridge 1972
F.H. Sandbach *The Stoics* London 1975
G. Santas *Socrates* London 1979
P.L. Schmidt 'Cicero's Place in Roman Philosophy' *Classical Journal* 74(1979), 115–27
D. Sedley 'On Signs' in Barnes *Science*, 39–72
C. Segal *Lucretius on Death and Anxiety* Princeton 1990
M. Schofield 'Aristo of Chios and the Unity of Virtue' *Ancient Philosophy* 4(1984), 83–96
  – and G. Striker eds. *The Norms of Nature: Studies in Hellenistic Ethics* Cambridge and Paris 1986
G.R. Stanton 'The Cosmopolitan Ideas of Epictetus and Marcus Aurelius' *Phronesis* 13(1968), 183–95
R. Starr 'The Circulation of Literary Texts in the Roman World' *Classical Quarterly* 37(1987) 213–33
D.L. Stockton *Cicero: A Political Biography* Oxford 1971
G. Striker 'The role of *oikeiosis* in Stoic Ethics' *Oxford Studies in Ancient Philosophy* 1(1983), 145–67
S. Sambursky *Physics of the Stoics* London 1959, repr. 1987
H. von Arnim *Stoicorum Veterum Fragmenta* (*SVF*) Leipsig 1903–4
N.P. White 'The Basis of Stoic Ethics' *Harvard Studies in Classical Philology* 83(1979), 143–78
  – 'Stoic Values' *The Monist* 73(1990)
M.R. Wright 'New Wine in New Bottles: Cicero *Fin* 3.4.15' *Liverpool Classical Monthly* 15(1990) 32

There are more specialised bibliographies in:
R. Epp ed. *Spindel Conference 1984, Southern Journal of Ancient Philosophy* suppl. 23 1985 ('Stoicism Bibliography')

and, in the above:
A.A. Long *Hellenistic Philosophy*, second edition ('Bibliographical Postscript 1985'), 257–268
Long and Sedley *The Hellenistic Philosophers* vol ii, 476–511
Griffin and Barnes *Philosophia Togata* (Bibliography compiled by Philippa Smith), 259–281

INDEX OF PASSAGES

INDEX OF NAMES